Lots of people dream of walking the path f~~~~~~~~~~~ed to entrepreneur, but Steve Glaveski's actually ᵈ~~~~~~~ took notes on what works and what doe~~~~~~~~~~~~~ how you how.

— **David Burkus**, ~~~~~~~~~~~ ᵣIEND

At its core, this book is about transl~~~~~~~~ ᵤd a conversation about how you work and make mone~~~~~ ~ guide to reimagining a life that you fully own.

— **Sherry Walling**, Ph.D., host of *ZenFounder* podcast, co-author of *The Entrepreneur's Guide to Keeping Your Sh*t Together*

Glaveski makes the case for entrepreneurship as the bastion that safeguards employment and meaningful contribution from the rapid encroachment of technologies that are disrupting every realm of traditional human work. He builds on that foundation with a framework to inspire aspiring innovators to make the leap — to evolve from employees/pawns of stagnant and dying corporations suffering 'paralysis by analysis', to successful entrepreneurs who can embrace the right risks, walk the edge of uncertainty with confidence and good judgement, avoid (most) beginner mistakes and turn the inevitable failures into future triumphs. An optimistic book, well-articulated and worthwhile; an antidote to doomsday prophecies about the future of work.

— **Whitney Johnson**, Thinkers50 Leading Management Thinkers, author of the bestselling *Build an A Team*, and critically-acclaimed *Disrupt Yourself*

Steve takes his personal learnings from years of doing the work and packages them up into one concise book — making his hard-won insights available to all of us.

— **Pascal Finette**, co-founder, radical Ventures, Chair for Entrepreneurship & Open Innovation, Singularity University

A must-read for anyone looking to make the transition from what Steve calls 'miserably comfortable' at a large organisation to the freedom and fulfilment that comes with entrepreneurship.

— **Cy Wakeman**, author of *No Ego: How Leaders Can Cut the Cost of Workplace Drama, End Entitlement and Drive Big Results*

EMPLOYEE

to

ENTREPRENEUR

EMPLOYEE
to
ENTREPRENEUR

HOW TO
EARN YOUR FREEDOM
AND DO WORK THAT MATTERS

STEVE GLAVESKI

WILEY

First published in 2019 by John Wiley & Sons Australia, Ltd
42 McDougall St, Milton Qld 4064

Office also in Melbourne

Typeset in 11.5/13.5 pt ITC Berkeley Oldstyle Std Medium

© John Wiley & Sons Australia, Ltd 2019

The moral rights of the author have been asserted

A catalogue record for this book is available from the National Library of Australia

Cover design: Wiley

Cover image: © art-4-art / iStockphoto

Opener graphics: © Sonic_S/Shutterstock

Printed in Singapore by C.O.S. Printers Pte Ltd

10 9 8 7 6 5 4 3 2 1

Disclaimer

The material in this publication is of the nature of general comment only, and does not represent professional advice. It is not intended to provide specific guidance for particular circumstances and it should not be relied on as the basis for any decision to take action or not take action on any matter which it covers. Readers should obtain professional advice where appropriate, before making any such decision. To the maximum extent permitted by law, the author and publisher disclaim all responsibility and liability to any person, arising directly or indirectly from any person taking or not taking action based on the information in this publication.

I dedicate this book to:

My brother Sašo who had so much potential and would often gaze at the night sky, dreaming of 'doing something that's never been done before', only to be taken away from us before he had the opportunity to make his dreams come true.

My father whose own struggles with and triumphs over adversity gave me the opportunity to write this book.

My mother whose resilience has been a lifelong inspiration.

CONTENTS

ABOUT THE AUTHOR

Steve Glaveski is on a mission to unlock the latent potential of organisations so they can create more impact for humanity and empower their people to lead more fulfilling lives.

Steve is the CEO of Collective Campus, a corporate innovation and startup accelerator originally established in Melbourne, Australia, that now works with large organisations from London to New York to help them find and adopt the mindsets, methods and tools they need to successfully navigate uncertainty in an era of rapid change.

Steve and his team have worked with the likes of Telstra, National Australia Bank, Clifford Chance, King & Wood Mallesons, BNP Paribas, Microsoft, Fox Sports, Village Digital, Charter Hall, Maddocks, Mills Oakley, Australian Unity, Ascendas-Singbridge, Singapore Pools and MetLife Insurance, among others.

Collective Campus has incubated and been home to more than 100 startups, which have raised more than US$25 million between them.

Aside from working with startups and large industry incumbents, Steve founded Lemonade Stand, a program that teaches children the fundamentals of entrepreneurial thinking. This program has been rolled out across Australia and in Singapore to more than a thousand children and at the time of writing was being developed into an online platform for the global English-speaking market.

Steve also wrote *The Innovation Manager's Handbook*, which was an Amazon bestseller across a number of its categories, including startups, management and technology. When he's not writing content, he's recording it. He hosts the *Future Squared* podcast, an iTunes Business chart mainstay that won an inaugural Australian

Podcasting Awards People's Choice award in 2017. Steve often shares his message with the world through keynote talks, having presented in locations as disparate as Perth, Singapore and Lincoln, Nebraska.

Steve previously founded the office-sharing platform Hotdesk and has worked for the likes of Westpac, Dun & Bradstreet, the Victorian Auditor-General's Office, EY (formerly Ernst & Young), KPMG and Macquarie Bank.

When he's not trying to help people unleash their potential, he can be found at the squat rack, skateboarding by the beach, cruising on his motorcycle, hiking (probably while listening to a podcast), catching a live gig or with his head buried in a book.

ACKNOWLEDGEMENTS

A number of times over the past few years I've found myself at the intersection of preparation and opportunity (some call this intersection 'luck').

Transitioning from roles in big corporate with the likes of EY and Macquarie Bank, in 2013 I found myself at the helm of a modestly funded tech startup, which gave me the opportunity to spend two years immersing myself in anything and everything relating to innovation and entrepreneurship. A subsequent stroke of serendipity led me to found Collective Campus, which has blessed me with the opportunity not only to do the kind of work I most enjoy, but to work with companies, individuals and kids—yes, kids, as part of our Lemonade Stand program—to unlock their potential to create more impact in the world and lead more fulfilling lives.

This experience has also enabled me to spend time on creative pursuits, such as hosting the podcast *Future Squared* since early 2016. I've now published more than 250 episodes and have had the pleasure of speaking with the likes of Adam Grant, Steve Blank, Tim Harford, David Allen, Grant Cardone, Brad Feld, Gretchen Rubin, Tyler Cowen, Rand Fishkin, Alec Ross, Jenny Blake, Karen Dillon and countless other thought leaders across a variety of disciplines. I've captured a number of my learnings from these conversations in this book.

I self-published my first two books online and struck a deal with Wiley for this book, my third in as many years. While it hasn't been easy to build a business from the ground up while also scratching various creative itches such as podcasting, blogging and book writing, it has been incredibly rewarding. I am eternally grateful and indebted to everyone who made it possible.

I'd like to take this opportunity to thank specifically:

My parents who left their own parents, siblings and extended family behind when they moved to distant Australia from what was then Yugoslavia in the early 1970s. They left home with very limited means, a modest education and zero command of the English language, but with a determination to give their children a better life, which they paid for with back-breaking factory work.

My sister Lidia, brother-in-law Peter and gorgeous nephews and niece, Nicholas, Thomas and Sasha, in whose presence the rest of the world just slips away.

My co-founder Sean Qian and the team at Collective Campus, Shay Namdarian, Charity De La Cruz, Bin Teo, Alec Sloman, Paulina Pinos and Frances Goh, all of whom have shared in what has been an incredible journey and promises to be even more exciting going forward. Thanks also to former CCer John van Noorden for helping to make this book happen.

You are the sum of the people you spend the most time with and I wouldn't be who I am today without the influence of different people at different stages of my life such as Daniel Nikolin, Nick Ivkovic, Carolyn Ng (thanks for the Starward and for reviewing the website!), Marjan Mladenovski, Steve Petkovski, James Nguyen, Bos and Cvet Corevska, Trinh Pham, Ivan Bozinovski, Lisa Du, Spiro Vladimiroski and last but not least, Onur Demir. If I missed your name, I am sorry—you know I love you.

My many awesome podcast guests, who represent a motley crew of authors, entrepreneurs, teachers, technologists, philosophers, economists, neuroscientists, psychologists, athletes, comedians, journalists, political commentators, investors and changemakers, for investing their valuable time to take part in the show and for teaching me a hell of a lot of new things. This list includes Adam Grant, Steve Blank, Kevin Kelly, Peter Diamandis, David Burkus, Tim O'Reilly, Adam Alter, Massimo Pigliucci, Whitney Johnson, Jeremy Bailenson, Alex Hutchinson, Bryan Caplan, Nicole Forsgren, Annie Duke, Arj Barker, Jeremy Heimans, Ben Yoskovitz, Rand Fishkin, Brad Feld, Scott Galloway, Perry Marshall, Lawrence Levy, Tyler Cowen, Jordan Harbinger, Sean Ellis, Andy Molinsky, Sam Walker, Andreas Antonopoulos, Brad Stulberg, Gretchen Rubin, Jason Calacanis, Neil

Patel, Karen Dillon, Brian Christian, Angela Maiers, Matthew E. May, Robert Kegan, Chris Kutarna, Leslie Barry, Dick Schmalensee, Pascal Finette, Ash Maurya, Parag Khanna, Ted Rubin, Oren Klaff, Ben Greenfield, Jeffrey Gitomer, Steve Hughes, Dan Toma, Larry Keeley, Peter Bregman, Chip Conley, Ajit Nawalkha, Richard de Crespigny, Bruce Tulgan, Ryan Blair, Marc Levinson, Susan David, Kevin Mulcahy, Paul Smith, Jamie Wheal, Alec Ross, Omar Zenhom, Jon Acuff, Carrie Green, Jacob Morgan, Mike Michalowicz, Emilie Wapnick, Jeb Blount, Cy Wakeman, Liz Wiseman, David Mead, Jennifer Kahnweiler, Primavera De Filippi, Erik Wahl, Eric Almquist, Jenny Blake, Rene Boer, Paul R. Williams, Gary Bolles, Evangelos Simoudis, Niel Robertson, Summer Howarth, Justin Lokitz and David Binetti.

A very special mention must go out to Tim Harford, who has not only supported my work but has also pointed me in the direction of invaluable resources to help secure a book deal.

I wouldn't be writing this book about entrepreneurship if it wasn't for my valued clients, many of whom took a leap of faith on us during our early days, while others have gone on to become great friends. Thank you for your vote of confidence: Aidan Coleman, Jon Satterley, Sean Hanrahan, Steve Brophy, John Kelly, Tobias Partridge, Balendran Thavarajah, Mac Korasani, Levent Shevki, John Nerurker, Michelle Mahoney, Shweta Babbar, Ramona Saligari, Jennifer Bednar, Matt Saraceni, Maria Crocker and last, but most definitely not least, Simon Quirk. These clients have all enabled my journey, as have the likes of Bill Petreski, Mick Williams, and Graham and Linda Huddy, whose contributions helped me keep the lights on and gave me the runway I needed to find my entrepreneurial mojo.

A big thanks to the startup and innovation ecosystems around the world, including Chris Joannou of Startup Grind, the teams at Startup Victoria and LaunchVic, Brian Ardinger and the team from Inside/Outside, Hans Balmaekers from Innov8rs, John Lee Dumas and Nathan Chan from Foundr.

Thanks also to the many thinkers who at the time of writing I had not yet had the pleasure of meeting but whose ideas have nonetheless helped to dramatically shape the way I think and show up every day. This list includes the likes of Tim Ferriss, Stephen Covey, Georges St Pierre, Joe Rogan, Sam Harris, Jocko Willink, Ryan Holiday, Jordan Peterson,

Seth Godin, Carol Dweck, Ray Dalio, Eric Ries, Clayton Christensen, Tim Urban, Yuval Noah Harari, Peter Thiel, Lewis Howes, Eckhart Tolle, Don Miguel Ruiz and those who are no longer with us such as Lucius Annaeus Seneca, Marcus Aurelius, Dale Carnegie and Zig Ziglar.

And of course, a huge thank you must go out to you, the reader and supporter of my work. That you're holding this book in your hands is testament to the fact that in business, as in life, every no gets you closer to a yes.

Thank you for choosing to give me your attention in such a crowded marketplace. At a time when on any given day hundreds of messages, through multiple different channels, vie for your attention, thank you for noticing and valuing mine.

I hope this book will give you both motivation and an actionable roadmap to help you realise your own potential in whatever area you choose.

Steve Glaveski

PREFACE

I was summoned to Human Resources on the 15th floor of a central Sydney office tower in the city's iconic Martin Place precinct, home to Macquarie Bank, the country's largest investment bank. Earlier that day I was featured in a one-page article in *The Australian* newspaper, in which I was referred to as an employee of the bank. Only it wasn't for anything I'd done for the bank. HR wanted to know how this media attention had come about. What a loaded question! My mind shifted back almost 12 months.

At the time I was working 800 kilometres away at EY in Melbourne. As a consultant for the big four accounting and professional services firms, I saw acres of vacant office space at almost every client site I visited, which prompted me to turn over the idea of an 'Airbnb for office space', connecting vacant office space with flexible workers, freelancers and business vagabonds. And the idea of Hotdesk was born.

I took the gig with Macquarie in April 2013, which meant moving to Sydney, but I kept working on Hotdesk, reading and learning everything I could about building a startup. I quickly realised how right Socrates was when he observed almost 2500 years ago that the more you know, the more you know you don't know.

I first tested customer appetite for the concept by posting a free advertisement for a non-executive director on the Australian Institute of Company Directors' website. At the time, I was interested in obtaining some guidance by bringing on a non-executive director; but what I ended up doing instead was learning what a number of people with business acumen thought about my idea.

Placing this free ad scored me about 25 meetings with both corporate executives from the commercial real estate industry and successful startup founders. They all asked me many questions that hadn't crossed my mind, all of which I used to go back to the drawing board and update my business model. The overwhelming consensus, however, was that I was 'onto something'.

Based on this early positive feedback, I decided that I'd build what Eric Ries, author of *The Lean Startup*, refers to as a 'minimum viable product', or MVP. This is, effectively, the simplest version of a product that creates sufficient value for customers that they are willing to pay for it. I hacked together a prototype, using a $500 online script that mimicked Airbnb's two-sided marketplace platform and an India-based web developer I'd found on the gig economy platform Freelancer.com. This bare-bones version of what I envisaged putting to market cost me a little under $2500 and took a couple of months to develop.

With prototype in hand, and with more than a hint of healthy naivety, I decided to Google 'how to write a press release' and try my hand at writing one. After working through a number of drafts, I mustered up the courage to send my final attempt to almost every email address I could find (or guess) belonging to technology, startup and commercial real estate journalists. Often I would glean these addresses from their Twitter profile. (Of course, today there are a number of online tools you can use to find email addresses, and we'll get to those later!)

The days went by and I heard ... nothing. The proverbial crickets, if you will.

Just when I had given up all hope and resigned myself to a career in banking, *one* journalist (out of almost one hundred I had emailed) got back to me. It happened to be a cadet journalist at *The Australian* by the name of Gina Rushton. The email went something like this: 'Hi Steve, thanks for this. Sounds interesting. Do you have a moment to chat?'

The next morning, after excusing myself from the office for a 'business meeting', I was interviewed over coffee, which for a wantrapreneur like me was quite the thrill. I thought I'd already made it! As I would later discover, this kind of foolish confidence makes and breaks many an entrepreneur. Gina contacted me again later that afternoon. 'We're going to run the story...but we need a photo. Are you free tomorrow at noon?'

What followed was a pretty elaborate photoshoot (for me anyway!) in the middle of Sydney's Martin Place, around the corner from Macquarie Bank's corporate HQ. Inevitably, given that the photoshoot took place at noon, I was spotted by a number of perplexed colleagues on their way to their respective lunch spots.

The article dropped the following day. Not only was it circulated nationwide to the paper's 300 000 readers, but it was also distributed through the 'Macquarie News', a daily compendium of press clippings mentioning the bank that was emailed to every one of the bank's 14 000 employees. So I wasn't surprised when my manager at the time asked for a word. I assured him this was just 'a little side project' that was not infringing on my work at the bank—which it wasn't. I found I could easily meet and even exceed daily expectations with two to three hours of solid effort a day (excluding meetings, of course, which were usually meetings to prepare for meetings, to revisit what was discussed during a previous meeting or to get out of actually doing work).

That's when I got the call from HR summoning me to the 15th floor.

I quickly dismissed the mention by the journalist that I was a Macquarie Bank employee as an irresponsible oversight on my part and swore it wouldn't happen again. They seemed satisfied. Less than three months later, thanks to the interest generated by this article, I had raised seed funding to the tune of US$120 000 and my 'little side project' was fast becoming a full-time pursuit.

Fast forward five years and Hotdesk has effectively evolved into Collective Campus, a team of entrepreneurs, designers, builders, thinkers, rebels, writers, teachers and modern-day philosophers working to unlock the latent potential of large organisations and startups alike. The venture has blossomed into a fast-growing, seven-figure business that works with brands such as Microsoft, Clifford Chance, Fox Sports, Village Roadshow, BNP Paribas, MetLife Insurance, Telstra, National Australia Bank, Charter Hall, King & Wood Mallesons, Maddocks, Mills Oakley, Asahi Beverages and Australian Unity.

During this time, I started my podcast, *Future Squared*, and found the time, inspiration, knowledge and desire to self-publish two books. Our team also spun off the children's entrepreneurship program Lemonade Stand to inspire a new generation of kids to leverage the power of the internet, not only as mindless consumers but as empowered producers.

I've lost count of the times I've been approached by corporate executives who have 'an idea', want to create meaningful change in their own lives and want to know how I did it. So I decided to distil the insights I've gathered over the past seven years in this book to help you unlock your potential to create more impact and lead a more fulfilling life. I hope you enjoy it.

Chapter 1
THE FUTURE IS HERE

'The only thing that is constant is change.'
Heraclitus

This isn't a book about building the next billion-dollar unicorn. I'm a first-generation Australian, the son of working-class Eastern European factory workers. I grew up in a socioeconomically challenged suburb in Melbourne's west, and went to public schools where illegal playground transactions were common. Several of my fellow alumni would be glorified on TV shows about Melbourne's underworld such as Nine Network's *Underbelly* series. I earned my bachelor's and master's degrees at universities that don't feature in the world's top 500. Despite this inauspicious start, I managed to hustle my way into gigs with powerhouses such as EY, KPMG and Macquarie Bank before starting and building my own business, hosting an award-winning podcast and writing books like this one.

In other words, if I can do it, *anyone* can.

This book is about earning your freedom, progressing from being miserably comfortable in a cushy corporate gig where the only thing getting you out of bed each morning is your salary, to running your own seven-figure business, all while doing something you love and find meaning in.

Let's go on a journey.

Exponential change

If you took a one-metre step today and doubled the distance every day for 30 days, how many metres do you think you might have walked by the end of the thirtieth day?

I've posed this question, inspired by XPRIZE founder Peter Diamandis, to corporate executives and entrepreneurs at some of my keynotes. Responses range from a self-censoring silence to guesstimates of 'thousands', '100 000', 'one million' or simply a playful 'lots'. I use this idea to illustrate Moore's law, which observes that computing power has been doubling every 18 to 24 months since the 1960s. In 1971, Intel released the world's first microprocessor, the 4004. The chip measured 12 square millimetres and contained just 2300 transistors. Today AMD's Epyc contains 19.2 billion transistors. Before you reach for your calculator, that's 8.3 million times more transistors than the 4004.

In the 18 months to December 2017, computer processor companies added about 10 billion transistors to a microchip. That's 10 times more in the past 18 months than we managed in *the entire decade of the noughties*, a time that also gave us the iPhone, *Borat* and Limp Bizkit's *Chocolate Starfish and the Hotdog Flavored Water* (human beings are fallible, after all).

This, then, is the difference between linear and exponential growth.

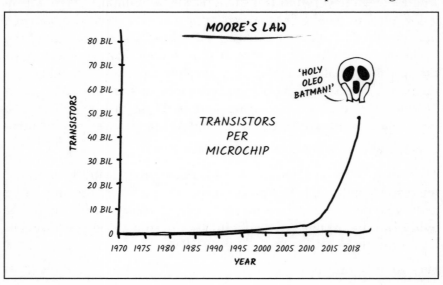

We've reached a major inflection point in human history—not so much in the quality of Top 40 music, as in the acceleration in technological development and the implications of this on society.

It's easy to write off Moore's law as just another buzzword, like *innovation*, *agile* and *disruption*. People overuse such terms because they conveniently encapsulate a phenomenon we simply can't ignore. It doesn't make them any less relevant or important. So, to put Moore's law into perspective, I ask the 30-steps question.

The answer?

One billion and seventy-three million metres. That's 1073000 kilometres, or about 666000 miles…sorry, I hope that number doesn't summon the beast! It's also the equivalent of walking around the world's circumference 26 times!

Remember the famous legend in which the grateful emperor of India asked the inventor of chess to name his reward? The inventor requested one grain of rice for the first square of the chess board and double the number of grains for each succeeding square. The emperor happily agreed to what he thought was a modest reward. It turned out that by the 64th square the inventor had earned nine quintillion grains of rice (that's nine million trillion), equivalent to over six trillion 50-kilo bags of rice, enough to cover all of India with bags of rice.

The power of exponential growth is essentially why ideas like immersive virtual reality environments, artificially intelligent systems, autonomous vehicles and multi-planetary humans are slowly but surely moving from science fiction to science fact. In many areas, these innovations are already being realised. As cyberpunk science fiction writer William Gibson famously noted, 'The future is already here—it's just not evenly distributed'.

What this means

Let's put science fiction aside for a second.

Twenty-five years ago, if someone had told you that you could enter a query into a computer form and generate an archive of thousands of results within a split second, you probably would have imagined it was some kind of magic box descended from the heavens (or perhaps from the fires of hell, depending on your religious persuasion). The more logical among you might have guessed that the trick involved a 'really big hard drive', rather than a search algorithm that effectively queries every indexed website in the world.

The search algorithm determines relevance before presenting you with the best fit-for-purpose results. If it relied purely on search terms, without filtering, you'd probably end up with what we had in the early days, when an innocent search for cars would generate a list of pornographic websites that featured the word 'cars' a thousand times over in black text on a black background in order to game the system. You probably wouldn't understand (any more than most of us do today) how that same search function handles 40 000 queries a second or 3.5 billion queries every single day. Google's capacity is something we take for granted.

Ten years ago, if someone had told you that you could push a button and within a couple of minutes your own private black car would pull up and take you to your destination, and charge you for it without your having to utter a single word to the driver or hand over any physical payment, you probably would have thought such a thing possible only for card-carrying Freemasons (or, for fans of *The Simpsons*, the Stonecutters). As an aside, I don't advocate not speaking to Uber drivers. I've had many fascinating conversations with them. On one occasion, I learned that my driver had escaped a detention camp in Iraq in a flurry of bullets, made for a camp in Saudi Arabia, and eventually claimed refugee status and safe passage to Australia.

Today we take ride-sharing services like Uber and Lyft or China's Didi Chuxing for granted, so much so that if the estimated wait time is longer than five minutes, we get annoyed. Damned annoyed! Infuriated even, though of course I'm not talking about myself.

For better or worse, Facebook's tentacles reach deep into many aspects of our lives, yet 12 years ago it was nothing more than a rather crude idea emanating from a Harvard college dorm room.

Today these things are a part of life. On average, each day we check our smartphone more than 80 times and spend more than 145 minutes engaged with our phone. We take Facebook, Instagram, Snapchat and other social media for granted, as we do video calls to our friends on the other side of the world.

Moore's law underpins this rapid change. It paved the way for the web, cloud computing, smartphones, connected devices, and game-changing platforms like Amazon and Google. It has changed the way we connect, consume and learn. And settle disagreements: 'Hey, Google … ?'

With these shifts has come massive disruption to incumbent organisations across almost every conceivable industry — and, by extension, to employees and their livelihoods. Historically, though, each wave of innovation ultimately created more jobs than it destroyed. The *first industrial revolution* gave us machines, chemical manufacturing, iron production, steam power and the factory system, giving rise to entirely new industries. The *second industrial revolution* gave us steel, petroleum, automobiles, mass production and the transition to electric power. Today the *third industrial revolution* has given us computers and the internet, new sources of energy and vast improvements in productivity, all helping to reduce the cost of producing and distributing goods and services virtually to zero. The total number of 'things' (including physical devices, software and electronic sensors) connected to the internet (IoT) is projected to reach 21 billion by 2020. Increasingly, this is changing the way we interact with our surroundings and even with each other.

Productivity is indeed increasing, However, median household income in the United States has stagnated since the turn of the century and in many regions, such as the Rust Belt (the US manufacturing heartland), median household income is actually decreasing. Mass discontent with this reality had a lot to do with why a certain Donald Trump came out on top in almost all these electorates. In the early 1970s, more than 45 per cent of the Rust Belt's population was employed in the manufacturing sector. As shown in figure 1.1, the decline of US manufacturing jobs over the past half century has left many without a reliable source of income. In Australia, manufacturing jobs dropped 24 per cent in the five years to 2016 alone.

Since 1999, productivity and income have not increased in lockstep, the first time in recorded history this link has been broken. It's happening because technology is becoming more 'intelligent' and is learning to do more of what we once thought only humans could do. After all, if you believe that intelligence is simply about processing information, then arguably a computer that can collect more information and process it faster than a human has the upper hand. As world-renowned economics professor and author Tyler Cowen comments, 'It's becoming increasingly clear that mechanised intelligence can solve a rapidly expanding repertoire of problems'.

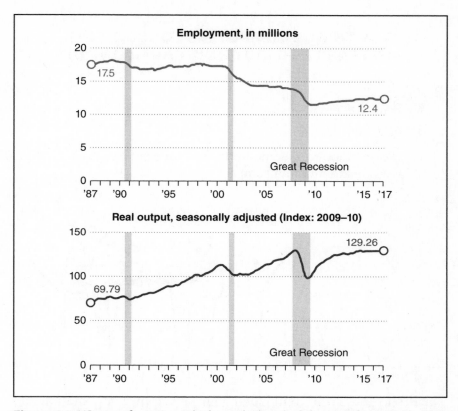

Figure 1.1: US manufacturing jobs have declined while manufacturing output has increased.

Source: Bureau of Labor Statistics

TEN THINGS COMPUTERS COULDN'T DO 10 YEARS AGO (BUT NOW CAN)

1. Play chess.
2. Write poetry.
3. Write and play emotionally engaging music.
4. Read human emotions.
5. Diagnose diseases.
6. Read lips.

(continued)

TEN THINGS COMPUTERS COULDN'T DO 10 YEARS AGO (BUT NOW CAN) *(CONT'D)*

7. Transcribe.

8. Read the news.

9. Customer service.

10. Create brand-new Rembrandts (see, for example, www.nextrembrandt.com).

The threat goes far beyond blue-collar jobs. Expert automation and augmentation software (EAAS) is expected to at first augment and eventually replace much of what today's lawyers, HR managers, marketers, sales clerks, researchers, consultants, accountants and auditors, compliance officers, reporters and editors, investment managers, teaching assistants and even software developers do.

The CEO of online investment platform Wealthfront, Andy Rachleff, writes that 'software is better than people … in just about every industry I know, software-based solutions deliver better functionality, convenience and speed than their human counterparts. There's no way people can keep up'.

At its peak in 2002, Blockbuster Video employed more than 60 000 staff worldwide and had a market capitalisation of US$5 billion. I remember during my teens gleefully making my way down to my local Blockbuster outlet to hire two overnight and three weekly rentals, immersing myself in cheesy early-1990's comedies like Mike Myers'

Wayne's World or Pauly Shore's *Encino Man* (don't judge). Nostalgia aside, at the time of writing (June 2018) Blockbuster's successor, media services provider Netflix, has amassed a market capitalisation of more than US$164 billion, all with just 5500 employees. If you divide its market cap by the number of employees, Netflix generates 357 times more value per employee!

BLOCKBUSTER

NETFLIX
357X MORE VALUE
PER EMPLOYEE

That's more than 32 times Blockbuster's peak valuation (unadjusted for inflation) with one-tenth of the employees. Which is to say nothing of the infrastructure and supply chain costs of a bricks-and-mortar business like Blockbuster's with physical inventory in the shape of video cassettes and DVDs. This starts to explain why the gap between household income and productivity is rising: companies are learning how to achieve more with less—less human capital, that is.

In the defence industry, an unmanned aerial vehicle (drone) costs one-tenth of a piloted jet. In education, the Khan Academy, with just 100 employees, is able to deliver high-calibre educational content to children and adults anywhere, so long as they have an internet connection and a cheap device. That's fewer staff than you'd find at your local high school!

THREE THINGS YOU SHOULD KNOW ABOUT ARTIFICIAL INTELLIGENCE

1. Narrow AI

Narrow AI is what we have today. Think: AI that is good at performing a single task, such as playing Go or chess, or forecasting the weather. Google Translate, self-driving car technology and image recognition software are all narrow AI.

2. General AI

General AI (or AGI) is often called human-level AI. Think: AI that can reason and understand its environment as a human would. As Tim Harford noted in *50 Things That Made the Modern Economy*, general AI has been '20 years away' since a 1956 workshop at Dartmouth College on 'machines that use language, form abstractions and concepts, solve kinds of problems now reserved for humans, and improve themselves'. General AI has been just over the horizon for about sixty years, and today, yes, experts say it's still about '20 years away'.

3. Artificial Superintelligence (ASI)

Finally, when AI becomes smarter than the best human brains at practically everything, including social skills, we'll have achieved what University of Oxford scholar and AI expert Nick Bostrom call artificial superintelligence.

How far are we really from human-level AI? With most accounts putting it somewhere between 20 and 70 years away, the general consensus is it'll definitely be this century. As for artificial superintelligence, some say once we hit AGI then ASI could happen in months, weeks or days, and once it happens there'll be no going back. The late Stephen Hawking believed full artificial intelligence represents an existential threat to humanity. Conversely, Demis Hassabis, the founder and CEO of AI company DeepMind, acquired by Google in 2014 for more than US$500 million, believes that AI will help humans solve intractable problems such as global warming, cure diseases and explore the universe.

No one knows for sure at this stage what ASI will bring, and chances are we won't know until it's here because, well, we simply aren't superintelligent and therefore cannot think or connect the dots in the same way ASI might.

WHAT DOES THIS MEAN FOR YOU?

As computers learn to do more of what humans currently do, we can ill afford to rely on our government or employers to ensure our basic human needs are met, to say nothing of our needs for belonging, self-esteem and self-actualisation. The next decade promises great upheaval brought on by the accelerating pace of change and adoption of emerging technologies. The seismic shift in technology is disrupting incumbent business models and will result in many of today's jobs simply ceasing to exist.

Optimists, as already noted, argue that this disruption will create more jobs than it destroys, citing studies that found technological innovation has traditionally done this over the past 140 years. Current employment indicators show little evidence that this trend will continue ad infinitum, however. We're already seeing elements of society push back against the harsh realities of automation, but town square protests, while admirable, usually do little to solve the problem of technology-led job displacement; only adapting to the changing environment does. In the 1810s, when the English Luddites destroyed machinery that threatened their livelihoods, it didn't halt or even delay the progress of the first industrial revolution.

While many Trump supporters seek to 'make America great again' by restoring its manufacturing heartland, Sweden's minister for employment and integration, Ylva Johansson, says the Scandinavian nation is approaching things a little differently. 'The jobs disappear, and then we train people for new jobs. We won't protect jobs. But we will protect workers.'

In *Blockchain Revolution*, co-author Alex Tapscott argues, 'The global financial crisis demonstrated the inability of the US government (and in fact the governments of the world) to identify and respond to threats in an increasingly complex and befuddling global financial system in a timely manner'. Tim O'Reilly, one of the founding fathers of the open source movement and co-founder of O'Reilly Media, writes in his 2017 book, *What's the Future and Why It's Up to Us*, that government continues to operate on 20th century infrastructure and ways of working.

To protect yourself you need to learn to adapt constantly to the changing environment. Don't expect government to make sense of all of these befuddling changes and offer you a lifeline, beyond a basic level of subsistence. If you want to live a meaningful life of financial freedom, growth and fulfilment, you'll have to take this bold mission into your own hands.

WHERE TO FROM HERE?

Chances are, if you're reading this, you're not only concerned by the looming threat to employment, but are probably not entirely happy with your existing job or circumstances. According to a recent study, more than half of the Australian workforce is dissatisfied at work, which echoes job satisfaction statistics from the US, UK and indeed most developed western economies.

Amid this growing discontent and uncertainty in the corporate workplace, entrepreneurship is thriving. Global venture capital (VC) funding alone jumped 50 per cent in 2017, to US$164.4 billion. Taking into account other sources of investment, 13 665 companies around the globe received capital injections in 2016. Entrepreneurs are in a unique position to take advantage of the economic and societal shifts because, to them, threats are simply opportunities we don't respond to in a timely way. In order to respond, one must embrace uncertainty, the very antithesis of how most large organisations and their executives operate. They choose instead to err on the side of caution and make decisions from a place of absolute certainty.

But here's the thing about certainty. Any decision you make from a place of absolute certainty is unlikely to foster a breakthrough idea. If all of the information is known and certain, then everyone else who looks can see it too. Innovation grounded in certainty results in uninspiring, incremental improvements and delivers marginal returns at best. There's a little thing in nature called the risk–return spectrum: the more return sought, the more risk one must take.

That's why most large organisations today are plagued by overplanning, meetings to prepare for meetings, political game playing, outsourced accountability, cost and schedule blowouts, and paralysis by analysis. The end result is a comfortably miserable existence for most people gainfully employed by a large, traditional organisation.

From employee to entrepreneur

The challenge is in the *how*. How do you make the leap from employee to entrepreneur? How do you go from a career of risk mitigation by comprehensive analysis and talking, to risk mitigation by building, testing and actually doing? How do you go from avoiding failure at all costs to embracing failures as a necessary obstacle on the path to valuable learnings and breakthroughs? How do you go from operating effectively under conditions of certainty to navigating extreme — what pundits today are calling, VUCA: volatility, uncertainty, complexity and ambiguity?

I often see first-time entrepreneurs, many of whom have come out of a big corporate, fall into the same old traps, such as:

- jumping to conclusions with the first idea that comes to mind (beware the optimist illusion or *optimism bias*; we're always more hopeful and positive about the future than we should be, just as people are more confident that *tomorrow* they'll get started on that diet)
- confusing the support of family and friends with market validation for their idea
- raising some initial seed funding from unsophisticated investors—and blowing it on team and marketing before honing their true value proposition
- spending inordinate amounts of money on software development agencies and in return getting a half-baked solution built by third-rate offshore developers the agency has subcontracted to, usually without the knowledge of the entrepreneur

- placing too much faith in their 'unique advantage', which it turns out is neither unique nor advantageous.

These are all sure-fire ways to plunge the stake through the heart of your entrepreneurial existence.

The chapters that follow are designed to help you:

- navigate the journey from employee to entrepreneur
- find more meaningful work and better use of your time
- avoid the common pitfalls faced by most first-time entrepreneurs
- fast-track your progress and increase your likelihood of success by distilling key learnings into a single book
- learn how to leverage traditional character attributes often found in the corporate world to your advantage
- become more conscious of and mitigate those character attributes that are detrimental to entrepreneurship
- gain access to a play-by-play framework so you can experiment more effectively and increase your chances of success
- develop the mindset you need to succeed as an entrepreneur.

This book not only elaborates on the 'why', but helps you identify *your* why, what and how. How do you go about finding your calling by using an actionable roadmap? It builds on not only my own learnings but those I've gathered from interviewing numerous thought leaders at the top of their field on the *Future Squared* podcast, meeting and working with countless entrepreneurs and corporate innovation teams, and what I have drawn from literally hundreds of books and podcasts on the topic of entrepreneurship, self-improvement, philosophy, health and more.

ENTREPRENEURSHIP IS A STATE OF MIND

Entrepreneur is far more than a job title — it's a state of mind and way of life. It's not enough to update your job description on LinkedIn, print some business cards proclaiming yourself 'managing director' and bask in your newfound title. While a lot of books focus on the how of entrepreneurship, so many neglect the most important ingredient—your state of mind. As Ben Horowitz, of VC firm Andreessen Horowitz, puts it, 'The most difficult skill a CEO has to learn is managing one's own psychology'.

Most of us have been brought up and socially indoctrinated with values that push us towards accepting the status quo. Go to school, get good grades, complete a college degree, land that job, climb the ladder, paint that picket fence white, be comfortable. This is the narrative that first found a home on our black-and-white television sets in the postwar world of the 1950s. Breaking the 'school, taxes, death' narrative takes time. Like culture change in a large company, it's a marathon and not a sprint. I broke the narrative in my own life through a somewhat serendipitous series of hops, skips and jumps, rather than an overnight epiphany.

Here's a summary of the past 14 years of my professional career:

1. 2005: Customer Service @ Westpac Bank
2. 2007: Administration @ Dun & Bradstreet
3. 2009: Completed master's degree in Professional Accounting
4. 2009: Financial Audit @ Victorian Auditor-General's Office
5. 2011: IT Risk @ EY
6. 2013: Founder of Madhouse heavy metal nightclub
7. 2013: Risk Management @ Macquarie Bank
8. 2013: Startup Founder @ Hotdesk
9. 2015–today: CEO/Co-founder @ Collective Campus, Co-founder @ Lemonade Stand, host of podcast *Future Squared*, keynote speaker and published author.

More and more people are finding themselves in unfulfilling roles. At the same time, many are becoming conscious of the fact that work doesn't need to suck and are seeking out purpose in addition to personal profit. For example, one-third of Australians have freelanced, with the number set to increase. This follows the US, where the freelance economy has been growing three times faster than the rest of the job economy since 2014. That's because the narrative is shifting, and it's time to shift with it.

'BUT IT'S NOT THE RIGHT TIME'

It will never be the 'right time'. University or work commitments, saving for vacations, children to take care of, mortgages to pay, bills, school fees, physical limitations... and so on. Whatever stage of life you're in, there will always be excuses. Choosing to overcome them by taking action is a choice, and everyone has that choice.

Jon Acuff, author of *Do Over*, argues, 'You don't need to go back in time to be awesome; you just have to start right now. Regretting that you didn't start earlier is a great distraction from moving on your dream today, and the reality is that today is earlier than tomorrow'. Conrad Hilton, founder of Hilton Hotels, was in his fifties before opening the very first Hilton Hotel outside of Texas. Today there are more than 5000 Hilton hotels in more than 100 countries. Jeff Bezos was in his thirties when he founded Amazon. Today Amazon is everywhere and Bezos' presence is even felt among the stars thanks to his Blue Origin spaceflight company. Research published in *Harvard Business*

Review while I was writing this chapter found that the average age of successful startup founders when starting their companies was 45.

Age aside, look no further than 32-year-old quadruple amputee Kyle Maynard on why the only obstacle between us and our goals is attitude. Maynard scaled Mount Kilimanjaro in just 10 days, totally unassisted. He competes in mixed martial arts, has opened a CrossFit gym and wrote the *New York Times* bestselling book *No Excuses: The True Story of a Congenital Amputee Who Became a Champion in Wrestling and in Life*.

'The species that survives', Charles Darwin contended, 'is the one that is able to adapt to and adjust best to the changing environment in which it finds itself'. Entrepreneurship is a vehicle for developing the mindset and skills we need to adapt and to overcome failures. You don't even need to become an entrepreneur per se, but by developing the underlying character attributes and mindset of one, you will give yourself the best shot of success in today's turbulent times, and the best chance of living a fulfilling and rewarding life.

'Inaction breeds doubt and fear,' Dale Carnegie wrote. 'Action breeds confidence and courage. If you want to conquer fear, do not sit at home and think about it. Go out and get busy.'

Let's get busy.

Call to action

1. Remind yourself why you picked up this book, and keep that reason front of mind both as you read it and on your entrepreneurial journey. Write it down if you have to. Make it visible. The act of getting it out of your head and onto the page will make it real and signal to your brain that it's beyond time to merely think about changing things up — it's time to start doing so.

2. Ask yourself which aspects of your job are process oriented and repeatable. Could they be performed by a sophisticated or even unsophisticated algorithm? Be objective. This will help determine the likelihood that your job will be replaced in the near to mid term, especially if you aren't a leader in your field.

3. If you haven't taken the leap yet, what's stopping you? Write this down too. Is this a legitimate reason or an excuse? Be objective. Identify what steps you might take to overcome the roadblock. Is it in fact a roadblock at all, or is there an underlying issue that you must first address?

4. Do you simply not have enough time? If so, what can you stop doing or do less of to free up some time? (See chapter 10 for guidance on getting your time back.) If you need to take care of dependents on top of your existing job, perhaps you can take small steps towards exploring entrepreneurship on the side. Where there's a will there's always a way, and we'll explore a number of ways in coming chapters.

Chapter 2
COLLECTING THE DOTS

*'The direction in which education starts a man
will determine his future in life.'*
Plato

In the past 10 years, I've worked across the public sector, at a big four consulting firm and at an investment bank, and I've founded a web startup. I completed a master's degree in accounting, got a certificate in journalism, earned project management and agile certifications, and completed a number of online courses on topics such as venture capital, design thinking, growth hacking and even stand-up comedy. I founded and ran a heavy metal nightclub, a corporate innovation consultancy and a children's entrepreneurship program. I published three books, hosted two podcasts and developed a software platform.

I rode a motorcycle, tried my hand at mixed martial arts, Brazilian jiu jitsu, boxing and, in Thailand, Muay Thai. I learned how to surf in Bali, *poorly*. I played guitar in an eighties glam metal tribute band, zebra-print pants and all—good luck finding the photos! 🐎. I jumped out of a plane at 15 000 feet, white water rafted in Indonesia, learned how to skateboard, took a Circus Trapeze class and gave Acroyoga a shot, braved the standup comedy stage, competed in a half marathon and a sprint triathlon and finished in the top 5 per cent of a Spartan Race in Melbourne.

I went to two World Cups (Germany 2006 and Brazil 2014 – I won't share which I thought was better so as not to offend my Brazilian friends) and to music festivals around the world including Germany's iconic Wacken Open Air, partied in Spain's Ibiza, explored different types of music from Beethoven and Johnny Cash to The Prodigy and Finland's Ensiferum, tried (with middling success) to learn Mandarin and Portuguese (my Portuguese was not 'muito bom'!), and visited favelas in Brazil, slums in India and rural villages in Vietnam. I learned how to make seriously good espresso, read and listened to hundreds of books and thousands of podcasts and met all kinds of people at functions and conferences across the globe.

This audit barely scratches the surface of a decade of my life but it does represent many dots that I'd later learn to connect, consciously or intuitively. As former World Series of Poker champion Annie Duke puts it, 'Your intuition is developed through past experiences and so in order to develop a better intuition and make better decisions, you've got to learn from diverse sources'.

Steve Blank, widely considered the 'Godfather of Silicon Valley' and the lean startup movement, believes people who are on top of their game are always curious about a lot of things—it's in their brain chemistry. When I spoke to Steve on my podcast he told me, 'We talk about resilience, we talk about agility, we talk about all the tactical things that make entrepreneurs go through walls, but I think the thing that makes them great and different is they're curious about more than just what you would think was their domain. They're *perpetually* curious—it doesn't stop'.

Collect the dots before you connect the dots

Too many people tell me they're unsure what their passion or purpose is. This isn't because they don't have one. They just haven't found it. Or, more to the point, they haven't been trained to *see* it.

This usually means they pursue business ideas purely for monetary gain or for the freedom of being their own boss. They'll stay the course begrudgingly, without truly believing in their work, because of the sunk cost investment they've already made, and come Friday morning it's 'TGIF' while Sunday nights are spent dreading the following morning. That's no way to live. Yet for so many it's become an accepted and unchallenged norm. These days I say TGIM and *still* enjoy my weekends.

How do you train yourself to find your purpose and passion? You collect and connect dots.

STEVE JOBS ON CONNECTING THE DOTS

At his famous Stanford commencement speech, Steve Jobs explained that 'you can't connect the dots looking forward; you can only connect them looking backwards. So, you have to trust that the dots will somehow connect in your future. You have to trust in something — your gut, destiny, life, karma, whatever. This approach has never let me down, and it has made all the difference in my life'.

What Jobs was talking about was broad experiences, in both a professional and a personal context, which often intertwine. In Jobs' case, his early interest in Zen Buddhism has been credited with influencing the simple minimalism of the Apple Mac and subsequent Apple products. Sitting in on calligraphy classes at Stanford (for which he wasn't enrolled) encouraged a love of typography that found expression in Apple typefaces. And who can forget his now infamous tour of Xerox's Palo Alto Research Centre (PARC), where he stumbled on a 'graphical user interface' that Xerox had little idea how to commercialise, so he 'borrowed' it for Apple. This was 1979, when all human-to-computer interaction was still performed through command line interfaces. (Are you old enough to remember the joys of typing in commands like 'DIR /W or perhaps, frantically, 'UNDELETE' in MS-DOS?)

Steve Jobs collected and connected a lot of dots on his road to creative and financial success.

Most successful entrepreneurs solve problems they connect with personally because they've observed them (collected the dots) and shortlisted potential solutions based on their research and understanding of business model and technology innovations (connected the dots). Think of:

- *Uber.* On a snowy Paris evening in 2008, Uber co-founders Travis Kalanick and Garrett Camp couldn't find a cab, so they came up with the concept for Uber: push a button, get a ride.
- *Airbnb.* Co-founders Brian Chesky and Joe Gebbia decided to rent out air mattresses in their apartment to attendees of a Silicon Valley conference because all the hotels were booked out.
- *Dropbox.* Drew Houston, Dropbox's founder, established the cloud storage company 'out of personal frustration'. He recalls 'carrying a thumb drive around and emailing myself files and all the things that we used to have to do'.

Often entrepreneurs connect the dots between seemingly disparate areas.

CLAYTON CHRISTENSEN ON CONNECTING THE DOTS

Harvard Business School professor Clayton Christensen, perhaps the world's foremost authority on disruptive innovation, defines connecting the dots as 'associational thinking' in his book *The Innovator's DNA*.

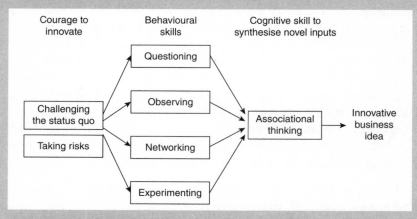

Figure 2.1 Associational thinking
Source: Clayton Christensen, The Innovator's DNA.

Associational thinking occurs when we synthesise and connect dots across unrelated fields or ideas. Swedish-American author Frans Johansson refers to this as 'the Medici effect', referring to a time in 15th century Florence when the Medici family patronised many poets, painters, philosophers, scientists, sculptors and architects, who created new ideas at the intersection of their respective disciplines. It was the beginning of the Renaissance, considered to this day one of the most creative periods in human history.

Connecting the dots with first principles thinking

Entrepreneurs such as Elon Musk, Jeff Bezos, Peter Thiel and Nobel Prize–winning physicist Richard Feynman credit much of their success to first principles thinking. Musk says, 'First principles is kind of a physics way of looking at the world. You boil things down to the most fundamental truths and say, "what are we sure is true?" ... and then reason up from there'.

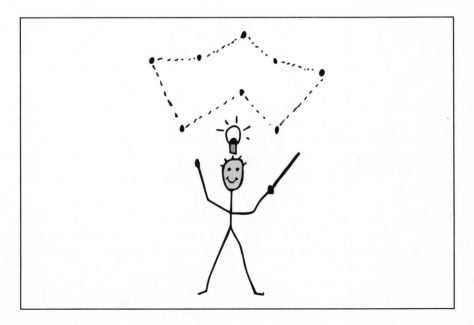

First principles thinking can help us move beyond incrementally improving what already exists towards fundamentally new, transformative ideas.

Consider the following thought experiment.

Imagine you have three things:

1. a skateboard
2. a bicycle
3. motorbike.

Break these parts down into their key constituent parts:

1. skateboard: deck, wheels, trucks
2. bicycle: handlebars, seat, frame, pedals, wheels, spokes, chain
3. motorbike: engine, oil tank, fender, exhaust, clutch, brakes, wheels, throttle.

How might you use these key parts to develop something new?

One option might be a motorised jetski, using the skateboard deck, the frame and seat from the bicycle and the throttle and engine from the motorbike. This is the process of first principles thinking. Deconstruct then reconstruct.

Like many things, first principles thinking sounds easy in theory but the practice is an entirely different proposition. We tend to optimise for form rather than function and have a predisposition towards incrementally improving what already exists. The suitcase is a classic example. In Ancient Rome mounted soldiers used leather messenger bags; for heavier loads they had wheeled wagons. Bernard Sadow had his breakthrough moment in 1970 when, while hauling two heavy suitcases across an airport concourse, he spotted a worker effortlessly rolling a heavy machine on a wheeled skid. So the first wheeled suitcase was invented more than five millennia after the wheel.

'Find value in unexpected places,' Peter Thiel advises, 'by thinking about business from first principles instead of formulas'. Many unsuccessful entrepreneurs fail to apply critical thinking and vision when identifying 'problems' and solutions because they are coming from a narrowly defined view of the world. Collecting as many dots as possible will help you expand your worldview, give you more sources from which to identify stories and themes that resonate to help you find your why, and ultimately help you identify genuine problems and opportunities worth exploring.

Where to collect dots?

Today there is no excuse for not learning something new every day. Peter Diamandis, founder of the XPRIZE and serial entrepreneur behind companies such as Singularity University and Human Longevity Inc., points out that a child with an internet connection today has access to more information than the President of the United States had 25 years ago. With the click of a button you can learn almost anything you want to. Recently I downloaded the introductory lessons I needed to finally start my motorcycle build project.

PODCASTS

Podcasts have changed the game. Not only are they disrupting traditional media, but they're paving the way for new, brain-expanding conversations around social norms and concerns, not to mention arguments around philosophy, religion, political affiliation, psychology, biological evolution and more. They're supporting the contest of ideas that mainstream media never could, or indeed wanted to, given their rigid focus on ratings and superficial soundbites. If you truly want to develop a greater appreciation of the world around you, and to listen to and join dialectic and intelligent conversations, you can't afford *not* to listen to podcasts.

Almost a quarter of all Americans listen to podcasts monthly, while 15 per cent listen to them weekly. That's five times more than go to the movies. As of this writing, Apple Podcasts had more than one billion subscriptions spread across 250 000 podcasts in more than 100 languages, with 8 million individual episodes. Podcasts run the gamut of discussion topics, from history and evolution to computer science and technology, from behavioural economics and neuroscience to popular culture and philosophy. Whatever your interest, whatever you're curious about or, perhaps more importantly, not yet curious about, you'll find podcasts you can access at any time for free.

The beauty of podcasts is that you can also listen to them anywhere. Your commute becomes learning time, whether you're walking, riding a bicycle or (in the spirit of the late, great John Candy) on a train, plane or automobile. Your workout becomes learning time. Quest Nutrition co-founder Tom Bilyeu told Quartz Media he listens to podcasts and audiobooks in transition moments. He also listens to audiobooks at *three times* the normal speed. That's three books in the time it normally takes to listen to one. I'm on 2X myself when it comes to podcasts and 3X on audiobooks.

Note: There's something to be said for giving your brain the space and time to reflect and just be quiet, as we'll explore in a later chapter, but making effective use of downtime to up your intellectual consumption is not a bad thing, so long as you're still giving your mind time to *just be*. It's the difference between mindfulness and what Aubrey Marcus, the founder of human performance company Onnit, calls 'mind*fill*ness'.

With 250 000 podcasts to choose from, you might be wondering where to start. That choice really is yours. In connecting the dots, it's when exploring disparate fields that magic often happens. As you're reading this book, though, it's a pretty safe bet that you have an interest in learning more about entrepreneurship, technology and reinventing yourself and your worldview.

For a list of my go-to podcasts across a number of disparate topics, check out **www.employeetoentrepreneur.io/podcasts/**.

BOOKS

A surprising number of people will admit, 'I haven't read a book since school'. In today's environment of accelerating change, if we don't want to be left behind we simply can't afford to stop learning when we graduate. Because we are all 'eternal newbies', a term coined by *Wired* magazine co-founder and futurist Kevin Kelly, the number one skill we all need is that of *learning how to learn*.

Books such as Tim Ferriss's *The 4-Hour Work Week*, Eric Ries's *The Lean Startup* and Marcus Aurelius's *Meditations*, a 1900-year-old collection of journals by the great Roman philosopher king, changed the way I respond to difficult situations and helped me win my freedom from the corporate world in a thoughtful, almost deliberate way.

Somewhere between 600 000 and a million books are published each year in the US alone. I'm shocked by how often I meet budding entrepreneurs who are treading water and have never taken the time to pick up a business or entrepreneurship book, or if they have, have failed to truly understand or, more importantly, *apply* the key concepts.

For a list of my favourite and most highly recommended books, check out **www.employeetoentrepreneur.io/books/**.

LEARNING HOW TO LEARN

'Tell me and I'll forget; show me and I may remember;
involve me and I'll understand.'
Chinese proverb

The key personality attributes needed to develop the mindset for learning anything new are:

- self-awareness

- resilience

- tolerance of ambiguity

- willingness to embrace failure

- disidentification with ego.

Such attributes help us negotiate the bumps in the road on any worthwhile journey, whether it's learning a new language, learning how to code or starting a new business.

What to learn

Your time is a finite resource, so before you decide to learn something new, you need to determine whether doing so is a worthwhile pursuit in the first place. If the subject is not a natural fit for you, are you wasting your time learning to be mediocre while it takes you away from your areas of strength?

If, for example, I'm looking to learn how to code so I can build an online store, I might want to consider some of the following questions:

- Is there someone I could pay to do this for me for a reasonable, non-prohibitive price?

- Are there custom, do-it-yourself solutions I could use instead (such as Shopify)?

- Do I *need* to understand all the technical elements or do I simply need a live and functioning online store?

- Can I better use the time in other ways, perhaps on getting to know my customers and marketing to them better? (Namely, what's the opportunity cost?)

- Most fundamentally, will this move me towards my goal faster than learning something else or having someone else do this for me?

How to learn

Once someone has the mindset required to support learning, they need to develop a process that works best for them. Usually it means focusing on the smallest possible input that will produce the largest possible output. I'm quite fond of Tim Ferriss's DiSSSCaFE method.

If I want to learn Japanese, I'd focus on the smallest unit of knowledge — words and phrases — and then focus on learning the top 20 per cent of words and phrases that show up 80 per cent of the time. Where possible, Ferriss advises the use of mnemonics to aid memory; 'SMART' is a popular mnemonic for specific, measurable, achievable, realistic and time-bound.

Here's what I do to remember and apply knowledge:

- Highlight sections, either digitally or with a good old-fashioned highlighter pen.

- Type out highlights into a Google Doc. (While e-reader and digital highlighters such as ScanMarker will do this for you automatically, the act of typing solidifies understanding and aids later recall.)

- Take notes as I listen to a podcast or audiobook on my smartphone or notepad.

(continued)

LEARNING HOW TO LEARN (*CONT'D*)

- Create mnemonics and visual associations to remember key concepts.

- Teach others (either as part of our daily team stand-ups, during our monthly team book club meeting or by writing a blog post).

- Run a workshop or webinar incorporating some of what I learned. (I did this in 2015 after going down the blockchain rabbit-hole. I ran a free one-hour session called Blockchain for Bankers and filled a room with 40 bankers ready to learn what I had discovered about blockchain, distilled into lay terms as best I could.)

- Experiment with and actually *apply* key concepts from books in the workplace or in my personal life.

By embracing a beginner's growth mindset and disassociating from ego, you will become better at determining what to learn, which sources to derive learning from and ultimately how to learn it. In this way you'll increase both your knowledge base and, more importantly, what you do with it and the impact you can make on both your life and the lives of others.

BLOGS

We're living in the information age, when almost everyone has the power to make their voice heard online, whether through posting on social media, blogging or in a growing number of cases, vlogging. This means there's a lot of noise in this domain, so learning how to cut through that noise to get to the information that will serve your mission best is key.

I use a content aggregation portal called Feedly to help me curate a personalised news feed of topics and publications of interest. This enables me to save time and be more deliberate about what I read by scrolling through the headlines until I come across a story I want to learn more about. This way I'm far less likely to go down click-baity rabbit-holes

('You Won't Believe What These 90s TV Stars Look Like Today!') that serve no purpose other than to hijack my logical brain so my reptilian brain can sit back and enjoy a short-term dopamine hit at the expense of my learning and growth. You might also enjoy the content aggregation app Flipboard and blogging platforms such as Medium.

When it comes to social media, you'll also want to be conscious of echo chambers and epistemic bubbles. C. Thi Nguyen explains: 'An epistemic bubble is when you don't hear people from the other side while an echo chamber is what happens when you don't trust people from the other side'. The 2016 US presidential election demonstrated how our online epistemic bubbles can harden us to particular belief systems. For example, left-leaning Facebook users were served up predominantly left-leaning news and reaffirming posts by left-leaning friends. Those on the political right received overwhelmingly right-leaning news feeds whose sentiments were echoed by right-leaning friends. As a result, many accused Facebook of influencing the outcome of the 2016 vote, with or without the 'help' of Russian hackers.

Similarly, if all of your news comes from one news source, such as Fox (Republican), CNN (Democrat) or any other single news network in the world, there is a good chance it is owned or otherwise influenced by large corporations with some kind of ideology or agenda.

If you've become an unsuspecting marionette — cut your strings! Today you can use services such as Google News or websites such as the Associated Press and Reuters to access impartial, uncensored news. If you're unsure whether your existing news sources are impartial, find out who owns the company and whether or not that organisation has made political donations and to whom. For example, News Corp donated $1 million to the Republican Governors Association in June 2017, drawing criticism from Democrats that a contribution of that magnitude casts a shadow on its media properties such as Fox News. This might be why Fox News presenters such as Sean Hannity are accused by the left of parroting Republican Party talking points.

Open your mind not only to different sources of information but to different points of view and different ideologies. Failure to do so ultimately limits your worldview and compromises your ability to empathise and collaborate with people who have different views and skill-sets.

Some of the most profound and impactful learnings I've had in the past couple of years that have had a tremendous impact on my approach to work and the culture of my team have come from books that had nothing to do with business, such as Marcus Aurelius's *Meditations*, Homer's *The Odyssey* and Paulo Coelho's *The Alchemist*.

STRONG OPINIONS, LOOSELY HELD

I cringe when I hear of school debates in which students are directed to argue a position whether or not they, or the facts, support it. Sadly, this misguided thinking pervades today's corporate and political arenas, where it often has a devastating effect on the common good.

As human beings, we default to putting things into neatly demarcated buckets; it's how we make sense of the world. However, as Robert Sapolsky noted in *Behave: The Biology of Humans at Our Best and Worst*, putting facts into buckets might have its advantages but it can wreak havoc on your ability to think about those facts. When you think categorically about left wing or right wing, red or blue, you have trouble seeing how similar or different two things really are, and if you pay lots of attention to where the boundaries are you end up paying less attention to complete pictures.

To counter this, regardless of what you read or learn, subscribe to the 'strong opinions, loosely held' school of thinking. Always be ready and open to having your opinion changed if the argument and evidence to the contrary are strong enough. Never confuse an attack on your position with a personal attack, which will only cause you to defend instead of understand. As Adam Grant put it in a tweet, 'When you're in a heated argument, stop and ask, "What evidence would change your mind?" If the answer is nothing, there's no point in continuing the debate. You can lead a horse to water, but you can't make it think'. Don't be the horse.

You might also want to use a free tool such as Google Alerts or the not free but effective BuzzSumo to ensure you don't miss a beat on topics of interest, particularly in core areas you're doubling down on. The more informed your conversation, the more you can put yourself forward as a thought leader and the more opportunities that will come your way.

NEWS

While consuming the news is a daily habit for hundreds of millions across the globe, advocates for *not* tuning into the news, such as Peter Diamandis, suggest that its overwhelmingly negative nature can infect us with cynicism (even though, as we'll learn later, we're living in the best times ever, at least at a macroeconomic level).

I choose to limit my news intake to mostly business and technology news. If something big and worth knowing happens, be it positive or negative, I'm sure I'll find out through other channels (because people will be talking about it for longer than a fleeting 24-hour news day).

If you must watch or read the news, perhaps limit it to news headlines and use aforementioned apps such as Flipboard or Feedly to filter out irrelevant news.

For a list of my go-to blogs and newsletter subscriptions, check out **www.employeetoentrepreneur.io/blogs/**.

TRAVEL

Gaining an appreciation of other cultures and innovations is a valuable source of inspiration and 'dots'. If you've spent your whole life surrounded by the comforts of a developed western economy, then your worldview will likely be somewhat narrow and would be rocked by a trip to a less developed country such as India. Such reality checks might make you more grateful for what you do have and less likely to complain over trivial first-world problems ('Gah, the train is five minutes late again!'). Replacing expectation with appreciation can shake us out of a victim mentality and move us towards a place of self-empowerment.

NEW PERSPECTIVES FUEL CREATIVITY

In the age of budget airlines, economics are not so much of a barrier to travel anymore. I tend to find travelling to 'developing' regions, such as South-East Asia, the Balkans or South America, provides more interesting insights than visiting another western country. Stepping off the plane or high-speed rail into a city, looking around to find the golden arches, Starbucks and the skyscrapers synonymous with big cities leaves me feeling like I never left home at all.

As with books, podcasts and blogs, choose a broad range of geographies and cultures. Whatever community you identify as, seek the opposite. And to paraphrase Abraham Lincoln (when he was speaking of the Southern states before the Civil War), don't criticise them, for they are just what we would be under similar circumstances. If you're a staunch conservative, believe in deregulation and are against unions, perhaps spend some time in socio-economically challenged areas or with tradespeople to try to better understand different points of view and why they might support unions such as the CFMEU.

I've been fortunate enough to travel to more than 20 countries and have drawn valuable life and business lessons from each country.

I'll never forget Hanoi, Vietnam, during the torrid summer of 2017, 42 degrees Celsius with 90 per cent humidity, sweating up a storm as soon as I left my blissfully air-conditioned apartment. As only a crazy person would, I had decided it was as good a day as any to go for a run, and as I forced myself into an uncomfortable jog I encountered a group of middle-aged street workers on their knees paving a new walkway. Despite the backbreaking work and the sweat streaming off them in the merciless heat, they were chatting away cheerfully, with much laughter. Whatever your situation, you always have a choice in how you respond. From an outsider's perspective, their lot might have seemed intolerable. But they were probably grateful to have a job that put food on the table, for the companionship and for a free lunch. Perspective distinguishes a disempowering mindset from a powerful one.

While working at Macquarie Bank, I visited the city of Gurgaon, southwest of New Delhi in India. On the road to my five-star hotel, through the windows of my chauffeured company car, I witnessed unbelievable poverty. The cognitive dissonance was palpable and perplexing. I saw babies that looked no more than nine months old crawling in the dirt in roadside slums. I saw families of four, or even five, crammed onto a 50cc motorbike made for one.

This trip not only fuelled my gratitude for the opportunities I'd been given, but also served as a catalyst for a deeper change in my thinking. I was determined to help make the world a better place in whatever way I could. These trips helped me find my purpose. Today much of the work that we do at Collective Campus is geared towards our mission to unlock people's potential to create impact not only in developed economies but in South-East Asia and eventually other underdeveloped regions of the world. We've planted our flag by setting up a base in Singapore and have already started navigating our way across the less developed countries of the region. Our journey won't be without its challenges, particularly of the cultural variety, but it will be well worth it.

The Republic of Macedonia, in South-East Europe's Balkan peninsula, is the land of my parents, grandparents and I imagine my ancestors going back numerous generations (although one can never be too sure when it comes to the Balkans, a region that has experienced more than its share of wars and population displacement across the centuries). My dad left behind three brothers and three sisters in 1971 when he took advantage of a change to Australia's migration policy to set sail for Australia. I was just 13 years old when I first visited the mother country in 1997 and remember my shock when I was presented with what I was told was a toilet in the village my mum had grown up in (the country's plumbing system has come a long way since then!).

On subsequent trips I found an unemployment rate of nearly 40 per cent, an average monthly wage of less than US$300 and many of my cousins struggling to find and hold down a job, even those with university degrees (which unfortunately are not recognised in most western nations). And I saw how people could be thrown out of their state-run jobs as soon as the political party they had voted for lost power. All of which helped me appreciate not only my dad's decision but the opportunities and freedoms I tended to take for granted.

It also helped me understand myself a little more. People often ask me, 'What got you into entrepreneurship?' Perhaps I didn't have a choice. I can't help but think of my dad and the six siblings he left behind. He saw it as an opportunity to build a better life for his family. That openness to opportunity perhaps runs through my veins.

Genetics are only as good as the environment in which they're regulated though, and growing up in a home where the head of the household was an opportunistic risk taker with a growth mindset (he later taught himself all about property investment) surely didn't hurt. Sadly, he succumbed to cancer in 2012. I miss him and his imposing and influential presence dearly.

Having said that, if you want to do something new but don't have a family history of risk-taking, the only thing stopping you from changing that is, well ... you.

Aside from building self-awareness and shaping your worldview, travel inspires creativity in your business life. Exposure to other cultures can be a fantastic source of inspiration, such as ideas you might be able to adapt and launch in your local market. Can't afford to take the time off to travel? Visit different communities in your own city. Spend some time in Chinatown in Sydney or Little Italy and Little Saigon in Melbourne, or perhaps feast on some Ethiopian gored gored in Footscray, Melbourne. If you're in a developed economy, chances are that an ethnic micro-neighbourhood isn't far away. New York City has 18 ethnic micro-neighbourhoods in its five boroughs, from the Little Dominican Republic in Washington Heights to Little Senegal in Harlem and Little Poland in Brooklyn.

GOING SOLO

On a number of occasions, I've taken trips on my own. When you travel with people you know you're far more likely simply to hang out with them and stay well within your comfort zone. Sure, going solo you could hike, ride a bicycle or simply walk around and sightsee, but eventually your desire for human connection will kick in. This will force you out of your comfort zone, especially if you're an introvert. You're more likely to take an interest in and strike up conversations with strangers. We often don't realise how underdeveloped certain aspects of our mindset and personality are, until we find ourselves in new environments without the social safety nets we take for granted at home.

On a recent three-day trip to Los Angeles, I quickly grew tired of walking around, spectating, and decided I wanted to participate. I consider myself an ambivert: if I have a role to play that requires me to come alive I'll play it, but I also need time alone to recharge.

Despite hosting a podcast and having delivered keynotes and facilitated workshops for thousands of people, the idea of joining a game of pickup basketball at Venice Beach with a bunch of guys who were much bigger and better at the game than me was confronting and forced me to fess up to some of my own personality weaknesses.

Despite that, the experience of playing pickup ball in LA left me on a high and built the momentum that saw me introducing myself and hanging out with strangers throughout the day, at the world-famous Muscle Beach Gym (Arnold is *still* numero uno), in restaurants and at bars. Stepping out of your comfort zone can truly be a transformative experience, serving to develop skills that are transferable into other aspects of your professional and personal life.

BREAK OUT OF YOUR COMFORT ZONE

We often default to the same holiday locations each year. Big cities, beach towns, comfortable and familiar surroundings. By doing so we miss out on the opportunity for personal growth. One reason I agreed to speak at an innovation conference in Nebraska in early 2018 was because that midwestern ('flyover') state is visited by few Australians — it actually ranks dead last in terms of tourism. The trip exposed me to a different way of life, different attitudes, political persuasions, economic realities and more. It also opened up new opportunities I would have been blind to if I had spent my time in more familiar environments on the west or east coast, which are often not too dissimilar from where I grew up and spend a lot of my time in Melbourne. I left Nebraska with new relationships, new opportunities and an expanded worldview, and shortly thereafter made plans to visit other parts of America's Midwest.

Experiencing new and unfamiliar places on your own also increases your tolerance of ambiguity and discomfort. Research suggests that people develop greater empathy when visiting unfamiliar places on their own because they are more likely to engage with and trust strangers. So next time you're making vacation plans, try somewhere new. Maybe try a few days on your own and encourage your team or colleagues to do the same.

CONFERENCES AND MEETUPS

Conferences can be expensive and a time drain, so if you're looking to meet lots of different people and learn lots of new things, check out Meetup.com to see what's happening in your part of the world.

Meetup is an online social networking service that helps people organise and/or join real-life group meetings. You might attend short, often free or really cheap, meetups related to startups, yoga, cooking, surfing, philosophy and pretty much any topic that commands any kind of following. Want to hang out with people to talk about the eighties TV show *Twin Peaks*? There's a meetup for that. Oh, there are also meetups for ambidextrous tennis players and bingo for singles, just in case you were wondering.

A word of warning on startup and entrepreneur meetups. It's easy to fall into the trap of going to meetup after meetup, but I've found that maybe one person in 20 is worthy of a subsequent conversation. That might sound uppity, *but it's true*. Most of the time you might spend at meetups could be better spent on other, more rewarding pursuits. As for the keynotes and panel talks you get to see, there's nothing you can't find on YouTube or Facebook at a time of your choosing.

It's easy to spend a disproportionate amount of time 'networking' instead of building your product or your marketing funnel. Sure, it makes you feel busy and you feel good connecting with lots of people, but is it moving you closer to your goal? Rather than spending all that time meeting people you'll never speak to again, perhaps you should focus more on your existing relationships — you know, the meaningful ones. Try limiting your attendance at such events to perhaps one per fortnight, and be intentional about mixing it up. When it comes to meetups, check the confirmed guest-list online for anyone of interest you'd like to meet, then prepare for those conversations and seek them out at the event so you waste less time on unproductive conversations that go nowhere and spend more time moving the needle.

BREAKING THE ICE

Not sure what to say to people when you attend a networking event? Instead of asking the usual 'What do you do?' question, leading management thinker David Burkus suggests, try something like, 'Who's your favourite superhero?' and follow up with 'Why?'. Have some fun with it. People will appreciate the unorthodox approach and conversation will flow more naturally.

Today's big go-to conferences and festivals for entrepreneurs include:

- SXSW in Austin, Texas
- TechCrunch Disrupt SF, San Francisco
- CES, Las Vegas
- PauseFest, Melbourne
- CeBIT, Sydney
- StartCon, Sydney
- London Tech Week
- Tech in Asia, Singapore
- Burning Man, Nevada (just because).

WEBINARS AND ONLINE COURSES

I recently completed a number of online courses on topics that I felt were holding me back. This lack of knowledge, I felt, could slow my progress in reaching my goals. Even if I chose to outsource in this area, a baseline of knowledge would enable me to better communicate, monitor and manage the work. There are thousands of micro and longer courses available online, usually free or for a small fee, through platforms such as Udacity, NovoEd, Udemy, EdX, Coursera and the Khan Academy, among many other platforms.

You'll also find loads of free webinars on emerging tech, trends and business practices, for example in relation to marketing, sales or design. Oh, and don't forget YouTube—just avoid the comments section, unless you enjoy scraping the bottom of the intellectual barrel. Sorry, ODoyleRules69.

Be intentional

Don't just wait for it to happen. Carve out the time but guard your time with your life. Set aside two hours, free from distraction, to consume useful content. It's easy to start off with the best of intentions and find yourself slipping very quickly. Track your progress at the end of each week and hold yourself accountable. Consider using a tool such as Rescue Time to determine how long you spend on particular learning applications on your desktop and mobile.

You'll find that positive feedback loops (better conversations, connecting the dots privately, identifying opportunities, closing a deal and moving the needle on your revenue) will keep you going back for more. It's just like seeing results in the gym: if you notice a slimmer waistline, a tighter booty, bigger biceps or visible abs, you'll be much more motivated to keep going.

In this chapter, we've reviewed just some of the many ways you might collect the dots to build your knowledge base. You're probably exploring some of them already, but it's far too easy to fall into the trap of consuming and doing the same old things where the number and variety of dots you collect remain small. Go wide and deep.

Call to action

1. Review the lists of resources referred to throughout this chapter.

2. Within the next 48 hours, subscribe to one of the podcasts mentioned and listen to an episode. Take notes and then share what you have learned with someone.

3. Carve out time in your calendar each week for learning; this could be during your commute, your gym time, a walk, before bed, early in the morning, during your lunch break ... 'I don't have time' is code for 'This isn't important enough to prioritise'. How much do you *really* want this?

If you take just one key message from a book or a piece of content, consuming it has been worthwhile. Don't underestimate the way consuming content feeds your understanding and intuition without you realising it.

Chapter 3
FINDING YOUR WHY

'Without a purpose, nothing should be done.'
Marcus Aurelius

I remember standing on a platform at Melbourne's Parliament railway station one evening after another day on another long-term consulting gig aimed at ensuring a large, heavily funded listed company complied with its regulatory obligations. This engagement, like so many before it, was plagued with politics and was painstakingly slow to progress. Often our recommendations to clients would go unheeded and we'd end up making the same recommendations the following year. Each day I found myself standing on that same platform and wondering to myself, 'What did I actually achieve or contribute today?'.

I was in my late twenties and I hadn't yet connected enough dots to truly know what I wanted to do, even though it was 10 years since I had to make the dreaded decision in high school. You know the one: 'So, what do you wanna do with your life, kiddo?' As if a 17-year-old has the requisite life experience to make such decisions, especially back in 2000 when information and people were nowhere near as accessible as today.

At 27, I lived for the weekend and what made for an alcohol-fuelled reprieve from the monotony of management consulting. I'd pursue the opposite sex in nightclubs not only to satisfy primal urges, but to feed my otherwise underdeveloped sense of self-worth. I'd do all the little things that serve to numb our pain and help us tolerate Monday mornings.

Looking around me, it was easy to see others following this same script. Smart and ambitious types who had been to good schools and physically took care of themselves, yet found themselves wasting their days playing office politics, sitting through multiple hour-long meetings and putting together exquisitely formatted PowerPoint presentations.

I'd submit a report to my Division Director for review that would come back heavily annotated with requested changes. I'd make said changes and push it up the chain for final review by the Managing Partner, who would duly annotate it back to what it originally looked like. The whole cycle would leave me feeling frustrated and bewildered. I knew that to find myself feeling a little more fulfilled at day's end, I needed to make a change.

Are you miserably comfortable?

When tackling the question *why*, you must first ask what your why is *right now*. Why did you pick up this book? What triggered it? Was it a single spark or a series of triggers over an extended time that impelled you to explore alternatives to the familiar, 'safe' path? (Of course, there's nothing safe about most notionally secure jobs anymore.)

It's easy for us to get sucked into the matrix to grind out work, day after day, to look around at our colleagues, all similarly immersed, and conclude that, well, this must be the way it's supposed to be. Mark Twain famously said, 'Whenever you find yourself on the side of the majority, stop and reflect'. So many people resign themselves to the false belief that work isn't supposed to be something they enjoy, without really taking the time to reflect on what would truly make them happy and fulfilled in their work, or whether those two words can usefully be paired to begin with.

THE 5 FS

Every few months I perform a sanity check to assess whether I need to make any changes to the kind of work I'm doing or how I'm doing it. Here I've found the '5 Fs' offer a helpful guide.

1. FREEDOM

Having the freedom to take on the projects you want to take on, to explore what you want to explore, to express yourself as you want to, to work wherever you want and to work with and for people you respect—who inspire you to new heights.

2. FINANCIAL INDEPENDENCE

We all want to do work we love, but we need to survive as well. You won't necessarily want to build the next billion-dollar unicorn. Your goal may be a lifestyle business that simply allows you to live a comfortable life, a position that ensures you are not a slave to someone or something else and are free to contribute to causes greater than yourself.

Dan Price, CEO of payments company Gravity, made headlines when he raised the company's minimum wage to US$70 000. He did so after reading a study conducted by Nobel Prize–winning economist

Angus Deaton and psychologist Daniel Kahneman, which found that emotional wellbeing rises with income up to about US\$75 000 a year, after which the law of diminishing returns kicks in and other non-monetary factors become more important (don't ask me why he stopped at \$70 000).

So how much money do *you* really need to be happy?

3. FULFILMENT

Are you doing work that matters, that makes a difference, that gets you out of bed in the morning with a spring in your step? Does your work make you feel excited about taking on the challenges of the day, because you know the pain and struggle is worth it? At day's end, do you feel proud of your accomplishment and the contribution you have made to the world?

4. FITNESS

Here I refer to fitness of both body and mind. Fitness has been a mainstay throughout my life. You have a much better chance of achieving the previous three Fs if you have a solid foundation of health and fitness. Success will mean little if you're physically sluggish, unhealthy and emotionally unstable.

THE CHOICE IS YOURS

'You have power over your mind, not external events,' wrote Marcus Aurelius in his journals. 'Realise this and you will find strength.' We all have choices in how we respond to and interpret the things that happen to us. To manage our emotions, we should align our responses with the person we *want* to be.

---

5. FAMILY AND FRIENDS

Finally, if you've managed to achieve everything on this list but find yourself with no time for socialising and spending time with family and friends, then perhaps you are over-investing in work.

TIME TO PLAY

Use an automation tool like Zapier and an outsourcing platform like Upwork to free yourself from mind-numbing and rudimentary process-oriented tasks and give yourself more time to play and live.

At the bank, I was strong on financials but felt far from fulfilled, so I made a change and haven't looked back since.

If you find yourself lacking in one or more of these five areas, then perhaps it's time to make a bold move. Understanding the motives behind your why is key to taking the next steps. Do some soul searching, but be objective. Ask yourself why five times to drill down to the root cause of what's prompting your dissatisfaction. Only then can you determine your next steps with confidence and clarity, rather than acting impulsively and irrationally in a way you'll later come to regret.

STOP DOING THE WRONG THINGS RIGHT WITH THE FIVE WHYS

The five whys provide a simple yet effective aid to help you get to the root cause of a decision. *Why is asking why five times so powerful?*

Here's an example that will no doubt resonate with Australian fans of the world game.

Problem statement: We are receiving a lot of complaints about our FIFA World Cup live stream.

1. Why? The stream is blurry and buffers a lot.
2. Why? Because there is an issue between the stream encoder and packager.
3. Why? Because we didn't perform end-to-end testing.
4. Why? Because our stream normally works well and we didn't anticipate an increase in demand.
5. Why? Because we didn't plan properly.

The five whys here point to not just taking the time to sort out the issue with the encoder and packager, but to a deeper systemic issue at this media company. Introducing better planning procedures for new broadcasts will not only help to resolve the current complaints but mitigate the likelihood of receiving such complaints in future and increase customer acquisition and retention by doing so.

In a professional context, what often starts out as a technical issue (such as insufficient bandwidth to support requests) quickly becomes a communication issue once why questions determine that 'the new guy' wasn't fully briefed on a new marketing campaign and therefore didn't prepare for the influx of traffic.

We only have one life, and it's a relatively short one, so to spend it in pursuit of solving the wrong problems, or surface-level issues that don't serve to move the needle much on personal or professional growth, is nothing short of tragic.

Were you prompted to pick up this book by an external trigger? Maybe you didn't get that promotion, or you had a tough day at the office, or someone you know was celebrated in the media for a startup they'd built, or you spotted another friend in an expensive sports car, or … whatever. When your emotions are running high, your amygdala—the primitive part of your brain and its emotional control centre—has hijacked your frontal cortex, the part of your brain responsible for emotional regulation and reasoning (and, incidentally, the last part of the human brain to develop as far as evolutionary biology is concerned).

Of course, it's easy to say and quite another thing to do, but you should try your best to make life decisions from a place of *voluntary* reason rather than *involuntary* reaction.

Your why

Now that we've established why you want to make a change, let's home in on your why or purpose.

PURPOSE

In AD 160 the philosopher king Marcus Aurelius noted in his journal, 'Without purpose, nothing should be done'. Nearly two millennia later, human performance coach and co-author of *Peak Performance*, Brad Stulberg, defined purpose as 'the world's greatest performance enhancer'.

You may be familiar with the story of Tom Boyle, the Arizonan motorist who saw a young cyclist dragged under a Chevy Camaro for '20 to 30 feet' before the unsuspecting driver came to a stop. Hearing the cries of the cyclist, Boyle ran over and without giving it a second thought lifted the front end of the Camaro off the ground, freeing the trapped rider. A Camaro weighs in at about 1500 kilograms, or one and a half tonnes, which is five times Boyle's body weight. Boyle's lift amounted to what powerlifters and gym rats like me call a deadlift. Most Olympic-level powerlifters deadlift somewhere between three and four times their bodyweight. Boyle managed *five*, not with a barbell designed for lifting, but with the greasy front end of a hot Chevy. This story speaks volumes about the power of purpose as a performance enhancer.

How much easier is it to maintain a workout regimen when you've had a serious health scare and doctor's orders have you swinging kettlebells or pounding the pavement? How much easier is it to cut sugar out of your diet when you've been diagnosed with a high risk of developing Type 2 diabetes? How much easier is it to work relentlessly towards finalising a business proposal when a six-figure contract hangs in the balance and you've got just seven hours to submit it?

That's because when we're given a compelling reason to do something and are operating within constraints, such as a tight deadline, we're far more likely to focus on getting things done. When it's life or death, win or fail, there's no *trying* to get in the zone. Jamie Wheal, co-founder of the Flow Genome Project, an organisation dedicated to reverse-engineering the genome of the flow state, cites environmental factors as one of the many triggers of flow, particularly environments with high consequences.

How much better would you perform with purpose at the centre of your work? How much easier would it be to get out of bed with a spring in your step each morning, ready to tackle the challenges of a new day? How much easier would it be to get into the flow each day and crank out lots of high-quality output? How much easier would it be to ride the inevitable lows in order to get to the highs? Life isn't about enjoying one high after another; it's about navigating the highs and enduring the inevitable lows and suffering that come with it. These lows become a lot easier to handle with purpose and meaning at the centre not just of your business but of your whole life.

RECALLING MASLOW'S HIERARCHY OF NEEDS

Psychologist Abraham Maslow first published his famous theory on human motivation in 1943 (see figure 3.1). For the purposes of his theory, Maslow proposed that human actions are motivated by a desire to fulfil certain needs. These he represented in a five-tier hierarchy. Once each level of need is fulfilled, we are motivated by those at the next level. The most basic levels cover *physiological needs* (air, water, food, clothing, shelter, sex) and *safety needs* (personal security, financial security, health and wellbeing). Next are interpersonal needs around *social belonging* (friendship, intimacy, family), followed by esteem or status needs (self-respect and the desire to be accepted, valued and respected by others). At the top is *self-actualisation* or the realisation of one's potential ('What a man can be, he must be').

He would later add a further dimension (*self-transcendence*) based on his belief that one can only find true actualisation by serving a higher goal outside oneself. This is ultimately about giving back to humanity and our environment.

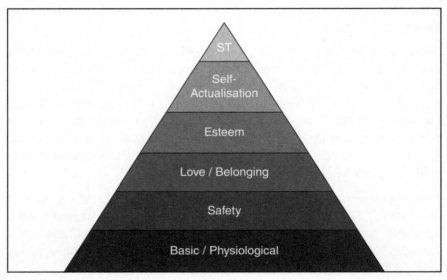

Figure 3.1: Maslow's hierarchy of needs
Source: Maslow (1943)

THE PURSUIT (*NOT* THE DESTINATION)

If you're reading this, chances are you're no longer treading water at the bottom of Maslow's pyramid, struggling to meet your basic physiological and safety needs, and are therefore focused on pursuing your higher order goals.

In *Man's Search for Meaning,* Holocaust survivor Viktor Frankl writes that 'success, like happiness, cannot be pursued; it must ensue, and it only does so as the unintended side-effect of one's personal dedication to a *cause greater than oneself'*. Again, purpose, self-transcendence and a worthwhile mission are at the heart of Frankl's famous assertion. Material possessions and accolades may give us pleasure, but they are not a source of enduring happiness. Only a life in pursuit of things that give us true esteem, and the opportunity to reach our potential and give back to others, can bring us true fulfilment.

Choosing work in which your levels of self-respect and self-assurance are high also changes the way you prioritise how you spend your days. Deriving your sense of self-worth from *within*, based on your actions and character, on being an interesting person rather than merely having accrued interesting possessions, also means you'll be far less likely to look for happiness or food for nourishment for your ego in all the wrong places, such as:

- getting blind drunk on weekends
- promiscuity and infidelity
- dropping hundreds if not thousands of dollars on retail therapy
- chasing fleeting comfort in the number of likes your photos get on Instagram
- feeling intense FOMO (fear of missing out) and dropping everything to join your friends for a drink
- complaining about everything and everyone instead of taking action.

I'm not advocating that you stop having fun and turn off that hedonist switch in your brain; heaven knows mine still flicks over from time to time. What I'm suggesting is that when you find your purpose, you're far less likely to spend a disproportionate amount of time pursuing such things, because you'll feel your time is better spent elsewhere.

'Retire into yourself as much as possible. Associate with people who are likely to improve you. Welcome those whom you are capable of improving. The process is a mutual one. People learn as they teach.'

Seneca the Younger

You have the opportunity, should you choose to take it (an enduring theme throughout this book), to climb towards the upper reaches of Maslow's pyramid.

WE'RE LIVING IN THE BEST TIMES EVER

Kevin Kelly, a renowned futurist and co-founder of *Wired* magazine, refers to the normalcy bias (the refusal to plan for, or react to, an unfolding disaster simply because it has never happened before) as the 'short-now'. We tend to base our beliefs and attitudes about the world on what we've known in our short experience. It's easy to forget that it has only been over the past century, the last 0.07 per cent of Homo sapiens' history, that we've developed automobiles, aeroplanes, computers, the internet, smartphones and other fundamentals of modern life. Life wasn't always like this, and tomorrow will be very different from today.

We should not only be grateful for the world of abundance in which we find ourselves but, building on the lessons of chapter 1, not imagine that the way things are today is the way they'll be 10 years from now. The following statistics demonstrate just how much the world can change when you take a longer view.

- The percentage of people living in absolute poverty has fallen from 53 per cent to under 17 per cent in the past 30 years.

- The United Nations Office on Drugs and Crime puts the international homicide rate at 7.6 deaths per 100 000 people (and 1.1 in Australia), a far cry from the 73 reported in 1450's Italy.

- Since 1800, global literacy has increased from 12 per cent to almost 90 per cent.

Finding something you truly believe in is key to sustainable contentment and happiness. It is also the key to doing work that truly shifts the needle, because if your work feeds your sense of self-worth and self-actualisation (those fundamental socio-cultural, emotional, intellectual and spiritual needs), then this creates a positive feedback loop. It feeds you and, as a result, you keep feeding it.

Organisational psychologist Edward Deci ran an experiment in the 1970s that demonstrated how students incentivised by money were actually less interested in working on solving given problems after they were paid. On the other hand, students who weren't incentivised by money maintained interest in solving the problems longer. Deci had stumbled on the difference between extrinsic and intrinsic motivation — that is, motivation that comes from without and from within.

In his 2011 book *Drive: The Surprising Truth About What Motivates Us*, Daniel Pink identifies autonomy, mastery and purpose as key to getting the best work out of people, providing they are paid fairly. This is where humans are at their best: they have a purpose but are also developing their abilities towards mastery in an environment offering sufficient challenge for personal growth. A 2009 study by Nakamura and Csikszentmihalyi found that psychological triggers, such as a challenge/skills ratio where tasks that are 4 per cent more challenging than our current skills can meet, strike a chord at the midline between boredom and anxiety and help us mentally get into the zone, where we do our best thinking and work. The opportunity to work autonomously in a self-managed environment where people are challenged to succeed can inspire actual, measurable change.

So, in light of all of these ideas, how do you go about finding your why, gaining autonomy and developing mastery? Remember all that dot collecting you did earlier and have been unknowingly doing your whole life? I like to use the following three steps, inspired by Simon Sinek's book *Find Your Why*:

1. Gather key stories about your life/work.
2. Identify and group common themes and patterns.
3. Draft and refine a why statement, in which you identify X (contribution) to achieve Y (impact).

When we went through this exercise as a team at Collective Campus, we effectively 'worked alone together'. First each of us was tasked with jotting down on Post-it notes as many key stories as we could remember that were pivotal to our time with the company. We then grouped the notes into common themes and extracted the key message, or the underlying reason this story resonated. From this we identified key motivators, such as impact and growth. Through multiple iterations and refinements we finally landed on a why statement that resonated with everyone:

> to unlock people's potential so that they can create more impact for humanity and lead more fulfilling lives.

From here we drilled down into our values. With a clear organisational purpose that everyone on the team helped to map, we aligned the company's why with our people's why, so it became clear not just *what* people did but why they did it. If purpose is the world's greatest performance enhancer, then my role as a leader is to inject as much of it as possible into the DNA of our company's culture.

For a comprehensive practical guide to discovering your and your team's why, check out Simon Sinek's book *Find Your Why*.

Today I no longer feel the need to live for the weekend or to numb my reality with alcohol. I barely drink anymore and look forward to Monday mornings as much as to Friday evenings.

WHAT'S THE WORST THAT COULD HAPPEN?

When Shay Namdarian, my friend and former colleague at EY, joined Collective Campus, I asked him why he walked away from the status and dollars he was enjoying in the management consulting world.

He told me that his desire to leave the corporate world was triggered a year earlier by a conversation he had with a colleague in the office kitchen. 'I asked how their day was going and the response shocked me, but it shouldn't have. It went something like, "Just counting down the days till the weekend". It was Tuesday. Only one-fifth of the work week had passed. It was at this moment that I recognised I needed to follow my passion and work with others who shared this passion.'

This incident triggered Shay's thought process, but what ultimately made him take the plunge and get past those self-doubts? *What will my friends and family think? How will I be able to afford my lifestyle? What if it doesn't work out? How can I give up a career I have invested so much time into? On and on ...*

Shay used the following questions to help light his way.

1. WHAT IS THE WORST POSSIBLE OUTCOME?

Embrace the fear—think of the absolute worst-case scenario. Most of the time this will not be as bad as you think. For Shay, it was to re-enter the corporate world if things didn't work out.

2. WHAT IS STOPPING YOU?

Perceived obligations pop up when considering this question. Are these obligations really holding you back? Human instinct encourages us to bring up reasons—often merely excuses, given we prefer to explore the path that is easiest and more comfortable. Rationalising is something we humans do well, but it often holds us back and prevents us from recognising our accountability for decisions and actions in life.

3. WHAT IS THE BEST POSSIBLE OUTCOME?

Two key impact areas are financial *and* emotional. Financially you may take a hit, but there is nothing stopping you from making some changes in your life to make it work. If you do something you love and are passionate about, the money will eventually come. Emotionally for Shay, 'it felt like shaking off handcuffs'.

4. ARE YOU SEEKING PERMISSION?

As Gary Bolles pointed out on my podcast, a key step in the process is to gain permission from an integral person in your life. This may be your partner, a family member or a close friend. Decide who you need to get permission from, then seek it.

5. WOULD YOU REGRET NOT TAKING ACTION?

If your working career ended today, would you be thrilled with the path you took? Would you regret not seizing an opportunity or following a path you had once dreamed of? Don't live with regrets, especially when you have control of your decisions.

When all else fails, summon your inner George Costanza. When confronted with the appearance of a beautiful woman in the famous Seinfeld gang's diner, George proclaims 'I used to sit here and do nothing, and regret it for the rest of the day, so now I will do the opposite, and I will do something!', before walking over to the woman and saying, 'Excuse me, I couldn't help but notice that you were looking in my direction'.

Rejection and failure are always better than cowardice and regret.

ONE MORE THING

The rewards are vastly greater when your why is a powerful one. One day in December 2017, I received the following email from an 11-year-old graduate of the Lemonade Stand program.

> Dear Steve
>
> I just wanted to let you know that I have finally got my online business up and running. It all took much longer than I thought, but it is finally live!
>
> I would never have thought I would be capable of doing anything like this if I had not done the Lemonade Stand course with you. It has opened my eyes to so many possibilities. I just wanted to thank you again for the inspiration and for helping me find this path.
>
> So, if you ever decide you would like to buy an inflatable paddle board, please take a look at my shop ... and even if you don't, please take a look anyway as I'd love to know what you think! Have a Merry Christmas and I hope 2017 is a great year for you guys.
>
> Thanks so much, Alex

Don't you just love the way he tried (successfully) to sell me on the way out? As you can imagine, I didn't have to think hard on 'What did I actually achieve or contribute today?' at the end of that particular day. I ended up buying a paddle from his site, and it's proudly displayed on a wall in our office, as a constant reminder of our why.

Call to action

1. Objectively rate yourself out of 10 across freedom, financial independence, fulfilment, fitness, and friends and family. By putting a number on these things, you can identify which aspect of your life to invest in and how work fits into this picture.

2. Apply the 'five whys' method to your reason for reading this book. You might have to do it a few times to get to the root cause, or causes, but once you're there you'll be able to solve the real underlying problem instead of apply a bandaid solution.

3. Use the 'find your why' method to help unlock your purpose. By working on something you truly believe in you'll be far more likely to stay the course than give up at the first sign of difficulty. For additional resources, visit startwithwhy.com/find-your-why.

4. Answer the questions Shay posed to help you crush your fears and excuses, and move forward with greater clarity and control.

5. Jerry Seinfeld suggests, 'If every instinct you have is wrong, then the opposite would have to be right'. Do the opposite of what you normally do and see what happens!

Chapter 4
EMBRACING YOUR WHAT

*'This action will advance me toward my goal, this
one will lead me nowhere.'*
Aristotle

When I began my entrepreneurial journey with Hotdesk, I identified what I thought was a gap in the market as more and more people transitioned from employee to freelancer. According to some sources, 40 per cent of the white collar workforce will freelance by 2020, and employees were taking advantage of growing opportunities to work flexibly and remotely.

When I wasn't straightening up my Windsor knot for my gig at Macquarie Bank, I was devouring books such as Eric Ries's *The Lean Startup* and Tim Ferriss's *The 4-Hour Work Week*. Inspired by these books, I embarked on my quest to build a minimum viable product (MVP) before quitting my day job. We'll get into specifics on the MVP later, but for now all you need to know is that most of this early effort was spent playing email ping pong with my India-based web developer. Over a few months my initial investment of $3000 in expenses led to a $150 000 capital injection, at which point I left the corporate world to work full time on building my startup.

Find your character, build a startup

In the 1987 film *Wall Street*, Lou Mannheim tells a young Bud Fox, played by Charlie Sheen, 'Man looks in the abyss, there's nothing staring back at him; at that moment, man finds his character and that's what keeps him out of the abyss'.

Entrepreneurship is a lot like this.

- You need to be thick skinned in order to survive.
- You need self-belief.
- You need to be able to accept rejection 99 times out of 100 and each time dust yourself off in order to move forward and get closer to that one 'yes'.
- You need to wake up after 'one of those days' with renewed vigour, focus and faith in the promise of a new day.
- If you fail to find your character in those dark moments, what many in entrepreneurial circles refer to as the 'trough of sorrow' or 'trough of disillusionment', you may just fall into the abyss.

I often doubted myself during the first couple of years and wondered whether I had made a grave mistake, knowing I could probably be making more money elsewhere, live more comfortably and keep up with the Joneses. But most decisions in life are reversible. I could always go back to the corporate world if I wanted to.

You do, however, need to know when to 'call it' and there is no shame, but courage, in doing so. Too many entrepreneurs get married to their idea and despite a multitude of signs pointing to the exit, they stay the course due to their emotional investment, and their talents and motivations can go to waste.

Whenever you find yourself staring into the abyss, ask yourself why you're doing what you're doing and look for that inner strength of character. You'll find that you will not only avoid the abyss, but you'll emerge with a renewed view of the world and your place in it. Whether it's a revitalised business model or a new personal path taken, you will emerge a stronger person for it.

Find your character, ask the right questions, implement your learnings and move forward.

Align your why and what

I endured two long, character-building years of absolutely devouring every piece of content I could find on entrepreneurship, marketing and sales, and I experimented relentlessly. At its peak, Hotdesk listed more than 1300 locations across Australia and Asia. As is commonly the case with two-sided marketplaces, though, it was no easy feat to build supply in lockstep with demand, and while supply (the easy bit) was rocking, demand was dwindling.

Building a *one-sided* market is hard enough. I discovered that building a two-sided marketplace is 10 times harder. Effectively, you have to align brand, distribution channels, price points and marketing efforts and grow both sides of the fence concurrently, as you can't afford too much supply with no demand, or demand with insufficient supply. Not that it can't be done. Uber, Airbnb and Deliveroo will attest to that, but for every successful marketplace, there are thousands that don't make it (Crunchbase lists more than 18000 marketplace startups globally).

After two years of learning and building out Hotdesk, I quit. My desire to invest the energy in the platform started tapering off about 12 months in, but I didn't know how to acknowledge that for what it was. So I kept on grinding away, and as employees do, I thought, 'Well, I guess this is what I'm supposed to do now, and I've taken a big risk, so I'd better keep going'.

Justifying increased investment in a decision based on cumulative prior investment, rather than objective analysis, perfectly illustrates the sunk cost fallacy. How many people has this fallacy kept from reaching their potential?

The reality was that I had little desire to become what amounted to a glorified real estate agent. There was no alignment between what I was doing and the greater purpose I believed in. To get the best out of yourself, your 'why' and 'what' need to align. The same holds true in organisations. If your employees or colleagues don't really buy into the mission of the organisation, if there's no values alignment, then they're hardly likely to give it 100 per cent. This misalignment meant it was harder to do my best work and much easier to quit.

Startups are really hard.

Award-winning author James N. Watkins once observed, 'A river cuts through rock, not because of its power, but because of its persistence'. Without alignment to your purpose, you ultimately won't persist long enough to cut through said rock. You won't get up early each morning with a spring in your step, eager to move that proverbial millimetre closer to your vision. I never regretted my Hotdesk journey, though. It was a beautiful butterfly moment that gave me a two-year personal MBA in entrepreneurship, and ultimately it helped me identify a why I could truly relate to and a what that aligned with it.

You need to trust that the journey will present you with new pathways.

Today I've fused the learnings I gained, and continue to build on every day, into the work I do with large companies that are themselves looking to become more entrepreneurial and innovative. Our mission is to unlock the potential of people working for large organisations and startups so they can create more impact and lead more fulfilling lives, something I care about deeply. For the business, this is showing up in our results and in the demeanour of my team.

How to make better decisions

Naturally you're interested in starting your own company. But is that really the answer? Could the issue be that you lack purpose, autonomy and mastery in your existing role? Could simply changing roles within the same organisation cure what ails you? Should you stay put and pursue creative or philanthropic opportunities outside of business hours?

Every day we're tasked with making decisions. Most of the time, these decisions are of minor importance (like whether or not to floss today). However, small things done consistently poorly over the long term can have a devastating impact on where you end up, whether in business or in life. It's like the power of compound interest. I'm no dentist, but it's pretty common knowledge that if every day you decide not to floss, then you're staring down the barrel of bleeding gums, halitosis and tooth decay (sorry for the mental image), not to mention the link made between flossing and cancer prevention.

Similarly, if I decide to check my email every 10 minutes it might seem like no big deal. 'It only takes a second!' But checking my email every 10 minutes, every single day, means I'm constantly distracted from my own priorities by responding to other people's demands on my time. It means that I never give my brain the space to 'get in the zone' and engage in what author Cal Newport calls 'deep work', which is where our best work is done. Over the long term this means I'm less likely to move the needle on any significant commercial or creative pursuit.

A SIMPLE FRAMEWORK FOR BETTER DECISION MAKING

How often do we truly think through our decisions rather than basing them on how we're feeling in that precise moment or on past experiences? How often do we jump to conclusions through groupthink, or choose whatever decision is easiest to make or requires the least thought, or fall victim to any one of the 100+ cognitive biases that plague our decision making?

Here I'll provide a simple framework on how we make decisions at Collective Campus. This approach works best in a team of at least three trustworthy, radically honest people who have enough experience to facilitate a constructive process.

That's not to say you can't use it when making your own decisions. I do all the time. As someone who suffers from FOMO, has a tendency to chase furry rabbits down rabbit-holes and struggles with the plethora of choices on a Thai restaurant menu, I have no choice but to use this method, and it's certainly proved a better approach than the way I've made most of my decisions during my first 30 years on this planet.

The process isn't perfect by any stretch, but it does mitigate many of the environmental and psychological pitfalls that plague decision making. It strikes a balance between making sensible, rational decisions and analysis by paralysis, something that a fast-moving, fast-growing company like ours can ill afford.

STEP 1: DECIDE WHICH DECISIONS TO MAKE

First, are you focusing on the right decision in the first place? Think about your life right now. How many decisions, both great and small, do you need to make today? I'm sure there are heaps, but how many of them are mission critical? How many of them require a great deal of effort or have major consequences?

You have choices:

- Outsource the decision where possible.
- Automate the decision if reliably repeatable.
- Make the decision now (more important).
- Delay the decision until later (less important).
- Do nothing.

Doing nothing is also a decision. People have a tendency to do nothing instead of something, but if doing nothing was put forward as an option, would you choose it? Make sure to include doing nothing on your decision-making board. Dietary requirements aside, if you had to choose between the chicken, the potato salad or the empty tray at a buffet, would you choose the empty tray? Sadly, that's what so many of us do, because it's easier than subjecting ourselves to the pain of having made what might be the wrong decision.

In my case, I've empowered my team to make most of the daily decisions and concern myself only with the big-ticket items. For example, we're exploring the establishment of a fund to support our corporate accelerator programs and we recently discussed a number of different fund structures, so it was important that I took part in this meeting. Deciding whether or not the colour of a button in an email we send out to mailing list subscribers is blue or green, not so much! I need to work *on* the business, not *in* the business.

STEP 2: MAKE A LIST (CHECK IT TWICE!)

When making such important decisions with my team, we always start with a list of options and detail the pros and cons of each to avoid cognitive biases (for more on biases see chapter 5). This is nowhere near enough, however. How often have you drawn up a list of pros and cons and by the end of it felt yourself paralysed, with just as many pros as cons on the page? You probably had no sense of which pros and cons were created equal and which more than likely weren't, and you defaulted to the path you were leaning towards originally despite the exercise you went through purely to make yourself feel better about your choice.

STEP 3: SELECT DECISION-MAKING CRITERIA AND WEIGHTING

To break out of your pro/con paralysis, determining your decision-making criteria can be helpful. For example, which key variables would underpin a positive outcome? If I'm evaluating startups to invest in, the obvious outcome being a return on investment, then I'll assess variables such as the management team's experience, traction, growth potential, uniqueness, strength of marketing strategy and so on.

When deciding between different pathways for establishing a venture fund for our corporate accelerator programs, the main variables that concerned us were time, confidence, ease and impact. We asked ourselves the following questions:

- *Time:* How long would it take us to explore and successfully establish a fund using option X?
- *Confidence:* How confident are we that we can successfully pursue option X?

- *Ease:* How easy is option X relative to other options?
- *Impact:* Does option X lend itself to creating more impact, in line with our mission, than the other options?

STEP 4: APPLY WEIGHTING

In this case, we simply applied a rating out of 10 to time, confidence and ease and a weighting of 1.1 for low impact, 1.2 for medium impact and 1.3 for high impact. This is a little arbitrary and you'll need to work out a weighting that makes sense for you and your respective decision. If you get the weighting wrong it could ultimately force you down the wrong path, so as I've stressed, having a radically honest dialogue and reaching a team consensus around these variables, ratings and weighting goes a long way. It's not about being data-driven. It's about being data-informed by pairing your professional judgement and intuition with data.

STEP 5: RATE AND DISCUSS

To avoid groupthink, I appropriate a method from agile project management called planning poker, where each person in the decision-making team privately writes down their rating out of 10 for each variable before they all reveal their ratings at the same time.

Any discrepancy greater than 1 (for example, one person selects 8 out of 10 while another selects 6 out of 10) will be discussed. Perhaps one person has more experience dealing with the nuances that underpin the option. For example, perhaps one person is more privy to how the regulations in that area might affect one of the variables.

STEP 6: REPEAT STEP 5 UNTIL CONSENSUS IS REACHED

After both parties have had an opportunity to weigh in with why they chose their ratings, we repeat step 5 until there is consensus (with a discrepancy of no more than 1 across the board); we tally up the scores, divide them by the number of participants to get the average, and apply a weighting to determine the final score and decide a way forward. It's critical that people on the decision-making team have the emotional awareness to seek truth over being 'right'. On the decision-making board shown in table 4.1, three team members (X, Y and Z) rated options (A, B and C) across three separate variables and then applied the weighting to arrive at their final scores.

Table 4.1: a decision-making board

Option	Variable 1			Avg.	Variable 2			Avg.	Variable 3			Avg.	Subtotal	Weight	Total	
	X	Y	Z		X	Y	Z		X	Y	Z					
A	9	8	8	8.3	7	8	7	7.3	6	5	6	5.66	21.26	1.2	**25.51**	☑
B	7	6	7	6.6	6	5	6	5.6	6	6	6	6	17.6	1.1	19.36	
C	5	6	5	5.3	5	5	5	5	8	7	8	8.3	18.6	1.3	24.18	

Apply a similar method to your big decisions, and where necessary pull in people you trust to help you make impartial, objective decisions. Ultimately, however, decisions about your career should be made by you alone and not influenced by people whose view of the world is different from yours.

THE INSTANT GRATIFICATION MONKEY

Tim Urban, curator of the incredibly popular *Wait But Why* blog, sees the rational decision maker in your brain as unwittingly coexisting with a pet he dubs the 'Instant Gratification Monkey' (see figure 4.1, overleaf). 'The monkey thinks only about the present, and he concerns himself entirely with maximizing the ease and pleasure of the current moment. Why would we ever use a computer for work when the internet is sitting right there waiting to be played with?' Don't let your Instant Gratification Monkey make big life decisions for you. And when all else fails, take a word of advice from entrepreneur Derek Sivers: 'If I'm not saying "hell yeah" to something then I say no'.

Figure 4.1: your Instant Gratification Monkey
Source: Tim Urban, Wait But Why (2015)

WATCH OUT FOR DECISION FATIGUE

Facebook CEO Mark Zuckerberg famously wears the same thing almost every day because he chooses not to waste his energy on such trivial decision making. Every decision we make depletes the energy we use to make more important decisions. Focusing on too many inconsequential decisions can ultimately cripple your performance.

Aim to schedule critical thinking and high-impact decision making early in the day, when your energy and willpower is at a premium (unless you didn't get much sleep after a big night out, or in, that is!). Ryan Blair, the founder of ViSalus and author of *Rock Bottom to Rock Star*, echoed these sentiments on my podcast. 'Seek simplicity. When you hear complexity, try to remove it, get it out of your life ... So [to reduce decision fatigue] just reduce the number of decisions you have to make in your life so you can focus on making quality decisions that actually have a long-term impact.'

Willpower follows a worthwhile purpose. It's much easier to *not* reach for those corn chips if you're trying to lose weight to fit into your wedding dress.

Lower barriers to entry = your opportunity

Until quite recently, setting up an eCommerce website could set you back tens of thousands of dollars, if not more. In the past 10 years, however, the cost of entry for starting up has come crashing down, thanks to the convergence of fast and affordable internet access and cloud computing. Today you can set up and maintain a website for that same eCommerce store for $29 a month, using an off-the-shelf, browser-based platform like Shopify, and cancel at any time. If you want to sell something to people who are literally on the other side of the world, all you need is an internet connection and a device. You don't have to worry much about technology infrastructure or establishing elaborate supply chains; you can outsource that stuff. Amazon Web Services' cloud platform, for example, gives you the ability to get started for free and scale up as your business grows. This supports your adaptation to changing business needs without overcommitting financially. It's a negligible cost compared with what data centres and fulfilment operations would have cost you 10 years ago to build a globally scalable business.

Take media production and distribution. I host a podcast that attracts thousands of listeners each month. Here's what I needed to get going:

- Macbook and an internet connection
- Skype (free)
- Audacity software (free)
- ECamm Call Recorder software ($40)
- GarageBand software (free)
- Logitech headset ($50).

Twenty years ago, I would have had to spend big on:

- recording studio time
- post-production costs
- distribution
- above-the-line marketing costs.

Even with a distribution deal, nowhere near as many people would have been able to tune in, as distribution would have been limited to specific geographic areas and device types. Today anyone with an internet connection can tune in to my show anywhere in the world, whether on their desktop, tablet, smartphone, smart voice assistant or smart TV or in their car (okay, maybe not in censored places like North Korea; perhaps I need to have a word with Dennis Rodman?).

'Knowledge is power.'
Sir Francis Bacon

Ninety per cent of the data in the world today was created in the past two years alone, yet instead of taking advantage of the new opportunities this revolution presents, the vast majority of people almost mindlessly consume content that others have created.

Former Google design ethicist Tristan Harris has called out the fact that sinister app design practices have us glued to our phones. Today's apps and websites have been engineered so that we maximise our screen time, and companies that manage to seize our attention are showered with profits. Harris has called our gut reactions to 'the attention economy' a 'race to the bottom of the brainstem'. He told *The Atlantic*, 'You could say that it's my responsibility to exert self-control when it comes to digital usage but that's not acknowledging that there's a thousand people on the other side of the screen whose job it is to break down whatever responsibility I can maintain'. Many people who think they control their phones are in reality controlled by them.

Phone addiction aside, if you're waiting for the 'right time' to explore entrepreneurship, then you'll be waiting a while because there's never been a better time, or a more necessary time, to develop the mindset and worldview of an entrepreneur, both of which will be critical to success in the volatile, uncertain and complex 21st century.

Lower barriers to entry have created new opportunities. Among the gigs that didn't exist in any meaningful way as recently as 15 years ago, we might include, for example, social media manager, data scientist, podcast producer, mobile app developer, anything to do with AI, anything to do with VR/AR, Uber driver, cloud architect, blogger, vlogger, SEO analyst, growth hacker, content moderator, virtual assistant and content marketer.

Beware old maps of the world

If you were to use a map from the 1500s to set sail from Europe for the beaches of Australia, then you might end up sailing in circles and growing old at sea (more likely you'd die of scurvy), because in medieval times Australia was quite literally uncharted territory and only luck or blind faith could possibly lead to its discovery.

OLD MENTAL MAPS

I once facilitated a workshop for a large law firm about the opportunities and threats the blockchain presented in the legal space. After we had introduced one another and got reasonably acquainted with the what, why and how of blockchain technology, I gave them some time to envisage applications of blockchain to their work.

Applications included taxation tracking, music royalties and real-time transaction settlements of trade on the blockchain. All plausible and all already being explored. A senior partner shot back at one of the proposed suggestions,

'Regulators would never stand for that!' But what if? What if regulation changed, as it so often does?

Did Uber put their plans on ice back in 2009 when they figured that taxi lobbies and regulators might not be exactly welcoming? No. They fought them. And look at them today. They are now one of the leading voices behind the on-demand movement (although not without their own cultural problems, which are beyond the scope of this book), which will slowly grow to influence almost every aspect of business and daily life. This movement is one of the key building blocks underpinning what prominent futurist and O'Reilly Media founder, Tim O'Reilly, calls the business model of the future.

In order to truly see and chase opportunities, we often need to understand and redraw our mental maps of the world.

When I left the high-flying world of investment banking, I took a massive step back in terms of remuneration (we're talking an 80 per cent pay cut here) and supposed social status to launch my own startup. But I was okay with that because I had redrawn my mental map in relation to my contentment and sense of self-worth.

Yes, like most people, I desire financial security and to live a comfortable lifestyle, but once I've got the basics, what's more important to me is doing work that matters—work that gives me freedom, growth and fulfilment. If you do important work, in time the money flows. I might have based my sense of self-worth on metrics such as how much money I made right now (which is often the most obvious and convenient measure, and therefore the one we default to as a society). But then I never would have been able to make that change and take the pay cut that gave me the runway (cash flow and time) I needed to pursue the opportunities that emerged years later.

Large companies are being disrupted by startups with a fraction of the resources. The former are ignoring the opportunities over the horizon because the market isn't big enough today or the technology isn't good enough today. To see how that story often turns out, refer to Blockbuster Video (see chapter 1).

If I had taken the investment I got and maintained the personal expenses I had while at Macquarie Bank, then my two-year runway with Hotdesk would have been slashed to three months, and no doubt I would soon have been back with the overwhelmingly indoctrinated at a large firm in order to survive. And I would have rationalised that 'I tried and it didn't work, but at least I gave it a shot and now, with no regrets, I'll just move on with my corporate career'. Such is the folly of the human mind, rationalising our own defeats. Interestingly, most perpetrators of theft or violence also rationalise. Whether we're doing harm to ourselves or to others, rationalising can often be our own worst enemy. Watch out for it!

I saw this play out recently when recruiting for Collective Campus.

Self-defeatist salary expectations and blunted risk appetite

We were on the hiring trail, looking for a customer relationship manager (a fancy title for sales rep), a product manager and a growth hacker (a fancy word for a really good, experiment-driven marketer). So many people I spoke to seemed to hate their existing jobs. When I asked why they wanted to join the company, they said it was because they loved what we stood for and wanted the opportunity to create real impact. In many cases, though, when the salary question was raised, they shot back with something like, 'Well, I'm on $150 000 now at [insert big corporate], so ideally I'd love a small increase, but I'm happy to start on that if necessary'.

We're effectively a startup, or an early stage 'rabbit' (real actual business building interesting things), which is to say we're a profitable, self-funded business that isn't reliant on external venture capital merely to survive. If you want to do game-changing work, in an emerging space, where you have the opportunity to inject your DNA into the company's, you'll usually have to take a step back in remuneration. Sometimes you can't; you might have other commitments (financial obligations and dependants). We'll explore ways around that later, but in most cases what's called for isn't more money but a new mental map of the world.

I remember climbing the corporate ladder, jumping from company to company, with salary the number one metric I cared about. If you think you need a 10 per cent pay rise to be comfortable and to justify a move, you'll limit your opportunities as starting a company or joining a fledgling startup is unlikely to generate great monetary rewards during its early days. But the trade-offs to look for are autonomy, learning and growth, meaningful relationships and meaningful work. If you make that sacrifice but end up without these things, and still find yourself playing politics more than creating value, then take a moment to reflect on said sacrifice.

Of course, you can join a well-funded startup or one that's four or five years into its lifecycle and command a six-figure salary. Your role and influence will likely be different from that of a super early-stage hire, but you might still reap the benefit and find fulfilment.

When the question of salary comes up, consider the words of the great Roman philosopher and statesman Seneca the Younger:

> 'It is not the man who has too little, but the man who craves more, that is poor. What does it matter how much a man has laid up in his safe, or in his warehouse, how large are his flocks and how fat his dividends, if he covets his neighbour's property, and reckons, not his past gains, but his hopes of gains to come? Do you ask what is the proper limit to wealth? It is, first, to have what is necessary, and, second, to have what is enough.'

In that round at Collective Campus, as in the past, I hired people who willingly took a 25 to 50 per cent pay cut to join us. Of course, there's also the promise that bonuses, regular salary increments and ownership in the company will kick in as quickly as possible to repay them extrinsically, but intrinsically it's about creating an environment in which they can find self-esteem and self-actualisation, an environment where their voices are heard, where they can do meaningful work and where they can build a business within our business—as we did with Lemonade Stand, our children's entrepreneurship program.

Another common misconception about starting a business is that it's 'too risky'. By understanding a risk you can learn how to mitigate it and so take calculated risks. Risk is simply a by-product of information asymmetry. For example, borrowers have much better information about their ability to repay a loan than lenders. As a result, they will be charged interest by the lenders to offset the ensuing risk. So in order to reduce your risk and make better decisions, you need to collect more information, quickly and cheaply. I'll elaborate on how you do this in chapter 8.

Is entrepreneurship the answer?

Finally, while it's easy to get drunk on the elixir of overnight success stories—say, Elon Musk waxing lyrical on yet another entrepreneurial venture (at the time of writing he's on the management team or board of Tesla, SpaceX, SolarCity, Neuralink, Open AI, the Musk Foundation, the XPRIZE Foundation and The Boring Company). The truth is that entrepreneurship is one of the most challenging pursuits one can embark upon. *Shark Tank* investor Lori Greiner quipped,

'Entrepreneurs are the only people who will work 80 hours a week to avoid working 40 hours a week'. I have my own views on the work-yourself-to-death narrative plaguing many startup ecosystems today, but Greiner's underlying point is true: you'll likely work at least twice as hard for half the reward, at least during the first few years.

Is entrepreneurship *really* the answer? If the only thing you want to do is make money, then you've got a much better chance of doing so—at least in the short term—by taking the more conventional path. Not everyone is cut out for it. As the following shortlist suggests, there are plenty of viable alternatives that just might offer you a shorter path to the contentment or fulfilment you're seeking.

1. Join an existing company where the environment aligns with your values.
2. Change roles within your existing company.
3. Assume a similar role in a different industry.
4. Take up learning and creative pursuits outside of work.
5. Change careers (without starting a new business).
6. Build a 'side hustle'.
7. Change your mindset and reframe your source of contentment.
8. Focus on building and nurturing relationships and extracurricular interests.
9. Move to part-time or contract work, and spend more time exploring life.
10. Become an intrapreneur.
11. Embrace creative freelancing.

Let's explore each of these options.

1. JOIN AN EXISTING COMPANY WHERE THE ENVIRONMENT ALIGNS WITH YOUR VALUES

Sheryl Sandberg, Facebook's COO and author of *Lean In*, didn't set her sights on starting her own show, despite having no doubt that she could. Instead she decided to join the up-and-coming startup Facebook. Similarly, my colleague, Shay Namdarian, on leaving his consulting career at global management consultancy Capgemini, didn't go off to start another entrepreneurial venture. Despite already having two modestly successful side hustles in Barnaby Socks and W Time Watches, he decided to join Collective Campus.

A quick search of the AngelList jobs directory showed me that more than 25 000 startups were hiring at the time of writing. Finally, who's to say you need to join a startup and not a more established or mature company that offers these incentives?

DETERMINE YOUR FIT FOR COMPANY

Here are some questions you might like to ask during the hiring process and of past or current employees:

- What's the culture like?
- What do you like most about working here?
- How are people empowered to try new things?
- How are people incentivised, aside from monetary rewards?
- What are the company's values?
- What is its purpose?
- What does success look like to you?
- Can I meet potential colleagues before I accept an offer?
- Where do you see the company in three years?
- What's your staff turnover rate?
- What's one story about the company that you're most proud of?
- If I have an idea, what next step can I take?
- What does the lifecycle of an employee's idea look like?
- Do you give people funding or time to explore things outside their core position description?
- Is the organisation open or siloed?

Such questions will give you a feel for the company's why, how actively that why is practised and celebrated, whether you'd fit the culture, and whether the company is serious about empowering its people to drive innovation and influence outcomes, or whether they just want you to be the proverbial cog in the machine. I'm guessing one of the reasons you picked up this book is because that's just what you *don't* want.

---

2. CHANGE ROLES WITHIN YOUR EXISTING COMPANY

We often default to making radical decisions when we're feeling emotionally overwhelmed or stuck. One in three Australian marriages ends in divorce, often because one or both partners sought something, whether emotional, financial, physical or intellectual, they weren't getting from their partner. Rather than talk these things through and seek reconciliation, many go looking for a quick fix outside of their marriage.

The point I want to make here is that we often don't need to look very far for what we're seeking. It's usually right in front of us. On our tendency to look for the silver bullet solution, Seneca the Younger wrote, 'If you really want to escape the things that harass you, what you're needing is not to be in a different place but to be a different person'. Perhaps being a different person within your company will do the trick.

You could always explore one of the following options before deciding to make the jump.

LATERAL MOVE

Making a sideways move or transfer to a new role in your organisation or to a new organisation with a similar title, pay and responsibility is effectively a lateral move and can pay off in the future. Early in my professional career I made three lateral moves that gave me a lot of experience and credibility, expanded my networks and opened previously locked doors.

First, while at the Victorian Auditor-General's Office (VAGO), I made an internal transfer from what I felt was the drab world of financial audit to the up-and-coming world of IT security risk, giving me a greater appreciation of technology stacks, cybersecurity and privacy risks. It was much more interesting for me at the time, even though it meant the same pay and a similar title. I then used my experience at VAGO to make a lateral move to EY's IT Risk department, which opened the door to working with large Fortune 500 organisations such as Toyota, BHP, Newcrest Mining and Air Liquide, exposing me to the inner workings of a world that would become critical to the work I would do in the corporate innovation space years later.

Lateral moves can also be a great way to boost your income. My move to earned me a 25 per cent pay rise; my lateral move to Macquarie Bank two years later earned me a 35 per cent pay rise. That additional income gives you more breathing space to invest in your side hustle and/or other creative pursuits.

BACKWARDS MOVE

Sometimes you might need to take one step backward to move two steps forward. For example, while I was working at Macquarie Bank I explored a transfer to Macquarie Capital. It would have meant my stepping back from a senior analyst role to a junior analyst role, but it would have brought me closer to becoming a fully-fledged investment banker, an option I was considering at the time. Depending on your goal, a 'backward' step with regard to your title and/or salary might be essential, because anything that brings you closer to your goals is in reality a forward step even though it may not seem like it at the time.

PROMOTION

It's a no-brainer that taking on more responsibility and greater decision-making authority will increase your sense of control and fulfilment. Of course, getting promoted is easier said than done, but if you're not happy with where you are right now, and a promotion might alleviate some of your stress, then perhaps you need to have a conversation with your manager or employer around how you might channel your efforts into earning that promotion in your current company.

BEWARE THE DANGLING CARROT

The way incentives and social structures work at most large, established organisations sadly rests in large part on what I call 'dangling the carrot'. You're told that if you meet your key performance indicators (KPIs) at annual or twice-yearly formal performance reviews, you'll earn a bonus or raise. This keeps you going above and beyond to meet those KPIs.

If you're lucky, meeting your KPIs will be rewarded with a promotion, but there is no guarantee of this. Many companies forgo promotions, pointing to external economic factors, internal restructures and other circumstances 'outside our control'. Sometimes a promotion will boost your existing salary by 5 per cent to 20 per cent. How much extra fulfilment or life satisfaction does that actually buy you? More money, a fancy new title, a more expensive business suit and a first-class airport lounge pass don't in themselves signify that you have fulfilled your potential. As hedge fund manager Ray Dalio says, 'Don't confuse the trappings of success with success itself'.

NEW DEPARTMENT

Perhaps you found yourself in a financial audit role out of university, after having decided to study accounting when you were just 17, almost a decade before your frontal cortex—the part of your brain responsible for executive function and longterm planning—is fully online. Now you realise that you tend to thrive through helping people rather than assisting large organisations to comply with regulations such as Sarbanes–Oxley (regulations that often give organisations a way to demonstrate that they're 'doing the right thing' while exploiting every loophole in the book). Perhaps a move into your organisation's Human Resources department will have you feeling more energised and fulfilled. Don't just mindlessly accept where you are as where you should be. You can change where you are. You always have a choice.

As Ryan Blair told me, when reflecting on his mom falling into a coma and his son being diagnosed with autism, the best way to dig yourself out of a hole is to take affirmative action. It sounds simple, but the vast majority of people fall into a fatalistic 'why me?' or 'this is the way things are' or 'this is just the way I am' mentality, and action is not part of the narrative. It's easier to rationalise than take action but it makes for an unfulfilling life.

NEW SKILLS

To make the move between departments or to access new opportunities in an organisation, you probably need to pick up some new skills.

Today that's never been easier. There are countless online courses available for next to nothing on virtually any topic you're interested in.

No doubt your organisation has training budgets you can take advantage of. However, many organisations will approve training requests for education only where they align with your current role and building your continuing professional education (CPE) credits. If your boss isn't willing to support your mid- to longer term goals, but expects you to work tirelessly to further *their* goals, then you probably need to reassess whether they are the kind of person you want to work for. This is especially true at a time when becoming adaptable and learning about different, emerging skill-sets outside your core duties will benefit your employer as well as you. If they don't recognise this, then consider reaching for the eject button.

3. ASSUME A SIMILAR ROLE IN A DIFFERENT INDUSTRY

Don't throw those professional qualifications out just yet. Perhaps the problem is not the type of work you're doing but where you're doing it. Different industries operate with different sets of values. The culture of a government department, for example, is quite different from that of, say, a management consultancy. In my time in government, I quickly tired of the slow-moving, bureaucratic nature of the office. They say you are the sum of the five people you spend the most time with, and I was convinced that most people I worked with were simply there because it was a secure government job. They could 'work' 9 to 5 and not a minute more (being physically present and working are not the same thing), and they were paid reasonably well given how unchallenging their jobs were. Ultimately, they lacked ambition and shied away from tension and adversity.

This was not a place where I could see myself growing. When I made the move to EY, I found myself surrounded by more ambitious and curious people who more often than not were reading white papers on emerging developments in, say, artificial intelligence, as opposed to reading *OK!* magazine or some such celebrity gossip rag.

Moving to EY offered me learning opportunities and a work-hard, play-hard culture that in my mid-to-late twenties suited me to a tee. Before you change roles, ask yourself whether it might be your organisation or your industry that's bringing you down. Have you considered a startup, a small business, professional services, publicly listed companies or government? Have you considered different vertical markets? Before you make a decision, inform yourself of your options and determine whether one or more might offer a feasible alternative and give you what you're seeking in entrepreneurship.

4. TAKE UP LEARNING AND CREATIVE PURSUITS OUTSIDE OF WORK

You're probably familiar with Google's (former) 20 per cent rule, which had permitted staff to spend 20 per cent of their time exploring side projects, based on the company's belief that the other 80 per cent of Googlers' time would then be used more effectively. A recent study by San Francisco State University psychology professor Dr Kevin Eschleman found that employees with outside hobbies feel more relaxed and in control.

According to Hiut Denim Co, side projects need to be low risk, low pressure and a labour of love.

I spent my last year at EY (Ernst & Young at the time) pursuing a side project that definitely met these conditions, when I co-founded a heavy metal night called Madhouse (named after the Anthrax song of the same name, for the headbangers who might be reading this). On the nights we tanked, fewer than 10 people showed up, whereas up to 150 would attend when we'd partnered up with a concert promoter to host the official after-party for a concert. We hosted after-parties for bands such as Alestorm and Cannibal Corpse, the latter having made a cameo appearance in Jim Carrey's *Ace Ventura*!

It was low risk. We struck a deal with a venue, who provided the space, sound system and drinks, making their money on the bar. We provided the marketing and the music, and made our money on the door after a venue minimum was reached, de-risking the partnership for them and leaving us several hundred dollars out of pocket on quiet nights.

Despite that, it was low pressure. I could still pay my bills if and when it failed. And it was a labour of love. I've been a heavy metal fan since I was 13. I got to DJ, MC and occasionally dance around the venue madly in a straitjacket and Eddie mask (that's Iron Maiden's undead mascot).

I also learned a lot about marketing from this gig, such as the value of partnerships with different players in your value chain. In our case, that meant DJs, bands, concert promoters and venues. During the time I hosted Madhouse, I felt more content at EY than I usually did, because I had a creative outlet that helped me recover psychologically and affirmed for me that there was more to life than just the grind of EY, that I was more than just another suit, that I had my own identity. It gave me licence to see myself as something of an enigmatic, Bruce Wayne type of character who suited up by day to consult to Fortune 500 companies but tore off his button-down shirt to reveal the Megadeth T-shirt beneath and DJ'd in dark clubs by night. That's how I liked to look at it; others might not have agreed, though I've no idea why.

While I never understood in those years why artists I admired, such as Mötley Crüe drummer Tommy Lee, would turn their backs on rock 'n' roll to go off and make hip hop and electro records, DJing at clubs in his spare time, today I get it. He got tired of playing a part, of recycling the same songs, night in, night out, for years on end. He needed another outlet, which was paradoxically one of the reasons why he decided to return to the band after a hiatus of several years.

Perhaps that's what you need too?

5. CHANGE CAREERS (WITHOUT STARTING A NEW BUSINESS)

Today this is no longer simply a choice you can make; it's more a matter of whether you're proactive or reactive about it. Long gone are the days of working for the same company for the whole of your career. A recent LinkedIn study found that US college graduates make an average of four job changes by the time they're 32! Maybe you'd rather not be stuck behind a desk and would prefer the great outdoors. If you want to meet more people, maybe you'd be better off in travel and hospitality? Sometimes career changes work out, sometimes they don't (just ask Michael Jordan about his foray into baseball's minor leagues in the mid nineties). But don't resign yourself to one line of work.

For TED speaker and author of *How to Be Everything*, Emilie Wapnick, who guested on the *Future Squared* podcast, the question we hear as children, 'What do you want to be when you grow up?', is problematic because it implies we can only be one thing. But we can be many things over the course of our lifetime, she insists. She has in fact coined a term for it: *multi-potentialite*.

If you feel like you've derived as much as you can from a particular line of work and it no longer leaves you feeling challenged, fulfilled or content, there's nothing wrong with leaving that profession in pursuit of something different. Remember the sunk cost fallacy and stop throwing good money and good energy after bad just because you've invested so much already. Past investment in a toxic relationship is hardly a good reason to stick around.

6. BUILD A 'SIDE HUSTLE'

Blogger and speaker Chris Guillebeau defines a side hustle as a way to make money without quitting your main job. It creates options, and the more options you have, the greater your sense of freedom and control.

In my mid twenties, I scratched my journalistic itch by becoming a freelance writer on the side for *Faster Louder*, an Australian online music publication. At the time, it paid me only in double passes to concerts and access to rock stars for interviews, which was more than enough for me. It created additional opportunities too, because while I didn't build a career as a music journalist, it laid the foundation for the podcasting, blogging and book writing I would do years later.

Your side hustle can stay a secondary interest, like my writing, or become your full-time gig, but relentlessly experimenting on the side is surely one of the more prudent paths for corporate employees looking to make the leap. Remaining gainfully employed and drawing a salary not only takes the financial pressure off but gives you a steady stream of income to invest into your side hustle. It will also show you that though you may have your shit sorted out in an established company, building something from scratch is an entirely different proposition with its own set of challenges.

Without knowing which options are really worth pursuing on both an extrinsic and an intrinsic level, you should start with an exploration mindset. Only once you've landed on something worth doubling down on will you want to consider turning your side hustle into your main gig. But remember, exploration never stops.

It's no different in the world outside work. On determining when to stop and exploit an opportunity, *Future Squared* guest and author of *Algorithms to Live By*, Brian Christian, offers a very specific formula: 'If you want the best odds of getting the best apartment, spend 37 per cent of your apartment hunt (eleven days, if you've given yourself a month for the search) noncommittally exploring options. Leave the checkbook at home; you're just calibrating. But after that point, be prepared to immediately commit, deposit and all, to the very first place you see that beats whatever you've already seen. This is not merely an intuitively satisfying compromise between looking and leaping. It is the provably optimal solution'.

7. CHANGE YOUR MINDSET AND REFRAME YOUR SOURCE OF CONTENTMENT

Many people define success purely based on criteria such as salary or title, and see anything short of this as failure. This is dangerous on at least two levels:

- When we reach it, we're still unhappy (this is the arrival fallacy, which I'll explain next).
- It also closes the door on other pursuits that might bring us happiness while in the short term not meeting our conventional view of success.

The amygdala is the primal part of our brain responsible for fear detection and our survival instincts. It is constantly on the lookout for negative experiences and stores them in our long-term memory *almost immediately*. On the other hand, we need to be aware of positive experiences for *more than 12 seconds* to store them in our long-term memory. Rick Hansen, author of *Hardwiring Happiness*, describes the brain as 'like Velcro for negative experiences but Teflon for positive ones'.

How might we combat this?

APPRECIATE WHAT YOU DO HAVE

Epicurus said that the things we really need are in reality few and easy to come by, but the things we can imagine are infinite, and if we build our notions of success around them we will never be satisfied. 'Do not spoil what you have by desiring what you have not,' was his advice.

Almost 2400 years later, we still tend to focus on what's missing from our lives, rather than what's right. A 2001 study published in the *Review of General Psychology*, 'Bad is Stronger than Good', concluded that negative experiences or the fear of them have a greater impact on people than positive experiences. 'Bad emotions, bad parents, and bad feedback have more impact than good ones.'

By paying more deliberate attention to all the good in our lives, we are less likely to be ambushed by irritation when the train keeps us waiting a few minutes, and we might actually take it in our stride because low and behold, we now have a little more time to be alone with our thoughts, to read an extra few pages of that book or chat with a friend. Here's a powerful question that came to me during an early morning kettlebell workout:

> What do you take for granted that, if it disappeared from your life, you would work incredibly hard to get back?

When I ask myself this question, my mind quickly rattles off a number of answers, including my health, professional and personal relationships, financial stability and freedom. That last one is worth emphasising because I now enjoy freedom in my work and I worked incredibly hard to build it. My perception of that freedom, like most things we enjoy, can quickly shift from appreciation to expectation—something motivational guru Tony Robbins warns against—which is of course one of the reasons many relationships fail.

By asking myself this question often, I don't lose sight or appreciation of what I do have in my life, what I have achieved. It is just one way I can help myself stay present and avoid the frustration of constantly shifting goal-posts.

REFRAME WHAT YOU DO

Perhaps you don't truly appreciate the difference or contribution you're making. Perhaps your employer has done a lousy job of communicating this and sharing stories.

If you're a garbage collector, it's easy to simply leave it at that. But you help keep our roads clean so children have somewhere to play. You play an important role in public health and social good, reducing the risk of preventable diseases. You perform a social service that not many people want to do.

We *all* contribute in some way, even though it might not always be obvious to us and it's easier to be self-deprecating. Identify how you're contributing and embrace that, and if, after genuine analysis, you're *still* struggling to identify how you're adding value, then perhaps it really is time for a change.

In his *Moral Letters to Lucilius*, Seneca wrote, 'What difference does it make how much there is laid away in a man's safe or in his barns, how many head of stock he grazes or how much capital he puts out at interest, if he is always after what is another's and only counts what he has yet to get, never what he has already'.

In our own time, Stephen Covey, in his bestseller *The 7 Habits of Highly Effective People*, recommends that we live a balanced, principle-centred life, rather than one based on too much attachment to work, money, family, friends, religion or pleasure. Firas Zahabi, a renowned mixed martial arts trainer to UFC champions such as Georges St-Pierre, was influenced heavily by Covey's book and insists that living a principle-centred life has helped keep him grounded and operating from a place of empowering reason, rather than debilitating emotion.

Perhaps it's not a change of work that you need, but a change of mindset.

THE ARRIVAL FALLACY

In his book *Happier*, Tal Ben-Shahar introduced the term *arrival fallacy* to refer to constantly shifting goal-posts that undermine declarations such as, 'If I can make an extra $20 000 a year, *then* I'll be happy', 'If I can get promoted to Partner, *then* I'll be happy', 'If I can just qualify for the Olympic track team, *then* I'll be happy'. The thing is that the high associated with the achievement of such goals is fleeting, and often pushes people to seek out distraction, often through mind-altering substances and experiences, in order to achieve comparable highs.

It's why rock stars, movie stars and athletes often find themselves depressed after reaching the pinnacle in their fields. They look around and think, 'Is this it?', and seek the dopamine highs of achievement through substance abuse. In *Black Vinyl, White Powder*, Simon Napier-Bell says 'most rock stars get hooked [on heroin] in order to escape a wretched existence, which for rock artists often means normal life as opposed to [the high of] being on-stage'. Rockers such as former KISS drummer Peter Criss have shared their own struggles to come down after performing. As clichéd as it sounds, Ben-Shahar concludes that 'it's the journey not the destination that teaches lessons, reveals simple pleasures, brings new people into our lives and instils in us a genuine, internal sense of contentment'.

Remember this the next time you're striving to kick one through those ever-shifting goal-posts.

ROCK STARDOM AND THE NEGATIVITY BIAS

A now-classic case study of this phenomenon can be found in the experience of Dave Mustaine, founder of the successful, platinum album–selling, heavy-metal band Megadeth.

Mustaine was an original member of Metallica but was kicked out of the band in 1983 for being a wild drunk (even though the band's self-imposed nickname was Alcoholica and co-founder and vocalist James Hetfield would later check into rehab to put his life back together, as related in the unflinching 2001 documentary *Some Kind of Monster*).

On being told he was out of the band Mustaine asked what time his flight back to California left, only to be told by bandmates that he wasn't flying home at all but was booked on a bus, a transcontinental journey that would take at least four days. And that the bus was leaving in an hour.

Mustaine wasn't beaten, though, and as Metallica's star ascended, he quickly put together his own band, along with now revered bass player Dave Ellefson. Megadeth would become one of the most successful and popular metal bands of all time, staking a claim as one of the big four of thrash metal alongside Anthrax, Slayer and, of course, Metallica.

Megadeth would sell more than 25 million albums worldwide and earn platinum certification for five of its 15 albums. However, the truth was that Metallica was way more commercially successful, having sold 110 million albums worldwide. This tore Mustaine up inside, until he quite literally drugged himself to death: after a heroin overdose his heart stopped for several minutes, but he was brought back to life by paramedics.

It would be almost thirty years before Mustaine would officially bury the hatchet, joining his former bandmates on stage in San Francisco in 2011, as part of Metallica's 30th anniversary celebrations.

8. FOCUS ON BUILDING AND NURTURING RELATIONSHIPS AND EXTRACURRICULAR INTERESTS

In his best-selling book of 2017, *Principles: Life and Work*, hedge fund manager Ray Dalio proposes that 'meaningful work + meaningful relationships = happiness'. Perhaps it's not meaningful work that you're lacking but meaningful relationships?

Human beings have six fundamental needs: social, physical, emotional, intellectual, sexual and love. You can satisfy many of these needs at work (although you might want to be very careful with one of them). But if you're not quite having the deep intellectual conversations or emotional connections you feel you need, whether in or outside the office, working on expanding these, rather than changing jobs, might be the cure for what ails you.

You might seek to give more to others, whether at work (by organising a fundraiser) or outside it (by volunteering). Often employers will actively support staff who take time off to contribute to such initiatives, especially if it can be traced back to the company (yes, I know, such corporate social responsibility efforts can seem transparently self-serving, but the rewards for you can be all the same).

Like side hustles and creative pursuits away from work, developing meaningful relationships can change the way you see your full-time gig, and of course the way you feel about and approach each day.

9. MOVE TO PART-TIME OR CONTRACT WORK, AND SPEND MORE TIME EXPLORING LIFE

You might be considering part-time or contract work, where the pressure to perform isn't quite as high and you can carve out more time and/or money to explore entrepreneurship.

Part-time work should free up more time without your sacrificing a stable source of income. Contract work, whether part time or full time, tends to pay more per hour than a permanent gig, but by its nature it is finite, with an end date. You are more or less freed from having to deal with the politics of a large organisation and will spend less time thinking about your day job after hours.

For the first seven months of Collective Campus, I took on a two-day-a-week contract with KPMG's innovation team in Melbourne. If you have considerable work experience and are willing to make some minor lifestyle adjustments, this level of commitment could amount to more than enough. As an aside, my time at KPMG also reminded me why I left the corporate world in the first place and made me even hungrier to ensure the Campus' survival.

A WORD OF WARNING ON CONTRACT GIGS

Contract work pays well. But note that there is often a ceiling to how much you can earn and how much intrinsic reward you can derive from contract gigs. There is also limited job security and a 'no play, no pay' reality to contract work: if you call in sick or for other reasons need to take a few days off, you won't be paid.

Use contract work as a means to an end rather than an end in itself.

---

10. BECOME AN INTRAPRENEUR

According to strategy consultancy Strategy&, the 1000 largest publicly listed corporate R&D spenders amassed a total of US$701 billion on R&D in 2017. Furthermore, research firm IDC predicted a US$1.2 trillion spend on digital transformation technologies worldwide in 2017. That spend alone is more than Australia's gross national product. This doesn't even account for culture change and capability-lifting initiatives that companies are embarking on to help them better navigate change.

That's a lot of money that organisations are spending on innovation and transformation.

It's also your opportunity.

So you've got the desire to create, to innovate, to explore how emerging technologies might apply in your industry and perhaps to build something from the ground up that you can point to later and say, 'I did that'. Or maybe you just want to enjoy what is often the most rewarding part—the journey, and all of the learning and growth that comes with it.

Whatever the impetus, today most large companies will have some kind of innovation function. But, having worked in the space of corporate innovation for a number of years, I will say that few have a legitimate innovation function and that many fall within the boundaries of what I call 'innovation theatre' (a topic for another book), so choose your organisation wisely.

Look at metrics such as the percentage of revenues the company generated this year from products that didn't exist five years ago. What is their internal process for empowering innovation across the organisation? Is there a budget for this? Are ideas not only encouraged but turned into experiments? How many experiments did they run last year? Is the culture open and agile and fast, or is it slow and bureaucratic? Does the company have a track record of partnering and/or otherwise investing in startups? Perhaps speak to some former employees with job titles involving 'innovation' and ask them for their thoughts. Determine if the job title was legitimate or simply token.

Before taking a gig as an 'innovation strategist' or 'chief disruptor', you'll want to be fairly confident that your role won't be marginalised, that the position wasn't created to demonstrate to the Board that the company is investing in innovation.

If it is a legitimate operation, you will find yourself with:

- access to budget and time
- opportunities to experiment with your ideas
- opportunities to partner with startups
- opportunities to learn about the methods that underpin entrepreneurship.

Some organisations are also realising that their most entrepreneurial talent will leave, so they're seeding them with investment so if they do leave, they can at least throw their weight behind the employee and gain some financial exposure to their venture.

The big plus? You're spending other people's money and are backed by the resources, domain expertise, distribution channels, assets and networks of a large company. Not a bad place to be if, and only if, those capabilities are being leveraged and not underutilised.

What's the downside?

- The mothership might deem that anything you work on while at the company is their intellectual property.
- You might find yourself on the wrong side of priority and resource reallocations as circumstances surrounding the company, both internally and externally, change.
- You might be limited as to the kinds of ideas you can explore—for example, only those that are strategically aligned with the mothership (which is fair enough).
- You might find yourself spending more time playing politics and trying to win buy-in to do stuff than actually doing stuff.
- The financial payoff if you strike oil is unlikely to be anywhere near what it would be for your own, independent venture.

Still, it's worth exploring whether you want to strike a balance between entrepreneur and employee, and try to incorporate the best of both worlds. Perhaps start by browsing innovative company indices. Maybe the organisation you work for right now has an innovation function or process. Engage with it, and see if it's anything more than just smoke and mirrors.

11. EMBRACE CREATIVE FREELANCING

Organisations are transitioning from closed and insular to open and collaborative structures, from long-term employment arrangements based on loyalty to the company to short-term stints based on current need. This phenomenon, together with (or due to) the globalisation of today's economy thanks in no small part to the internet, has opened the door to the gig or freelance economy. According to Upwork, one-third of both the Australian and US workforces do some sort of freelancing, and this number is set to rise.

If you've got skills and the ability to market yourself online through platforms such as Upwork, Freelancer, Fiverr or Expert360, then you've got a distribution channel to potential financial freedom and fulfilment, particularly if, like most people, you enjoy variety and want to perform creative or intellectual work.

Web development, graphic and UI design, copy writing and blogging, consulting, putting together financial risk management frameworks, driving for Uber or Deliveroo, performing recruitment functions, doing PR or even developing a smart contract—you'll find no shortage of opportunities, both locally and globally, online. Like most third-party platforms, it's not a matter of just creating a profile on a freelancing platform and then watching the job offers stream in. As with launching crowdfunding campaigns on Kickstarter, you need to promote your presence on the platform effectively in order to build up a steady stream of recurring income.

You might at first find it difficult to compete with millions of registered freelancers jockeying for position globally. Like listing an apartment on Airbnb, or selling stuff on eBay, initially buyers might be hesitant to deal with someone who has no reviews or testimonials behind them. When browsing listings on Airbnb, I've often passed over the opportunity to stay at, say, an apparently impeccably presented apartment in the centre of town because of an overwhelming sense of uncertainty. But people *will* take a chance on you if you try hard enough, and as the positive reviews slowly start trickling in you'll find that the momentum will build, as will confidence in your abilities. If you've already got a solid portfolio of work and client testimonials to point to, then you should find it easier to make a walking start.

Freelancing, like contracting, comes with few strings attached for buyers, who can usually cancel engagements at any time and don't have to make contributions to your retirement fund. Typically they don't pay you for sick days, maternity or paternity leave, or annual holidays. You need to ensure that you get your house in order and make contributions towards your financial freedom and future, rather than just living hand to mouth on whatever gigs you manage to secure.

If you really enjoy being in the trenches of creative work in particular *and* you can handle the responsibility of managing your own affairs, then freelancing might be the path for you. If you can justify paying a virtual assistant $10 an hour to support your work, do it.

On the other hand, if you're creative or enjoy getting on the tools, entrepreneurship might end your fun. Do you enjoy designing? Do you love coding? Do you prefer the more creative aspects of your work? Is this where you truly get into flow and feel fulfilled and buzzing once you're done? If so, entrepreneurship might not be for you. Especially during the early stages, entrepreneurship calls for you to wear many hats. You will do the creative work, but you'll no doubt also have marketing, sales, legal, bookkeeping, operational and customer support duties.

If you enjoy some early success and build a small team around you, then your focus will need to shift towards leadership, business development and strategy. As the business grows, your role as a leader will be to work *on* the business, not *in* the business, which means less, if not *no* creative work, and more time running the show and drawing the best out of your team. Is this something you'll find fulfilling?

In a delightful blog post titled 'If Management is the Only Way Up, We're All F***'d', Moz founder Rand Fishkin put it like this: 'Our corporate culture and the world of "business" has created the expectation that unless you manage people, your influence, salary, benefits, title, and self-worth won't increase...basically, if you love getting stuff done and doing a great job at it, you should be a contributor (not a people manager)'.

If you still want to 'be your own boss', then consider bringing on board someone who has the capacity to lead and free you up to do a little more of the creative work you enjoy. A classic example is Steve Wozniak and Steve Jobs, the former a techie, the latter a leader. Whatever the case, as the business grows, you might find yourself transitioning from doing the coding to overseeing and managing a team of coders.

In the 2015 biopic on Steve Jobs, featuring the delightful Seth Rogen as Wozniak, Steve Jobs made the distinction between Wozniak and himself by arguing that while Wozniak might play an instrument, Steve plays the orchestra.

That's essentially what your job is as an entrepreneur, as a team leader — to play the orchestra. Whether you start out as a tech co-founder or as the business guy, success will necessitate that you do less instrument playing and more orchestra playing. Are you happy with that as the price of success?

Entrepreneurship is not easy. If you truly derive fulfilment from creative work, why not just explore freelancing? Building up a credible profile as a freelancer means you will be able to do nothing but creative work, choose your projects, work on a variety of them and get paid. You won't be beholden to anyone or have to pay staff (or face sleepless nights when unable to do so). Once you're done with a project you can move on to the next fresh challenge.

As Guy Kawasaki said in *The Art of the Start*, entrepreneurship isn't a job title, it's a state of mind. Perhaps this state of mind is more nature than nurture. Some people have a less active amygdala, which lowers their fear and anxiety signals and makes them much more predisposed to taking risks. How are you wired?

DON'T JUMP TO CONCLUSIONS

One of the critical flaws in human thinking is our tendency to jump to conclusions. When things aren't going our way, we often persuade ourselves that the grass is greener on the other side and make irrational decisions based on this. We favour action because it makes us feel like we're moving in the right direction, when in many cases we might just be digging ourselves a larger hole.

The underlying point here is that whatever your decision, think through not just the first, but as Ray Dalio puts it in his book *Principles*, the second- and third-order consequences. People who overemphasise the immediate consequences of a decision and ignore the subsequent consequences are thought to rarely reach their goals. Don't quit your job just because you hate your boss, only to find yourself working for an equally loathsome person elsewhere. Think through the longer-term consequences before making a decision. This will help you make rational decisions, rather than ones offering instant gratification but no long-term benefit.

Call to action

1. Develop a shortlist of potential 'whats' that align with the whys you identified in the previous chapter: why you picked up this book and the why underpinning your purpose.

2. Consider the proposed alternatives to entrepreneurship and add to your shortlist.

3. Apply the decision-making framework given to help you make an informed, rational decision between options.

4. Consider how you might 'dip your toes in the water' to test personal suitability to any given path and avoid overcommitting.

5. Review your values and your 'map of the world'; do any of your values hold you back and if so, how might you reframe them in order to empower rather than inhibit your personal growth?

Chapter 5

AN ENTREPRENEURIAL MINDSET

*'Nothing in this world can take the place of persistence.
Talent will not: nothing is more common than unsuccessful men
with talent. Genius will not; unrewarded genius is almost a proverb.
Education will not: the world is full of educated derelicts.
Persistence and determination alone are omnipotent.'*
Calvin Coolidge, 30th President of the United States

Mindset shows up often in this book. That's because it is more important than any other factor in differentiating success from failure. I cannot stress this point enough. The right mindset is critical for creating the conditions to help you find success and fulfilment in both your professional and your personal life.

It comes down to how you show up and respond to adversity each and every day.

When I started Collective Campus, it was just me and my co-founder, Sean. We had no brand, no content, no marketing or distribution channels, and little to no track record. Yet we were positioning ourselves to sell to large enterprise clients. I'll never forget those first few months. We set up literally hundreds of meetings and calls between us (according to my Google Calendar history we took more than 500 in the first three months). How? We asked. We did all manner of things, from sending messages to people on LinkedIn who we thought were in our target audience, to guessing people's email addresses and requesting introductions in the odd case that we had a mutual connection.

These weren't sales meetings. They were learning and relationship development meetings. By reframing the purpose of these early meetings, not only were we more likely to secure more meetings because we didn't come across as 'salesy', but we were less likely to get discouraged because we weren't trying to sell anything. It was almost impossible to walk away from these initial meetings without successfully learning something, provided we asked good questions. We made it clear in our outreach that we were simply looking to make a connection and that we were genuinely interested in learning more about the role, industry, objectives and challenges faced by those we approached so we might eventually be able to help them in one way or another. More often than not, people were happy to give up 20 to 30 minutes over a coffee to share some insights and hear us out.

Of course, the 'can I buy you a coffee to pick your brain?' approach rarely works if you're targeting genuinely busy people, so you've got to have some angle that makes it about what you might be able to do for them. Here's a typical email to our target market that dates from before we had yet adopted the Collective Campus moniker.

Hi Chris

I understand you are an expert in the L&D space.

I'm from Queens Collective, one of Melbourne's tech startup co-working spaces.

I thought I'd reach out as we're developing a corporate innovation school called <u>Collective Campus</u> and would love to get your insights on the space.

I'm not trying to sell you anything, I'm just trying to learn so that I can help you. If you've got 20 minutes you can spare, perhaps over a quick coffee or a short phone call, so that I can gain a better understanding of the objectives and challenges of your role, I'd really appreciate it.

The purpose of the campus is to not only provide large organisations and their employees with the right tools to tackle the dilemma of innovation, but also to improve employee engagement and retention through empowering employees to become more creative and innovative in their day to day jobs.

102

We envisage delivering short modules but also co-location at one of Melbourne's most exciting tech co-working spaces, where employees would have the chance to mix it with hot startups across various industries. This, as you might imagine, is particularly important in keeping the growing Gen-Y workforce engaged and happy.

You can find out a little bit more about Collective Campus and our prospective syllabus here.

If you're too busy or not the right person to speak to, can you please point me in the right direction?

Thank you.

If I was to rewrite this email today, it would look quite different and be much shorter and more to the point, but it did enough to secure said meetings.

Corporate experience can be a serious advantage when it comes to opening doors. By then I had more than eight years' experience working for the likes of EY, KPMG and Macquarie Bank. I had a half-decent LinkedIn profile, and my co-founder Sean had been running Queens Collective as a co-working space in Melbourne's CBD (which was doing okay by 2015's definitions of success for such a space, pre-WeWork's arrival of course) after a stint in event promotion including having brought Neil deGrasse Tyson to Australia.

A good LinkedIn profile is something anyone can build quickly and painlessly, and it makes all the difference to whether someone accepts or rejects a request to meet.

We made thousands of meeting requests and ended up buying a hell of a lot of the brown stuff during those first few months. We should have had some kind of loyalty membership and our own table at Bond St Café (our local haunt for those early meetings, conveniently located at the foot of our building). While we like to pretend that we were strategic about who we met, the truth is we met with almost anyone who would give us the time of day, if for nothing other than to help expand our worldview of the corporate innovation space.

We would conclude later that many of the people we met with were themselves miserably comfortable corporate professionals who hated the daily grind and took meetings with guys like us to escape from the office drudgery and add some light entertainment to their day. This is something you should be wary of as an entrepreneur selling to large companies. Ultimately pointless meetings are par for the course in large companies, so don't jump to conclusions, thinking that because someone agrees to a meeting they are seriously considering doing business with you, or that they even have the decision-making authority or budget to further your cause.

So that was a hell of a lot of meetings that went nowhere, right? Well, no. The initial flurry of meetings helped us sharpen our meeting game and our sense of what the market does and doesn't want. It helped us get our name out there, improved our subsequent outreach (better defined target industry, target job titles and marketing channels) and, most importantly and practically, it helped us understand our market and tailor our value proposition accordingly. Remember, explore *then* exploit.

When I look at our client list today, only three (3) of the initial 500 people we met with ended up becoming paying customers (and they did so more than 12 months after the initial meeting—not exactly the world's fastest sales cycle). In case you're wondering, a 0.6 per cent conversion rate is hardly great, unless those customers are high-dollar-value clients (which these three weren't). But we took the learnings from our time in the field and applied them to our work. We decided we'd run some initial lean startup workshops for corporates because it was clear that one of the pain points big corporates were experiencing, and continue to experience, is that they come up with lots of ideas that go nowhere.

We promoted our 'lean startup for corporates' free one-hour workshop on a number of third-party event marketing platforms such as Eventbrite, WeTeachMe and Meetup, as well as our own website (not that anyone was visiting it at the time, but anyway). We'd shoot emails to many of the people we'd previously met. We'd post on LinkedIn, Facebook and Twitter and in those early days managed to rustle up more than 50 RSVPs to most of these initial events.

I'd prepare the material, rehearse my moves and prime myself for the workshops. I'll never forget one of the early ones. We were so excited to have more than 50 people RSVP and we prepared meticulously, setting out 50 chairs neatly, lining up just the right music (no, it wasn't

Metallica ... it was AC/DC). As these events were scheduled for 6 pm, we even put some beers on ice and got out the Shiraz and Riesling.

In the end, *four* people turned up.

Something I learned in those early days was that whether it's four, 40 or 400 people, you put in the same amount of effort you would if 4000 showed up. Not only does that prepare you for bigger audiences, but if just one person in the audience has influence then it can open doors to all kinds of opportunities.

Staring at a room full of empty seats, it would have been easy to give up there and then, but we used this to identify what went wrong. What were we missing? We took ownership of every failure. Rather than make excuses or complain that 'people don't know what's good for them', this forced us to have a chat with reality and ask questions of:

- the topic and/or workshop title
- the marketing channel, branding and promotion (and the all-important event reminder emails)
- the timing and duration of workshops
- customer problems and pain points.

Understanding which factors determined the success or failure of a workshop helped inform our testing choices, such as alternative topics or workshop titles that would be more compelling. For example, 'How to Think Like a Startup' is way more compelling and puts more bums on seats than 'The Innovator's Mindset'.

What we got during that intensive trial by fire was lots of learning. We only made enough money to keep the lights on and paid ourselves nothing, zero, zilch for the first six months. Failure is inseparable from success, especially if you want to do something bold and new. You need to maintain a sense of self-worth that comes from something other than external validation in order to stay grounded, maintain belief and keep moving forward towards your objectives.

The trough of despair

In entrepreneurship, you will inevitably visit the 'trough of despair' or the 'trough of disillusionment'. Life, in the words of the great Rocky Balboa, 'is about how hard you can get hit and keep moving forward'—it's just the same with entrepreneurship.

One of my favourite stories is Homer's *The Odyssey*, an epic poem that is among the oldest works of western literature. The story tracks the journey of the Greek warrior king Odysseus who, after spending 10 years fighting in the Trojan Wars, spends another 10 cruel years finding his way home to his wife and son. During the journey he must fight mythical creatures; face the wrath of the gods, shipwreck, cannibals and enslavement; and overcome many other terrible trials. When he eventually gets home, he has to fight off numerous suitors for his long-suffering wife's hand, and then convince her of his identity, because 20 years of conquest and enslavement left him unrecognisable.

An entrepreneur's journey is not unlike *The Odyssey* (without the man-eating Cyclops) and requires the same level of commitment and perseverance to overcome the trough. If, like Odysseus, you are driven by a greater purpose, you are much more likely to stay the course. You just need to recognise that darkness and find your own way of dealing with it. Anita Campbell, founder of the Small Business Trends media company, says, 'The best antidote [to the trough of despair] is to get some exercise, a bike ride or a run, or some similar activity. Get a good night's sleep. It helps. It really does.

In the morning things often seem better. I've had the worst day of the year and the best day of the year happen in the same month'.

'Finish each day and be done with it. You have done what you could ... Tomorrow is a new day; begin it well and serenely and with too high a spirit to be encumbered with your old nonsense.'
Ralph Waldo Emerson

Tomorrow really is a new day.

The process of rapid experimentation, learning and adaptation that characterised our early days became a part of our core values at Collective Campus, and in time we started getting not only more than four people attending our free workshops, but people and large companies actually paying us for the privilege. To get to that point, however, we had to make friends with discomfort. This is something too many people aren't willing to do.

Recently we ran a digital readiness workshop for a client in the banking industry, and some young up-and-coming bankers told me how they had used the online platform Code Academy to try to learn coding, but as soon as it got a little too difficult they legged it. Why? Because the feeling of discomfort and the threat to their ego this raised became too much to handle.

We tend to avoid what threatens our identity. Zig Ziglar said, 'Anything worth doing is worth doing poorly until you can do it well'. But it's hard, especially when society keeps telling you you're crazy. Parents, significant others, friends—they probably won't get it. Author and *Future Squared* guest Whitney Johnson observes in her book *Disrupt Yourself*, 'disrupting yourself *should* feel lonely'.

Foundr magazine's Nathan Chan found bucking society's expectations 'extremely challenging'. In an email he told me, 'None of my friends or family are entrepreneurs or business owners, so they thought I was an idiot and many laughed at me. I just didn't listen to them and did what was best for me, not them, or what they thought was best for me'.

Entrepreneurship can indeed feel lonely, especially in the early days. But through discomfort comes growth. When discussing the growth of the lean startup movement with Steve Blank on my podcast, Blank said of his own experience, 'It started when there was a total market of *one*. And when I convinced Eric Ries it was a good idea, I doubled the market size, but let me tell you it was a pretty lonely place to be, telling everybody we're building startups and teaching entrepreneurship the wrong way! If you cared a lot you would not do that and if you care what other people think, you're going to have a hard time being a founder, because a founder by definition is *an artist who is creating something that doesn't yet exist*'.

In my case, had I not reframed my mental map (see chapter 4), had I not made friends with discomfort and placed purpose at the core of what I was doing, I would have quit. But despite all of the initial setbacks and signals telling me to give up, I still believed. Without belief, it is difficult to follow through with sustained, needle-moving effort.

If you can get better at making friends with discomfort and less than desirable outcomes and choose to empower yourself to respond to them, rather than play the victim card, then you are setting yourself up for success.

An operating system for success

I'll now introduce a number of tools and philosophies that offer you what amounts to an 'operating system for success', not only in entrepreneurship, but in life, because life is full of unexpected twists and turns and what we get doesn't always align with what we want, need or expect.

GROWTH MINDSET

In her best-selling book *Mindset*, psychologist Carol Dweck argues that people have either a fixed mindset or a growth mindset.

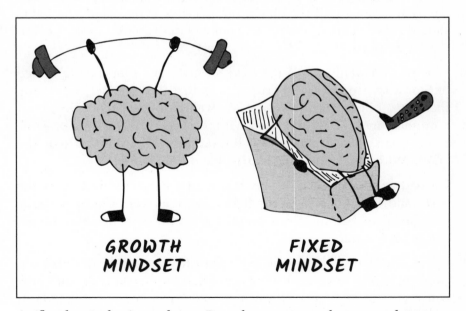

GROWTH
MINDSET

FIXED
MINDSET

A 'fixed mindset', explains Dweck, assumes that our character, intelligence and creative ability are static, and success is the affirmation of that inherent intelligence.

On the other hand, a 'growth mindset' embraces challenges and sees failure as a valuable form of feedback that helps us grow. With a growth mindset, your capacity for happiness is abundant; without it, it is limited.

To succeed at anything new, having a growth mindset is paramount.

I recently got my motorcycle licence, after 18 years of driving nothing but automatic transmission cars. Not only was I moving from four wheels to two but the entire concept of a manual transmission was foreign to me.

In my home state of Victoria, you're required to participate in a two-day motorcycle course before sitting your learner permit test, and once you've passed the brief written and practical test you're out on your own. You're set free, having learned about 10 per cent of what you end up learning in those first few months on the road, either through riding experience or through trawling online motorcycle forums for answers to noob questions like, 'Can I drop more than one gear when I pull the clutch in?' or 'How soon before the lights should I start gearing down?'. Of course, I didn't need to ask either of these questions. ¯_(ツ)_/¯

When I first went out on the road on my own, after having forked out for a Hyosung GV650 cruiser, I stalled the bike before turning the corner of my street *five times*. My frustration was mounting, but I reminded myself that this was a natural part of the learning process, rather than some fundamental limitation on my own part or the bike's. With every mistake, I learned and I got better.

If I had approached the experience with a fixed mindset, after the first handful of stalls at traffic lights where a river of horn-honking cars piled up behind me, I might have traded in my bike for an automatic scooter.

Adam Grant told me on *Future Squared*, 'We wander around not wanting to hurt anyone's feelings, and that's understandable, it's how you maintain smooth relationships and harmony, but it stands in the way of people really learning, growing and improving'. You will doubtless receive constructive criticism in your work and outside of it. Embrace it, ask for it. Surrounding yourself with 'yes' people and nice people might make you feel good in the moment, but in the long term, not hearing (or listening to) actionable feedback will only hold you back.

Hedge fund Bridgewater Associates uses what it calls a challenge network, a group of people who tell you the things you don't want to hear but need to hear, and if you recognise that they're doing it because they care about you and they want to foster your development, it doesn't sound like they're stabbing you in your back. At Bridgewater they call it front-stabbing, because they're saying it to your face. Seek opportunities to be front-stabbed, unless you'd prefer to be back-stabbed and blind to what's holding you back.

A growth mindset is absolutely fundamental to success in the ever-changing 21st century where learning and adaptability will need to be constant.

HOW TO SPOT A FIXED MINDSET

Some people say things like 'I'm just no good at it' or 'It's just the way I am'. Is that you? Time to change that conversation with yourself to 'I'm not yet good at it because I haven't put in enough time'. The stories we tell ourselves about ourselves dictate our behaviours and results.

DARKEST BEFORE THE DAWN

All my life I have been a reasonably high achiever. I say *reasonably* because my average grade in university bounced between credits, distinctions and the rare high distinction, so I wasn't exceptional academically by any stretch, but I had a satisfactory record. After spending the better part of my teens and early twenties working as a sales assistant at Target and as a bank teller at Westpac, I completed my Bachelor of Business degree. It was time for me to get my first 'real' job. At this stage I still had long hair, a hangover from my time playing in a heavy metal band. I'd tie it up nice and neat for job interviews. But time after time, no matter how well I performed, I got nowhere. So eventually, and perhaps against the contrarian spirit of this book, I cut it, and the very first interview

I scored with short hair led to a job offer. Interestingly, the person who hired me later made it clear that if I had turned up with long hair I more than likely would *not* have got the job. So much for diversity!

This was a gig with Dun & Bradstreet (D&B) as an information administrator, whatever that meant, in their upstart consumer credit bureau (it was as fun as it sounds). The bureau was a relatively new part of the organisation, consisting of a small team of fewer than 10 people and not much by way of processes or procedures, which can be the kind of environment I thrive in now, but back then, as a fresh-faced 21-year-old, I needed a little more direction.

This was before ubiquitous, fast and affordable internet access. In fact, it was before smartphones. What do you get when you combine a 21-year-old, a lack of process or direction, and free high-speed internet access at a time when it wasn't cheap? A complete misallocation of attention and resources — my attention and resources, that is. While I wasn't a complete degenerate in the role, and I did enough to get by, I didn't do enough to move forward, and after two years, and several warnings for abuse of internet access — no, not that kind of abuse — the general manager pulled me aside and told me I would be 'let go'.

As someone who hadn't read any significant motivational books and knew nothing of self-awareness or stoicism, this hit me like a sledgehammer, and I had to fight back the tears as I sat there in his dimly lit office, watching his lips move but no longer hearing the words.

As far as I was concerned, I had failed. I was a failure. I couldn't hold down a job that, at the time, was paying me a pittance — little more than $30 000.

After the dust had settled, I wondered what I would do next.

I had really enjoyed studying English and writing in high school and remembered my English teacher urging me to study journalism. While working at D&B, I had completed a certificate in writing from the Australian College of Journalism, so this was one path I pondered.

I also strongly considered becoming a high-school teacher myself. I could surely teach English, I thought, and I'd enjoy 10 weeks of leave each year.

Until then I had looked to carve out a career in the corporate world. It was probably largely social expectations and notions of status that pushed me towards a life in a suit, but whatever the backstory, it seemed like a copout to now turn my back on that and become a teacher. As is often the case in life (and product development!), not jumping to conclusions and giving yourself time for the cobwebs to clear will often pave the way to our best decisions.

I scored a part-time gig at a call centre to keep me going while I figured out exactly what it was I was going to do with my life. As it happened, the call centre was located in the middle of Melbourne's legal and financial precinct. I'll never forget how one day on my way to work, still down over my recent firing, I first started noticing what could have only been lawyers and management consultants making their way to their respective offices, dressed to the nines, carrying briefcases and what looked to my untrained eye like 'important' paperwork. Something about this spoke to my ego. If they can do it, I remember thinking, so can I.

Shortly thereafter, I enrolled in a master of accounting, a degree I would complete remotely in 12 short months while working 25 hours a week at the call centre. Opting to study accounting, which has little to do with how I spend my time today, was in retrospect one of the best decisions of my life. And while I had no luck scoring a graduate gig with a big four accounting firm straight out of the blocks, it opened the door to a grad role with the Victorian Auditor-General's Office, which, as I've discussed, would open the door at a big four accounting firm less than two years later.

Almost a decade later, Collective Campus had its darkest moment when we had just $1000 in our bank account and a $12 500 rental payment due the next day. Obviously, we survived to tell the tale, and I now speak fondly of that time with my co-founder as it served to make us stronger and more appreciative of what we have today. It's indeed always darkest before the dawn!

IF YOU ASK A GOLDFISH TO CLIMB A WALL, IT'LL SPEND ITS WHOLE LIFE THINKING IT'S STUPID

When Michael Jordan turned his back on basketball in 1994 to pursue a career with the Chicago White Sox baseball outfit, he did so after closing out a 'three-peat' with the Chicago Bulls — that's three consecutive championships, the last of which was against my beloved Phoenix Suns. He had won the coveted MVP award three times and was a nine-times NBA All-Star.

The move was also triggered by the then recent murder of his father, who had always dreamed of him playing major league baseball. After a season with the Double-A minor league affiliate of the White Sox, the Birmingham Barons, Jordan finished with less than impeccable stats. He mustered a batting average of .202 (number of hits divided by bats) and managed just three home runs. For the uninitiated, a batting average of below .200 is generally considered unacceptable.

In 1995, Jordan announced his return to basketball and he went on to complete another three-peat, win two more MVP awards and appear in another five NBA All-Star games before retiring in 2003. He is still considered the GOAT (greatest basketballer of all time), and in May 2017 *Forbes* put his net worth at US$1.31 billion. Sorry, LeBron and Kobe. Despite his illustrious status, though, he's not immune to being a target for meme trolls. :~(

If Jordan had originally pursued baseball instead of basketball, would he have carved out a career in the *major* leagues? Doubtful, but we'll never know for sure. Would he have done so in the *minor* leagues? Possibly. After all, he did manage a batting average of .252 during a stint for the Scottsdale Scorpions in the Arizona Fall League. Would he have scaled the summit the way he did in basketball to become an all-time great? It's fair to say it would be highly improbable.

Just because you don't thrive in one environment it doesn't mean you won't thrive in another. The *fundamental attribution error* is a cognitive bias referring to our tendency to judge people and ignore their environment when assessing performance, but those situational factors hugely impact performance. If you find yourself in an environment that isn't conducive to bringing out the best in you, change your environment.

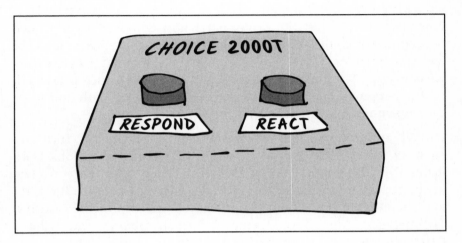

Here are some of the other lessons I learned from this experience in my early twenties:

- You always have options when choosing how to interpret and respond to anything that happens to you.
- Adopt empowered thinking ('If they can do it, so can I') rather than thinking of yourself as a victim ('Why them and not me?').
- Don't jump to conclusions when making big decisions.
- Leverage stepping stones.
- Don't shy away from junior titles if the role moves you closer to your goal (one step back, two steps forward is more than just a catchy saying).
- And, perhaps most profoundly, it's always darkest before the dawn. It's usually in the darkest or most challenging moments of our lives that we evolve into a better version of ourselves.

Looking back after all these years, I am immensely grateful that I was sacked from my first real job. If you're reading this, you know who you are — *thank you so much* for firing me.

SOCRATIC THOUGHT

Through *Future Squared* I've been fortunate enough to speak with almost one hundred thought leaders, and what is remarkable is how, just like the rest of us, no matter how educated, experienced or accomplished, they often hold contradictory views. Our views are coloured by the circles we move in, our associates and the information we consume. We make decisions based on the evidence presented, past experience, the belief systems we've grown up with and more than one hundred other cognitive biases.

On AI and automation taking our jobs, I've heard futurists such as Kevin Kelly argue that AI will create more jobs than it destroys. Economists such as Tyler Cowen paint a grim view of the future, pointing to the growing gap between productivity and the median household income since the turn of the century. Technologist Alec Ross, formerly Barack Obama and Hillary Clinton's adviser on innovation (he insists he did not hack her email), argued that as we increasingly embrace technology, there will be no room for mediocrity, suggesting a future for humanity shaped by an almost Darwinian 'survival of the fittest' standard. Since that conversation, I have spent time chatting with technologist Tim O'Reilly, who spearheads the open-source movement. Tim disagreed with Alec's sentiments, arguing instead that the growing gap between productivity and income is more to do with resource allocation choices than with the technology itself. He pointed to innovations we take for granted today that were unimaginable 25 years ago and proposed that companies redesign their businesses around a new business model and create new customers based on building the unimaginable. This, he believed, would then free people up to work on more value-adding and fulfilling work.

To make informed decisions, seek out evidence to support your assumption but also counter-evidence that refutes it. Ray Dalio recommends hunting down as many 'believable' people as possible.

If you've assembled five credible people on a topic and they all draw the same conclusions, then to contradict them might not seem prudent.

Then, just when you were thinking 'that makes a lot of sense', someone of Peter Thiel's calibre throws the following contrarian challenge at job candidates and startups seeking investment: 'Tell me something that's true, that almost nobody agrees with you on'. As he told *Business Insider*, this 'sort of tests for originality of thinking' because 'most people think originality is easy, but I think it's actually really hard, and when you find it, it's really valuable'.

Hosting *Future Squared* has brought home to me how important it is to truly understand the other person's point of view and why they think what they think, and to empathise with that position if we are to truly collaborate, have an informed conversation, make informed decisions and move forward in a meaningful way. This applies not only to business and technology but also to our own personal relationships.

Form your own worldview. Never forget that the other person has not walked in your shoes. They probably didn't grow up in the same kind of household, go to the same school, study the same topics, work in the same industry, travel to the same places, consume the same content or mix with the same people, so don't be baffled when they have different opinions from you.

Perhaps the two most important things I've learned are best captured by two sages separated by two and a half millennia. Socrates said, 'The only true wisdom is in knowing that you know nothing'. Stephen Covey writes, 'Seek first to understand, then to be understood'.

STOICISM AND SELF-CONTROL

Stoicism is a Hellenistic philosophy strongly influenced by Socrates. Centring on logic and the idea that virtue, as the highest good, is based on knowledge, it teaches the value of being responsive rather than reactive to external events. Thinking clearly in challenging times is key to responding effectively and, to use an old adage, turning lemons into lemonade.

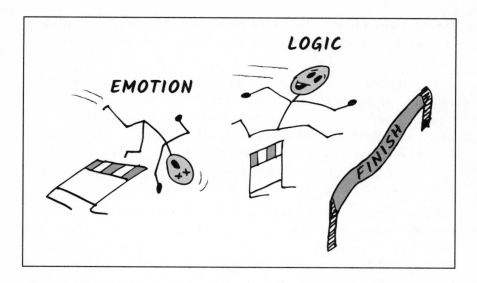

The power of a Stoic outlook may be best encapsulated by the following journal entry from Marcus Aurelius:

> Remove the judgement and you have removed the thought 'I am hurt'; remove the thought 'I am hurt' and the hurt itself is removed.

It's also about focusing on what you have control over and not sweating over what you don't. Professor of philosophy and scholar, Massimo Pigliucci, puts it this way: 'One of the first lessons from Stoicism, then, is to focus our attention and efforts where we have the most power and then let the universe run as it will. This will save us both a lot of energy and a lot of worry'.

As an introduction to Stoicism, check out Seneca's *Moral Letters to Lucelius* and Marcus Aurelius's *Meditations* or, for a modern take, *The Obstacle Is the Way* by Ryan Holiday.

TAKING OWNERSHIP

Jocko Willink, a former Navy Seal, podcast host, founder of leadership consultancy Echelon Front and author of books such as *Discipline Equals Freedom* and *Extreme Ownership*, posts a photo of his wristwatch on Instagram at 4.30 each morning to prove he is up early to work out and seize the day.

As his sometime co-author, Leif Babin, sees it, 'Taking ownership instead of blaming others, finding excuses, or maybe even denying that problems exist … a lot of that is about checking your ego'. Taking ownership is empowering yourself to do something about it. Making excuses is disempowering and cedes control to the randomness of the world around you.

Which side will you take?

DERAILED BY EGO

If you're looking to identify new opportunities, have meaningful conversations, build better relationships, innovate and create real value in the world, then the one thing that is almost sure to get in the way is your ego.

Check your ego at the door.

Why? Because ego either lulls us into a false sense of superiority, which results in our not really listening, or it prevents us from putting ourselves out there in fear of being judged or having our ego hurt.

As the late Zig Ziglar put it, 'You are who you *think* people think you are'.

Our egos are just one example of our subconscious at play, and while it is not always a bad thing—a healthy dose of ego can provide the impetus for you to leave the starting mark—too much ego, or ego applied poorly, can derail your plans, big time. Abundance of one thing means there is scarcity of another; if you have too much ego then you will be short on reason. But there *is* value in balance.

Here are seven cognitive biases that can inhibit our decision making, especially when it comes to entrepreneurship. Remember, there are many more examples of subconscious biases, but becoming aware of them is the first step to doing something about them.

SEVEN COGNITIVE BIASES THAT INHIBIT ENTREPRENEURSHIP

Human beings are prone to more than one hundred biases that shape our behaviour and inform our decisions. Becoming more aware of them is step one in engineering workarounds so you're not misallocating resources and sacrificing your potential for success in the process. I've chosen to zoom in on just seven cognitive biases that can stifle your foray into entrepreneurship and have suggested how they might affect your efforts, offering workarounds for each.

1. Ambiguity effect
The tendency to avoid options where information asymmetry creates too much uncertainty.

'If you fail to plan you plan to fail' is an old adage. A certain amount of planning is necessary for any venture, but overplanning in order to feel in control is something that traditional project management methods such as

Waterfall, PRINCE2 and Stage-Gate teach us. Business cases are designed with this in mind, to give decision makers a sense of control and certainty. To feel in control is an innate human need.

The problem with this is that it supports pursuing only what we can reliably predict and see, and it doesn't lend itself to taking something new to the world. To truly innovate and stand a chance of surviving in a constantly changing environment, getting better at embracing uncertainty is key.

Workaround: Get more comfortable with experimentation. More on this in chapter 8!

2. Anchoring

The tendency to 'anchor' our opinions or ideas on the first piece of information we acquired.

This is notoriously common in run-of-the-mill brainstorming sessions, particularly where dominant personalities speak up first. What usually happens is everyone else anchors their ideas on this first 'big idea' rather than coming up with new ones.

Workaround: To combat this, ensure people 'work alone together' by first writing down their ideas individually, then grouping similar ideas and silently voting on them before finally engaging in a wider group discussion. If you're working alone, seek out conflicting opinions or ask open-ended questions like 'How might you solve this?' rather than closed ones like 'Do you think the solution I'm proposing is a good one?'.

3. Backfire effect

The reaction to disconfirming evidence by strengthening one's previous beliefs.

Working in the corporate innovation space, I've lost count of the number of times we've run experiments that disprove a corporate executive's initial thinking. More often than not, they take this in their stride and pivot accordingly. However,

(continued)

SEVEN COGNITIVE BIASES THAT INHIBIT ENTREPRENEURSHIP (*CONT'D*)

every now and again, after a company has engaged us to test their assumptions with target customers — and invested considerable time and money in doing so — we hear something like this (an anonymised quote from an actual email I received from a large, listed company):

'Company X has decided to accelerate its efforts in respect of product X and create an enterprise-wide program that will touch every facet of our business above and beyond: product and pricing design, operations, corporate social responsibility, brand and reputation, employee engagement and legal and regulatory lobbying.'

What?! We just learned that the market has no appetite for your idea and you're not only going ahead with it, but ramping up its size and complexity significantly? This is not too far removed from an echo chamber, where people surround themselves with information that confirms their views and any evidence to the contrary is not only dismissed but actually serves to harden their pre-existing beliefs.

Workaround: Establish a truth-seeking group or a 'brain trust' and use the decision-making framework introduced in chapter 4 to help keep your biases in check.

4. Confirmation bias

The tendency to search for, interpret, focus on and remember information in a way that confirms one's own preconceptions.

Whatever your opinion about the topic, you'll find data to support it. However, you could probably find lots of disproving data too. In most cases, there will be a correlation between X and Y in the data, but that doesn't necessarily mean that X causes Y.

Workaround: When building experiments to test your assumptions, always ensure that your hypotheses:

- are SMART (specific, measurable, actionable, realistic, time-bound)
- are testable (can you actually run an experiment to prove or disprove your hypothesis?)
- answer what, why, where and who.

5. Congruence bias

The tendency to test one hypothesis exclusively through direct testing, instead of testing possible alternative hypotheses.

An example of this might be testing a subscription pricing model of $10 a month. You discover that 7 per cent of your website visitors agree to pay this, and with a target metric of 3 per cent you're ready to move on and implement this pricing model.

Or *are you*? Have you tested other price-points? Maybe people are willing to pay $20 or even $50 a month for the value your product delivers? Or perhaps there's a better pricing model? Up-front pricing, value-added pricing, scaled transactions, freemium, licencing, metered use, membership and countless other models might be more financially rewarding in the long run.

Workaround: Identify all key and high-risk assumptions underpinning your idea or business model and test these assumptions before drawing any conclusions on the best path forward.

6. Courtesy bias

The tendency to give an opinion that is more socially correct than one's true opinion, so as to avoid offending anyone.

(continued)

SEVEN COGNITIVE BIASES THAT INHIBIT ENTREPRENEURSHIP (*CONT'D*)

Similar to Bridgewater's challenger networks, Ed Catmull and the gang at Pixar have set up what they call a 'brain trust', whereby key people come together to give brutally honest feedback about a film they're working on, where feelings aren't spared and there is no fear of reprisal. They credit this with being an essential part of the creative process and of Pixar's success as an animation studio.

Workaround: Create a safe environment or process for giving honest, unfiltered feedback that supports the creative process.

7. Fundamental attribution error
The tendency for people to overemphasise personality-based explanations for behaviours observed in others while underemphasising the role and power of situational influences on the same behaviour.

If you're expecting your team to behave like Elon Musk but your processes are more attuned to Dilbert, then you can't blame them for not coming up with or developing the next breakthrough business model or idea.

Workaround: If you want to get a certain behaviour out of people, you need to create a supporting environment.

I've only just scratched the surface with these seven biases; for an additional 29 cognitive biases that plague entrepreneurship, visit **www.employeetoentrepreneur.io/cognitivebiases/**.

Meditation

The days of meditation being perceived by the mainstream as 'new age mumbo jumbo' are long gone. Today, thanks in part to smartphone apps such as Headspace and Calm, it has well and truly hit the mainstream. At least 10 per cent of people I associate with meditate daily, and most of them (myself included) have never been to an ashram or gone on a meditation retreat.

The benefits of meditation are wide-ranging: it can reduce ageing and stress, increase your attention span and immunity, improve your metabolism and brain function, help you build better relationships, increase your appreciation of life, help you get a good night's rest and make you, and by extension the people around you, happier.

On the physical side, meditation lowers high blood pressure and reduces anxiety attacks, tension-related pain, ulcers, insomnia, and muscle and joint problems, while increasing serotonin production, which improves mood and behaviour, strengthening the immune system and increasing energy levels as you gain an inner source of energy. Above all, though, meditation supports personal transformation, emotional steadiness and harmony with the world.

If you think you're 'doing it wrong' or 'I tried it once, but it doesn't work for me!', remember that no one gets good at anything or builds a habit after one attempt. If you think your mind is too noisy to meditate, you need it more than you think. Start by taking a single deep breath.

The list of influencers and power players who meditate is long and includes personalities such as legendary music producer Rick Rubin, Tim Ferriss, Ray Dalio, Jerry Seinfeld, all The Beatles, Oprah Winfrey, Ellen DeGeneres, Martin Scorsese, George Lucas, Flea (Red Hot Chilli Peppers), Eddie Vedder (Pearl Jam), Russell Simmons (founder of Def Jam Records) and of course, Steve Jobs.

I began my own daily meditative practice four years ago and haven't looked back. Each day, after my morning workout, I simply take five to ten minutes to focus on my breathing and present environment, and cycle through the mantras I've developed around gratitude, presence, self-awareness, forgiveness and compassion.

It leaves me feeling mentally sharp and makes me much less likely to get stressed out by little things that would otherwise distract me. It helps me make better decisions throughout the day, which has a huge cumulative, compound impact. It's not just the big decisions but the little choices you make every day that add up to big outcomes. On top of that, I believe it makes me a better, more pleasant person who prefers to share, understand, listen and learn; to have actual conversations, rather than argue and point-score.

Popular meditation practices include mindfulness, Heart Rhythm Meditation (HRM), Transcendental Meditation™ and visualisation. Two mindfulness apps are Headspace and Calm.

Being calm and relatively content won't kill your drive or ambition. It will make you less reactive and help you develop your relationships and make better, less emotion-charged decisions.

Break things down to their smallest possible units to see them for what they really are—nothing more than your own subjective interpretations. For example, to fight FOMO when you should be working, recognise that a large crowd is just lots of individual people drawn together, often succumbing to their own FOMO and in the process sacrificing their own work.

Try stargazing to get perspective on your problems. The stars we see in the night sky were there for billions of years before we arrived and will remain for billions of years after we're gone. The brightest star in the sky is just over eight light years away. The most distant star visible to the naked eye is about 1600 light years away from Earth. What does that mean? They are very, *very* far away. Not only that, but there are more stars in our universe than grains of sand on all the world's beaches. Take a moment to process that last one. It will help you put your own challenges and perceived sacredness into perspective!

Perhaps counterintuitively, I'll close this chapter by channelling Oscar Wilde: 'Life is too important to be taken seriously'.

Call to action

1. For the next 21 days, notice any negative emotions or anger you feel, or any reactive state you fall into. Stop yourself from simply reacting and consciously choose your response. You'll find that, like building muscle, the more you do this, the stronger your ability to control your response becomes. You have a choice in how you interpret and respond to things that happen to you. The better you get at making the right choice, the better will be your decisions in business and in life.

2. Read some philosophy (I recommend the likes of Marcus Aurelius, Epictetus and Seneca, or for a more modern twist, Friedrich Nietzsche, Alain de Botton, Jordan Peterson and Sam Harris), or if you're looking for a gateway drug, check out a blog such as *Brain Pickings* or an online magazine such as *New Philosopher*.

3. Start using a meditation app, even if for just a few minutes a day. At the very least, take six long, conscious breaths daily, preferably in the morning before you take on the day.

4. For at least seven consecutive days, write down three things you are grateful for, and see what it does for your mental equilibrium.

Chapter 6
TAKING ACTION

'The key to success is action.'
Sun Yat-sen

So many people tell me they've got a great idea, but they never do anything with it. Maybe they fear failure or fear that other people will steal the idea. It's what they do with it that counts—and that, my friends, is the hard bit. As Michael Dell, founder and CEO of Dell Technologies, puts it, 'Ideas are a commodity, execution of them is not'. Some people get started and blow their entire savings on a full-blown product it took countless months to develop in what they call 'stealth mode', or it all becomes a little too hard and they give up. Others never try, insisting it's just not the right time yet.

Today taking action doesn't need to be hard or expensive, especially if all you want to do is test an idea, which is what you should be doing when it is still just an idea. As with staring at an intimidating blank page, writing down the first few words is the most difficult bit; with each step you will learn, move and gain momentum.

When my team decided to explore running a children's entrepreneurship program (an idea that bore fruit in Lemonade Stand), we didn't reach out to schools, hire a K12 teacher to help us develop the content, set up an elaborate website and marketing campaign or announce classes all over Australia from day one.

No, we had to test our idea before committing scarce resources to it. We had to design experiments to observe what the market wanted, rather than just ask them or assume what they wanted.

Our initial test cost us little more than $100 and a few hours to set up. How? We created a simple event listing for a 'kids school holiday business workshop in Melbourne' on Eventbrite with some workshop copy I'd mocked up in under an hour. We spent $100 on Facebook ads targeting 'people who like' mum blogger Facebook groups and pages.

Within two weeks we'd sold 12 tickets at just under $500 a pop. This was enough to justify running the pilot workshop, particularly given that our cost of customer acquisition was $9 (ad clicks cost us 45 cents each and for every 20 clicks one person would buy a ticket).

It was by no means smooth sailing. Our first workshop had one child act out, throw a chair, bang his head against the wall and burst into tears, though he was all smiles after he pitched his idea at the end of the day. We could have taken this trial by fire as reason enough to give up there and then (and we almost did), but again, as you learned in the previous chapter, it's about being responsive and taking ownership — learning how we could have mitigated the risks and what we could do better next time. I'm happy to say we haven't had any such incident since!

We also received some critical feedback from concerned parents that helped us to improve our offering. Sign-in and sign-out forms, first aid qualifications for staff, clearances for working with children, media release forms — as well as being prepared for allergies and peanut reactions — were among the many areas we needed to address if we were serious about taking Lemonade Stand to the next level. We have since learned, adapted, iterated and improved.

With any idea, there's financial risk (will it make money?), technical risk (can we build it?) and market risk (will people want it?).

Perhaps:

- the problem you're solving isn't big enough
- the solution fails to hit the sweet spot
- your branding and marketing aren't effective
- your distribution channel isn't the right one
- your costs exceed your revenues
- your current model isn't scalable

- other products are vying for your target market's attention and dollars
- the target customers are more or less happy with the way they do things now.

Lemonade Stand didn't start with global ambitions. We started with a free event listing and $100 of Facebook ads. Business coach and author Dan Sullivan puts it in a nutshell: 'Don't get ready, get started'.

Inspiration without action is entertainment

Entrepreneurial boot camps and self-help seminars are full of people who turn up, get inspired and then walk away, do nothing, come back a year later, get inspired, walk away, feel good for a little while, do nothing ... and so the cycle continues.

Often when people get inspired but give up shortly thereafter, it's because they lack an effective roadmap or don't know where or how to begin. Getting started can be exhilarating, but also overwhelming.

WHY NEW YEAR'S RESOLUTIONS FAIL (AND MOST BUSINESS IDEAS NEVER GET OFF THE GROUND)

Many of us make bold promises to ourselves in the form of New Year's resolutions. According to research carried out by StatisticBrain, almost one-third of these resolutions come unstuck in the first two weeks of the new year. Almost half of us make New Year's resolutions; 92 per cent of them have failed by year's end.

Why do we fail at something that means so much to us? Clearly we feel that the changes we aspire to make will improve us or our lives, whether financially, physically, emotionally or professionally. We make resolutions because we know we could be better in certain ways (we can *always* be better).

(continued)

WHY NEW YEAR'S RESOLUTIONS FAIL (AND MOST BUSINESS IDEAS NEVER GET OFF THE GROUND) (*CONT'D*)

In the chaotic euphoria of the festive season, we forget about everything that held us back during the previous year and pledge that the new year will be different. Just as every new day begins with the promise and excitement of possibility, only to end with us slumped in front of the television, anxious about the next day's meetings, the dawn of the new year also presents endless possibility. Our initial optimism drives us to make bold proclamations and set the bar high.

Why then do most resolutions fail? Here are a few possibilities you may recognise:

- You didn't have time to go to the gym (translation: you didn't *prioritise* it).

- Your hectic travel schedule prevented you from getting into the habit of regular yoga or boxing classes.

- You said 'yes' to too many new projects, which meant working into the night and over the weekend, so you didn't spend enough time with your family.

- You didn't perform as well as you would have liked in the office because your sleeping patterns and diet are all over the shop, leaving you feeling spent by early afternoon.

- You have a bad attitude that needs working on.

It's all very well resolving to get fit, spend more time with family, or become the office superman or wonder woman, but if we don't change the underlying behaviours and blockers that prevented us from doing these things the previous year, then all the wishing and hoping in the world won't help us.

Once you've identified what you want to change, prioritise. Do you *really* want to get fit or do you place more value on an extra hour of sleep in the morning?

Maybe there are other resolutions you could make where your circumstances are more likely to result in success. Ever wanted to learn a language? Maybe you can use Duolingo for 20 minutes a day during your morning commute. Time? Work? Sleep? Money? None is an issue here. This is just one example of how considering the blockers and enablers underpinning your resolution can help you make resolutions you'll actually keep.

Some may say that this is a lax approach to resolutions, and they may be right. If you really have set your sights on losing weight and getting fit, and your disablers are many while your enablers, the things that help you achieve your goals, are few, then you will have to change that. Perhaps you can learn to say no to some jobs and work more effectively by focusing on what actually adds value rather than sweating the small stuff.

Spending too long on the morning commute? Perhaps you can negotiate working remotely a couple of days a week? Overwhelmed with tasks and errands? Consider outsourcing creative tasks through Upwork or Freelancer and everyday errands through AirTasker or TaskRabbit. If you're not outsourcing, chances are you're wasting time doing what someone else could do for a fraction of the cost. Not only that, but it's time you could better spend on becoming the person you want to be.

Perhaps you can get a better night's rest by staying away from the blue light of your smartphone for an hour before bed so getting up for that morning gym session doesn't become such a Herculean effort.

Whatever your disablers, there are numerous ways they can be overcome. So before you break your resolution, identify what will prevent their achievement and how you'll overcome that, then get to work on becoming one of the 8 per cent of people who successfully achieve their resolutions.

What about securing my financial future?

I'll begin by stressing that I am not a financial adviser, and you should consider seeking independent legal, financial, taxation or other advice to determine how this information relates to your particular circumstances. What worked for me, or anyone else for that matter, might not work for you.

Walking away from a six-figure salary and stepping into the brave new world of entrepreneurship, where you might earn and save very little in the first few years, can be daunting. But it doesn't need to be an all-or-nothing proposition.

Before I left Macquarie Bank, I received pre-approval for a property investment loan. I ended up purchasing a property for $420 000, which required a deposit of just $42 000 (most of which I was able to draw from the equity I had built in my first investment property, purchased five years earlier). The property is now valued at $600 000. That's a capital gain of $180 000 in just over four years. Of course, owning an investment property comes with expenses, including interest, insurance, council rates, property management, maintenance, strata, water and tax. However, being positively geared means that my tenants' rent covers the interest and some of these expenses.

The average American saves just 2.2 per cent of their income each year; the average Australian saves just $427 each month (that's $5124 annually, or 36 years to save $180 000). Those who are a little more fiscally savvy, or are simply in a position where they can save a little more, might manage to save 10 to 20 per cent of their salary each year. Assuming a $120 000 salary and an annual saving of 20 per cent, or $24 000, I would have saved only $96 000 in the four years since I purchased my property, just over half the capital gain my investment made. And I didn't need to work for the $180 000 capital gain. I engage a property manager (who receives just 6 per cent of the rent). All I really have to do is sit back and (fingers crossed) watch the value of the property increase each year. If I had just saved the average of $5124 each year, I'd have banked little more than $20 000, the cash value of which would be rapidly deteriorating as inflation drives the cost of goods upwards.

By taking this approach, I was able to focus on building my business over the three- to five-year time horizon without feeling like I was jeopardising my financial future and being tempted back into a J.O.B. because of it. The business is now in a position where I can draw on the equity in this property and purchase another should I choose to. Where does it stop, though? Three properties? Ten? Fifty? Nothing should be done without purpose, and more assets won't necessarily mean more happiness, contentment or fulfilment. What matters most to me is having enough so I don't have to worry about covering the basics and losing my freedom to explore. As Seneca put it, 'You ask what is the proper limit to a person's wealth? First, having what is essential, and second, having what is enough'.

This method is just one of many ways you might explore to offset the hit to your savings. Even if you choose not to do something like this, forgoing a handsome salary or saving for several years in pursuit of your dreams is a perfectly reasonable trade-off to make.

A word of warning on property investment. The Australian residential property market has been relatively stable thanks to stringent lending requirements and other factors that helped Australia weather the global financial crisis of 2008. Unlike the property crisis that befell the US economy in 2008, Australia does not face high government debt and high budget deficits, making it less vulnerable to adverse economic shocks. That's not to say that Australia is immune from the kind of bloodletting we saw in the US housing market in 2008, when ninja loans (loans given to people with no income, job or assets) artificially inflated the market, so when the bubble eventually burst, many property valuations fell by 50 per cent, resulting in foreclosures of more than 860 000 homes in 2008 and a subsequent 5.5 million through to 2014, leaving countless Americans without a home. In times of economic turbulence, interest rates can skyrocket and what was a positively geared loan can become a negatively geared one that you're unable to service. Australia has not had a recession since the early 1990s, but that doesn't mean the country will avoid one indefinitely.

Wherever you are in the world, whatever investment you're deciding on, ensure you have adequately informed yourself of the risks. Once you know the score, it's your call on whether you choose to accept the risk, hedge or mitigate against the risk, or avoid it altogether by not pursuing said investment.

On procrastination

If you're struggling to do that something you keep putting off, my best advice is just to start. If it's writing, aim to do the bare minimum — 'just a crappy 200 words a day'. You'll find that the act of writing just 200 words makes getting into the zone and writing the subsequent 2000 so much easier.

Regularly doing at least the bare minimum, in whatever challenge you set yourself, delivers a small sense of achievement and a hit of serotonin. Getting up and going to the gym is the hard bit — once you're there, it's much easier! Signing up to that online course you've been putting off or watching a lecture seems onerous, until you hit the play button, hear a couple of interesting ideas, and get hooked. Heck, even going out for a carefree night on the town with friends can sometimes seem like an effort when your butt is parked in the comfort of your living room!

When I sat down to write this book, the last thing I wanted to be thinking was, 'Oh shit, I need to write 75 000 words'. No, in the spirit of Homer Simpson, I think, 'Okay brain, I'm just asking for a crappy 200 words, let's do this and we can get back to drinking Laphroaig whisky, riding motorcycles and listening to podcasts'. Sure enough, I've tricked the brain into giving me a few thousand words by the end of the session.

Remember, it's okay to fail, so long as you fail small, learn and survive to fight, and improve another day. A $50 000 failure, where you've effectively wasted your life savings on building an app without having done *any* testing — and had it fall flat the day you exposed it to the big bad world — must be avoided at all costs. A $50 failure, testing one of your problem statements using, say, Facebook ads, is a very cheap way to learn.

Today you can test your idea for a few hundred dollars, often at virtually no cost (more on that in chapter 8). Yet so many 'wantrapreneurs' still engage web or app development agencies to build an untested concept for $50 000 or more, assuming they have all the pieces of the puzzle in place. Shortly thereafter they go out of 'business' (it's only a business if it makes money), having failed big financially and collected some emotional baggage, and they never recover to try again.

In the next couple of chapters, we'll deep dive into the *how* underpinning the modern startup.

Call to action

1. Before you embark on your entrepreneurial journey, take a moment to reflect on what might get in your way and how you might mitigate or overcome this blocker.

2. What's your equivalent of 'a crappy 200 words a day' — the smallest possible step you can take to start building momentum? Take this step *today* and back it up every subsequent day with another small step! You'll soon find those steps getting bigger.

3. What's the smallest step you can take today to give you some confidence that the market also thinks your idea is worth pursuing?

4. If it matters to you, identify and take steps to give you peace of mind and a buffer, as far as your financial situation is concerned. This will free up your mental capacity to focus on moving the needle on your ambitions instead of worrying about bills piling up or about emerging from entrepreneurship after several years without a dollar to your name.

Chapter 7
KNOWING YOUR HOW

'If I have seen further it is by standing on the shoulders of giants.'
Isaac Newton

Today I work with many entrepreneurs to help them validate market appetite for their ideas before they go off and build them. I always begin with one simple question: 'How is this problem currently being solved?' They'll usually fire back with something like their idea being *a little bit better* or *a little bit cheaper* or having some 'killer' feature. But being *a little bit* better or *a little bit cheaper* is usually a fatal combination for a business entering an established market. Not being *remarkably* better sets you up for a race to the bottom in what becomes a blood red ocean.

One night I was on a judging panel at a startup pitching event in Melbourne, where I had to provide constructive feedback to up-and-coming entrepreneurs who had decided to share their idea in front of 100 people. One idea was for a YouTube content parental control system, and my conversation with its promoter went something like this.

'How is this problem currently being solved?'

'Well, YouTube has its own built-in parental control system, and there are a number of competitors out there, but none of them do what we do.'

'Oh, and what's that?'

'We make it easier to configure.'

'Okay, great, so you're a little bit better at configuration.'

'Yes ...'

'Do you think that in this world of marketing messages and demands on our attention, being *a little bit better* than YouTube's built-in system will get people interested enough to fork out their hard-earned cash for something they currently don't pay for?'

'When you put it that way, probably *not*.'

I'm all for supporting entrepreneurs and encouraging wild ideas, but by nipping certain ideas in the bud early, hopefully before thousands of dollars have been poured into its commercialisation, we're giving them more time and money to focus on products that will really resonate with people.

I've also run a number of what we call '14-Hour Startup' workshops. I walk would-be entrepreneurs through the gamut of ideation, problem and solution validation, business model development, prototyping, customer acquisition, growth hacking, capital raising and scaling. A fair chunk of our time is spent on problem and solution fit, because without this, most of the other stuff doesn't matter. As Lincoln said, 'Give me six hours to chop down a tree and I will spend the first four sharpening the axe'.

Many entrepreneurs have approached me after having paid $50 000 to a software development agency (90 per cent upfront!), to show me a product that looks like it was outsourced to a cut-rate software house in a developing nation. The platforms often have zero design or UX ethos, don't work properly, are buggy as all hell, contain code from other clients the agency has worked with, and ultimately have to be rebuilt from the ground up.

The worst bit? What they end up developing isn't designed to observe and identify what the market really wants. They don't help the budding entrepreneur learn something important about their target market. Prototypes and early-stage apps should help you test the underlying building blocks of an idea and business model such as the problem, solution, marketing channel, price point, distributional channel, customer segment and so on.

Given that you can effectively test these for next to nothing, what many (not *all*) web and app development agencies do is almost criminal. They underdeliver, overcharge and seriously compromise the financial runway and psyche of would-be entrepreneurs, who instead of earning their freedom and creating meaningful contributions to the world, end up chasing their losses and falling victim to that little voice in their heads urging them to quit and get a 'real job'.

In an age of unparalleled change, there are many untested assumptions underpinning almost every new idea. The best way to learn what people really want is to take lots of small bets across these assumptions. And fortunately today that is easier than ever.

Place lots of small bets

'I have not failed. I have just found 1000 ways that don't work.'
Thomas Edison

During the 2018 Melbourne International Comedy Festival, I had the opportunity to see Arj Barker perform live in front of almost 1500 people. His set contained lots of anecdotes about how technology pervades our lives, so I asked him to appear on my podcast. I've found that there are parallels between making it in all kinds of creative pursuits and in entrepreneurship. When it comes to placing lots of small bets, Arj does a 'work-in-progress run' at tiny clubs under the alias Keeper or Crapper. 'There's no pressure on me during that week. I road-test the show. I record it each night, listen to it most days and improve it a little each night.' He jokes during his set that people should ask their friends to come along, because by the end of the festival they'd be getting the very best show!

Experimentation and iteration are fundamental to progress in science, in innovation, in comedy, in animation and in music. The script for *Toy Story* was scrapped multiple times, once halfway through production, before it became a game-changing animation feature film that was nominated for three Oscars and grossed US$361.9 million at the box office for Pixar.

To give yourself the best chance of success and avoid overinvesting financially, emotionally, mentally or physically, you've got to empower yourself by testing as many different opportunities as possible before deciding what to double down on.

Ninety-five per cent of startups fail. The main causes, according to data collected by CB Insights, come down to:

- market failure (42 per cent)
- running out of cash (associated with market failure) (29 per cent)

- pricing and cost issues (associated with market failure) (18 per cent)
- lack of need or ineffective business model (associated with market failure) (17 per cent).

You get my point. Building stuff that the market doesn't want will kill your business more than anything else.

If your problem and solution are off, you'll find no joy in painstakingly trying to optimise your marketing or pricing strategies. If you spend a little more time getting the first principles right, everything you do thereafter will be significantly easier. For example, if you've found product/market fit, then it's easier to attract people, your cost of customer acquisition drops, the retention and virality of your product increases, partners want to work with you—things just flow. But if you don't have it, then it becomes an uphill battle. Sales and marketing expert Perry Marshall told me on *Future Squared* that 'It's not a marketing problem [when startups fail]; it's a value proposition problem'.

'But what if people steal my idea?'

You might be thinking, if I'm experimenting and putting my idea in the public domain, am I not sharing my intellectual property? Won't someone steal my magic formula?

First, I'm not going to say there isn't a chance in hell that someone else will steal your idea and successfully commercialise it. But I will say that the chances of that happening are as good as a retired Shaquille O'Neal hitting five free throws in a row.

The reality is this:

1. In their initial form, ideas are a dime a dozen and are very rarely 'good'.
2. Execution is everything, and that's the hard bit. Anyone can come up with ideas but how many are willing to spend the next two, three, four or five years of their life doing the heavy lifting to successfully commercialise those ideas and deal with the financial and emotional barriers we've discussed?
3. If someone wants to fall in love with your idea and commit to it, then good luck to them, but does that really sound like something people will do? It can be hard enough scheduling time with people for fun social events!
4. Finally, protecting an idea is a little like protecting an unfertilised egg and expecting baby chicks to hatch. For ideas to 'incubate', you've got to share them, run experiments, learn, improve and iterate on the idea to discover what works.

Lifestyle business versus unicorn

It seems like everyone wants to build the next Uber, the next billion-dollar unicorn, but do you need to? Would you not be happy generating a six-figure income doing what you love and having the freedom to make your own decisions, and not having to report to a boss whose current position is due mainly to political manoeuvring or length of tenure?

You've got to be clear about defining what kind of business you want to build. Most readers of this book will likely have set their sights on one of the following:

1. a global behemoth with hundreds of millions in revenue and a 10-figure valuation
2. a lifestyle business that earns you a comfortable six-figure income and gives you freedom over how you live your professional and personal life
3. somewhere in between (most established companies live here).

The path you take depends on your why and your what. Some ideas will lend themselves to one type of business more than another. The dynamics of a service-based business are more aligned with options 2 and 3 than option 1 (although the latter is not impossible; it just requires lots of human resources, time and money to scale up).

The fundamentals underpinning the business model, team, path to scale, investment and so on will depend on the type of business you're building. For example, if you were building a lifestyle business with a view to generating several hundred thousand dollars in revenue, then you probably wouldn't need to, nor be able to, raise angel investment or venture capital.

Funding

As at the time of writing this book, I've secured $156 000 in funding from angel investors and $685 000 in government grants (half of which has been realised). I've bootstrapped Collective Campus and Lemonade Stand and helped a pool of startups raise millions through crowdfunding platforms, angel investments and blockchain-based ICOs (initial coin offerings).

I've also interviewed prominent venture capitalists on my podcast, such as Brad Feld of the Foundry Group, which has invested in companies such as Moz, Techstars, YesWare, SendGrid, Sphero and About.me, and prominent angel investors such as Jason Calacanis, author of *How to Invest in Technology Startups*.

5 WAYS INVESTMENT CAN KILL INNOVATION

Depending on the type of business you're starting, you may want to raise funding. But before I go any further, I'd like to offer some words of warning.

Collective Campus, unlike other like businesses, many of which have come and gone, didn't start out with fundraising as a key priority and it still isn't. We started by and continue to focus on our value proposition and being cashflow positive. Over the course of the first 18 months, with a team of just four people, we built a seven-figure business.

By not tapping into funding early, we were operating in a constrained environment. We didn't pay ourselves anything in the first six months, relying instead on side gigs and part-time jobs to keep the lights on. We had to be creative with hiring, incentivisation and marketing, opting for quid pro quo arrangements where possible.

Most of all, we ran countless short and fast experiments across our entire business model, and we still do this today. We never assumed anything about our product, target market, distribution channels, price points, marketing channels, target geographies, sales strategies or messaging in order to land on a model that worked. Because we hadn't taken on external funding, we had the freedom to try different things, which meant we basically decided one day to change the direction of the company entirely by ditching public workshops and instead focusing on corporate innovation training and accelerator programs.

Funding can be a blessing, but it can also be a curse for the following reasons.

1. False validation

Where many entrepreneurs come unstuck is that they confuse raising capital with validation for their idea or concept. Raising

(continued)

5 WAYS INVESTMENT CAN KILL INNOVATION (*CONT'D*)

capital ≠ 'we made it'. For the investor on the other side of that transaction, the startup usually represents one of many bets in a diversified portfolio, most of which they don't expect a return on.

2. Overinvesting in the product, marketing and team

'Now we've raised $1 million, let's hire 10 new employees — designers, UXers, front-end web developers, back-end web developers, a barista, a masseuse, a spiritual guide and a certified moustache curler.' In reality you probably don't need all these people (except maybe the moustache curler).

Unless these people create value above and beyond what they consume, you are better off holding out on hiring. First find something resembling product/market fit and a repeatable way to turn one dollar into one dollar fifty.

3. ROI demands of investors

VCs aim for a 20 per cent return a year, or a 30 per cent net return on capital invested to investors in their fund, or 'limited partners' in the fund's lifetime. Some investors can prematurely push their startups to scale, even though they haven't yet found product/market fit. The problem with this approach is a rapidly rising cost of customer acquisition that customer lifetime value struggles to keep pace with. Venture capitalists, like many in positions of power, can be the lifeblood or ring the death knell of great ideas and teams.

Eric Paley, a managing partner at Founder Collective, recently spoke out about this toxic problem in a TechCrunch article titled 'Toxic VC and the Marginal-Dollar Problem'. VCs are accountable to investors. Often they will try to push a startup that is weighing up a purchase offer to hold out for a larger offer (perhaps blocking smaller offers) because they think the startup has the potential to grow and generate the returns the fund's investors desire. The growth and the bigger offer don't come, so what could have been a multimillion-dollar payday for a founder who invested years of sweat and tears in the company can wind up being much smaller, if anything at all. Taking into account liquidation preferences, investors can sometimes wind up with several times their initial investment before the founder sees a single cent!

4. Lack of testing

Startups that raise big bags of money are far more likely to load up on Facebook ads than they are to diligently test across hundreds of marketing opportunities to see where the most value can be derived. This tendency leads to premature spending on the wrong things (such as team members you don't need and marketing campaigns that go nowhere). Worse still, it also applies to testing the key building blocks underpinning the idea: trying to scale a product without market fit is like rolling a boulder uphill; scaling with market fit is like finding what legendary military strategist Sun Tzu referred to as *shih*, a position of potential force — the position of a boulder perched on a hilltop.

5. Lack of constraints

Operating within constraints forces us to make more diligent decisions. It also encourages us to make lots of small bets, obtain rapid feedback and iterate based on this until we figure out what customers want, because, well, we have no other choice short of betting everything we have on black.

In 2017, my team secured $550 000 from the Australian federal government, but this wasn't to find product/market fit; it was to scale up our corporate accelerator programs, having incubated over 50 startups at the time and run the Mills Oakley Accelerator, Asia–Pacific's first legal–tech focused program. We had something worth scaling.

(continued)

5 WAYS INVESTMENT CAN KILL INNOVATION (*CONT'D*)

Typical startup investment lifecycle

When startups seek investment, they do so based on different factors, and from different people, at different stages of their lifecycle (see table 7.1). I should note, though, that today it's not uncommon for founders to secure significant investment off the back of an idea, but it's usually if they have a track record or (at the time of writing) are doing an ICO.

Table 7.1: example startup investment lifecycle*

Product development	Investment stage	Source of funds	Example metrics	Investment amount
Validate problem	Bootstrap	Under your pillow	User feedback	$0–$25 000
Validate solution	Seed	Family and friends Crowdfunding	User feedback Website sign-ups	$0–$500 000
Validate business model	Seed	Crowdfunding Angels Venture capital	Sales and pre-orders Engagement rate NPS CPA v LTV	$250 000–$1 million
Feature development	Series A	Venture capital Private equity	Monthly recurring revenue growth	$2 million+
Scale	Series B+	Venture capital Private equity IPO	All of the above	$5 million+

* indicative only and may vary based on type of idea and geographic region

SOURCES OF FUNDING

Here are the main sources of funding for startups.

BOOTSTRAPPING

Bootstrapping means financing your startup's growth without the assistance of external investors. Invest small amounts of your own money and try building a customer-driven, cash-flow-positive business (at least in the early stages). Frugal founders tend to make better decisions about where each dollar goes and are less likely to overinvest in team members they don't need or features their customers don't need. It also means that should you choose to eventually seek investment, you will have developed a business that is profitable, and you can therefore raise at a higher valuation, give away less of your business and become more compelling to smart money investors whose powerful networks and experience can help you as much as, if not more than, their money can.

Some entrepreneurs shun investment in favour of maintaining control over their business, and while this might come at the cost of scale, it means they are effectively doing things on their own terms, rather than being held accountable to external investors who may have engineered a deal to have control.

Jane Lu, founder of Sydney-based online fashion e-commerce platform ShowPo, aims to build her business into a $100 million juggernaut by 2020 without external funding. Sure, she could probably have done it more quickly with external support, but at what cost? The ShowPo crew work nine to five; if people are being stretched, Lu says, they hire additional resources. Fridays in the office mean beer and rosé on tap. If scale comes at the cost of work/life balance and ShowPo's fun work culture, then Lu, based on what she values, has made the right decision.

Pros: You maintain full ownership and control, you become better with your money and avoid prematurely scaling the business to death.

Cons: You miss out on the revenue growth, scale, networks and credibility that investment might bring.

Where to source: Under your pillow (or your bank account).

CUSTOMER FINANCED

The best source of financing, in my opinion, is always going to be your customers. At the time of writing, my team was developing a piece of software that aims to productise much of what innovation consultants actually do. But as a lean operation that practises what I preach in this book, we're not about to drop $200 000 on design, development and marketing, and hire a sales team to build the product. We've approached this problem by getting a key client on board to pay us to do it. We effectively sold it before there was anything to sell.

We're now in the process of building this product and it hasn't cost us a dollar of our own money. We get validation. We get customer-informed product development. We get funding. We get a case study. We get a testimonial.

Size: $50 000 – $250 000 (ballpark).

Pros: You don't end up in the red. You gain market validation, case studies and testimonials to build on.

Cons: Customers might not want to work with other parties during the design and build phase, as they may be interested only in what works for them or exclusive deals. What works for them might not necessarily work for other companies in your target segment. You're only as fast as what's in front of you, so such deals might inhibit your speed and growth (especially if the customer is a slow-moving beast).

Where to source: Your prospects, existing customers and companies/ people who look like them.

BONUS: HOW TO STRUCTURE PRE-SALE DEALS

If you're building an enterprise product that you're looking to sell later to the mass market, consider taking a leaf out of the world of agile contract management to increase your chances of getting the product off the ground and avoid overspending on developing features you don't need.

If the product is going to cost, say, $100 000, then tell your very first buyer that you will charge them in four instalments of $25 000, with each subsequent payment contingent on development milestones having been met. Throw in an early termination clause whereby the client pays just 20 per cent of the remaining contract value if they pull the plug early. For example, if the customer decides they've received most of the value they need after the first instalment of $25 000, and they pull the plug then, they need pay only 20 per cent of the remaining $75 000 ($40 000 in total).

This saves you lots of time you might have spent on building out subsequent features that aren't of value (consider the Pareto Principle). It also gives you a higher margin for your efforts and means you can now start to sell the product to the mass market, and build in features as you go based on mass market feedback, rather than the feedback of one customer.

By developing a product in partnership with a client who is a good representation of what your target customer looks like, you might also spare yourself an MVP (minimum viable product) hangover, particularly if your market is small, your prospects expect bells and whistles, and they aren't too fond of second chances.

CREDIT CARDS AND PERSONAL LOANS

You may have heard the story of how Airbnb co-founders Joe Gebbia and Brian Chesky worked up credit card debt worth tens of thousands of dollars in the company's early days. 'You know those binders that you put baseball cards in? We put credit cards in them,' says Chesky. The company famously made only $200 a week for most of 2008. It wasn't until they developed 'their own' line of cereal (called Obama O's and Captain McCain's; actually they simply repackaged an existing cereal) during the US presidential campaign that they made enough to cover their debt and gain the attention of Paul Graham, founder of startup accelerator Y-Combinator, setting them on a path to much, much more than a $200 a week company. Today Airbnb is worth more than US$30 billion.

In a world where testing your idea, bootstrapping and relying on customer funds to build out your business are all viable options, it doesn't make a great deal of sense to pay upwards of 15 per cent in interest and dig yourself into debt through credit cards and personal loans. If you've got product/market fit, then customers should be able to provide the initial runway. If you haven't, then it's hardly advisable to be going into debt to test your assumptions.

Should building out a $75 000 feature put you in pole position to do a million dollars' worth of recurring revenue deals and a personal loan is the fastest way to it (raising funding through angels and VCs takes a lot longer and is generally for larger amounts), then maybe this pathway makes sense. In some cases, small overdrafts might mean the difference between paying your staff long enough to get over the proverbial hump or closing the blinds on your business.

Size: $5000 – $95 000.

Pros: You maintain ownership; a fast source of funding.

Cons: High interest repayments; personal liability.

Where to source: Your local bank or financial institution, as well as online peer-to-peer platforms such as Lending Club and Society One.

FAMILY, FRIENDS AND FOOLS

If you need an initial investment into your business, one of the first places you should look is family, friends and fools. Fools because investing in an early stage business is incredibly risky and is unlikely to deliver a return on investment. That's just the truth, folks.

Size: $5000 – $250 000 (ballpark).

Pros: You have less control but they are generally more supportive — they want to see you succeed; a fast source of funding in most cases.

Cons: This is generally dumb money; you give away ownership (unless they are willing to *loan* you the money); it can undermine relationships if handled poorly and if things don't work out, so it's important to be honest and transparent. These initial investments, if handled poorly, can also make you an unattractive prospect for more sophisticated investors and VCs down the line.

Where to source: Your contacts, LinkedIn, investor networking, meetup events, your Facebook friends list and so on.

ANGEL INVESTMENT

Angel investors either make one-time investments into early-stage companies or deliver ongoing injections of capital to carry the company through its difficult early stages.

Size: $100 000 – $1 000 000 (ballpark).

Pros: Networks, smart money (usually).

Cons: You give up some ownership (generally 10 to 25 per cent) and control; slow to secure (a rule of thumb is three to six months of about 50 per cent of your time).

Where to source: Naval Ravikant's AngelList.com is a good place to start, but industry websites and networking and investor events in your home town are a common go-to. Also search 'angel investor' on LinkedIn and see if you have any mutual connections. If so, ask for a warm introduction.

VENTURE CAPITAL

Taking on VC can make or break you, and as Brad Feld said on *Future Squared*, 'There really are only two key things that matter in the actual term sheet negotiation: economics and control'. Don't get them wrong.

Size: Anywhere from $500 000 to billions. Seriously large VCs such as Softbank don't baulk at investing US$2 billion in on-demand services such as Grab in South-East Asia or US$1.4 billion in Flipkart. Of course, the majority of deals are at the lower end of this spectrum.

Pros: VCs are well networked and can open doors; they understand startups and can provide expert guidance; they can usually invest in subsequent funding rounds and give your company credibility.

Cons: You might give up considerable ownership *and* control; you might be forced to scale prematurely or fall into a number of other VC traps that might not be quite so self-evident when signing a term sheet.

Where to source: Mutual connections on LinkedIn and in your network, AngelList, Crunchbase, CB Insights, your local venture capital networking and pitching events—really, just Google 'how to find venture capital'.

EQUITY CROWDFUNDING

Depending on what corner of the globe you find yourself in, equity crowdfunding may be an option. In principle it's similar to crowdfunding platforms such as Kickstarter, except rather than repaying your supporters with a copy of your finished product, you offer them equity in your company.

Equity crowdfunding is effectively aiming to democratise startup investment as it opens the door to everyday people investing as little as $1000 in an early stage startup at a post-money valuation of, say, $500 000 for 0.2 per cent of the business.

Such arrangements have usually been restricted to the 'sophisticated investor', who meets a minimum annual income or net wealth threshold, as opposed to the everyday retail investor. These restrictions are mostly about protecting retail investors, but a consequence of this is that it effectively increases the gap between the haves and have nots, as the wealthy consolidate their wealth by getting in early on in companies such as Uber, for example.

Size: $100 000 – $1 million (ballpark).

Pros: With no major investors, you can maintain more control; faster; offers social good.

Cons: There are lots of people to be accountable to and report to; dumb money and (usually) limited networks.

Where to source: Platforms such as New Zealand's Equitise, WeFunder and LocalStake are good places to start.

GOVERNMENT GRANTS

Depending on the nature of your product, you may qualify for a number of government grants. For example, Collective Campus has benefited from three government grants totalling $685 000:

- $550 000 dollar-for-dollar matching for our accelerator programs
- $100 000 for Lemonade Stand, our children's entrepreneurship program
- $35 000 for an Entrepreneur-in-Residence grant.

Depending on your business, I suggest Googling 'startup business grants in [your city/country]', because each jurisdiction will likely have its own programs at local, state and federal level.

Size: Anywhere from $5000 to millions.

Pros: You don't give up any equity and tap into government networks.

Cons: Depending on the size of the grant, there might be accountability and rigid reporting requirements to contend with (grants tend to be milestone based and these milestones are usually determined up front, which can inhibit your flexibility to adapt your strategy).

Where to source: Google; local, state and federal government websites offer a wealth of resources.

INITIAL COIN OFFERINGS (ICOs)

You might have read about ICOs, the funding mechanism driven by the blockchain and cryptocurrency. Currently, this funding model is most plausible for blockchain-based startups. ICOs provide startups with investment capital, without the oversight of an angel investor syndicate, bank or venture capitalist, and while they can be a force for good and—like equity crowdfunding—democratise early-stage startup investment, they have also attracted a lot of people looking to make a quick buck.

Many ICOs, up until late 2018, required nothing more than a flashy white paper to successfully raise millions, often in minutes, from unsophisticated investors looking to cash in on the crypto hype-cycle. Such startups have been referred to as 'slideware', pointing to the fact that their entire business is based on a PowerPoint slide deck, rather than revenue, customers or traction. They tend to be littered with 'what we will do' promises, rather than 'what we have done'. ICOs can be a legitimate source of funding for your business, and I have personally been involved in ICOs for legitimate companies. Just be aware that they have a relatively bad name because numerous scammers have used them to get rich quick and disappear. For example, the startup Prodeum promised to 'revolutionise the fruit and vegetable industry', but duped its ICO investors by leaving behind a website with only one word on it—'penis'—shortly after raising millions.

Size: $500000 to millions.

Pros: Social good (if you're legitimate, you're aiding the democratisation of startup investment); you maintain control (most coins offered don't come with ownership or control); they are liquid (you can sell out on the secondary market at any time). Also, you can share the underlying codebase and transfer control to other players much more easily than a traditional finance-backed business.

Cons: They currently have a bad name, which might reflect on your company and hopes for future investment from more legitimate sources such as VCs, securities regulation risks (still a grey area), volatility around price (for example, high-profile ICO Bancor raised US$156 million and crashed by 56 per cent shortly after).

Where to source: Blockstarter, ICOBOX, Crypterium, Lykke, Ethereum, NEM and more (Google ICO platform for an extensive list).

TWO TERMS YOU NEED TO KNOW

Your **burn rate** is the amount of money that you are effectively 'burning' through each month. Your **runway** is the amount of months you've got before you run out of money to 'burn' — essentially, your cash at bank divided by your burn rate.

Do I need a team?

I'm often asked this question. The conventional 'wisdom' in the startup world is that you need a hacker (web developer), hipster (designer, UX, marketer) and hustler (for sales and strategy, the business brain) on your team to do anything meaningful. I dare say this is an oversimplification. As mentioned in chapter 4, in the early stages of your journey, whether it is finding out *what* to do or figuring out your product, you'll want to explore before you exploit.

Josh Kaufman, author of *The Personal MBA*, asks, 'To build a skill from scratch, you need to know how to climb a ladder but how do you know which ladder to climb?' When *The Lean Startup*'s Eric Ries met with senior Toyota executives to talk about both Toyota's lean production system and Ries's much-celebrated philosophy, Ries held forth enthusiastically but respectfully (after all, the lean startup evolved out of Toyota's 'kaizen' approach to business) about how the lean startup could be applied in large organisations such as Toyota. After a brief pause, one of the executives turned to Ries and said, 'This is the missing piece ... we have a system for efficiently taking products to market, but we don't have a system for deciding *what* to take to market to begin with'.

GETTING THE RIGHT PEOPLE ON THE BUS

Long ago, in his genre-defining book *Good to Great*, Jim Collins explained that in order to be great, companies need to start by getting the right people on the bus, the wrong people off the bus, and the right people in the right seats.

When what you're working on is a mere kernel of an idea, putting a team together can be a premature step, unless you're what author Gretchen Rubin dubs an 'obliger'—that is, you perform better when you're accountable to other people, you enjoy the energy of working in a team and you won't get anything done without one! If you have a strong sense of accountability to yourself, then you might want to figure out the basics before you bring on a team.

What if you lack design, marketing or development skills? Today finding freelancers to help you at a very competitive rate is a click away through platforms such as Upwork, Freelancer or Fiverr.

Once you've closed in on what it is you're actually building, then perhaps you can recruit complementary skill-sets to help you where needed.

When I started Hotdesk, I spent the first year going it alone. In retrospect, I should have brought on my first hire, Lambert, much sooner. Not only were we able to get way more done, but we could bounce ideas off each other, complement each other's skill-set and perhaps most crucially, provide each other with moral support to keep digging deep while rolling the proverbial boulder uphill.

In short, and depending on the nature of the business, if you must start with a team, it will usually be prudent to start with one complementary co-founder. This is also something that startup investors will look for, because they appreciate how difficult it is to build a startup and that one person simply can't go it alone. Be absolutely diligent about getting the right people on the bus, especially when equity, ownership and decision-making authority are involved. One bad egg can ruin it for everyone.

I've seen *pre-revenue* startups legally give up 20 per cent of any future profits to an ex-founder over an intellectual dispute. Bringing a co-founder on board is a little like getting married. You probably wouldn't put a ring on the first person you meet after a couple of dates, so why would you make a comparable commitment when it comes to your business partner?

First hire for attitude and factors such as development potential and coachability, then look at experience and skill-set. Often a generous starting salary brings you experienced talent, but it can also bring you a stifling 'I know best' mindset and someone who, when things get tough, will quit at the drop of a hat in search of 'better' opportunities elsewhere.

You'll want to hire people who share your vision, people who believe in what you're trying to build, whose purpose is aligned with the company's. Otherwise, when the going gets tough, there's not a tough person to be found. I've often hired people who were willing to take a pay cut to join our team, demonstrating that they're driven by more than just money and giving me the confidence that they'll be in it for the long haul.

In short, explore while you're figuring out what to build, use freelancers to help you, and once you've figured it out, look to bring on a co-founder. To help you on your journey, table 7.2 catalogues some of the pros and cons of bringing on team members early.

Table 7.2: pros and cons of bringing on team members early

Pros	Cons
More ideas and honest feedback (which can lead to better decision making!)	Misaligned values and vision
Motivate each other	Increase operational costs
Emotional support	Might not be enough work to go around, so you're wasting money
Many hands make lighter work	Potential legal disputes
Complement each other's skill-sets	Incongruence between team members
Go further *and* faster	
Easier to raise funds	
Leverage each other's networks	

Whatever the case, if you operate solo then there's a pretty low ceiling on how far you can go. If you've got what Jim Collins calls a Big Hairy

Audacious Goal (BHAG), then you'll eventually need to build a team around you so you can focus on value creation, rather than spreading yourself too thin across every facet of the business, doing a half-baked job of it and burning out in the process.

Getting the wrong people *off* the bus

The problem with many startups trying to do great things is that the wrong people are on the bus and they're distracting the driver.

Tell-tale signs of having the wrong people on the bus include the following:

- People default to 'I'm so busy' whenever asked how they are.
- People watch the clock.
- People are more concerned with how much they get paid than with their work.
- People are always looking to get away with doing as little work as possible.
- People's values aren't aligned with the organisation's.
- People have other priorities (such as watching reality television).

If you or your teammates demonstrate these values, stop, reflect and take action.

A CHAMPION TEAM OR A TEAM OF CHAMPIONS?

A winning team is always much greater than the sum of its parts. Sam Walker, *Wall Street Journal* sports journalist and author of *The Captain Class*, researched thousands of champion teams across the globe, and found that some of the best teams in sporting history could be described as a 'group of individuals who were unremarkable alone, but together—potent, magical'.

If you have a purpose or mission that inspires people, if you create an environment that gives them autonomy and challenges them to get better every day, and perhaps most importantly, if you develop a system that enables ordinary people to achieve extraordinary things, then you don't need to worry about finding extraordinary people.

Not only will this minimise financial strain on the business and extend your runway, but it will also leave your workforce feeling gratified by the journey.

MONEYBALL

In the film *Moneyball* (based on the book of the same name by Michael Lewis), Brad Pitt plays the Oakland Athletics coach. The film focuses on the analytical, data-informed approach that the team took to compete, despite having a fraction of the funds of marquee teams such as the Yankees. The 2002 Athletics, or 'the A's', had a successful season, having spent only US$44 million on salaries, compared with the likes of the New York Yankees whose equivalent payroll was more than US$125. Not only that, but the team's brand of analytics has since been adopted by many major league teams, including the Yankees, the Red Sox and the Mets, and was fundamental in helping the underfunded Mets reach the 2015 World Series.

Of course, if you have bags of money you could take the Netflix approach of hiring top of market, but something tells me that if you're reading this book you probably don't have this luxury.

Models

One of the best ways to avoid making common mistakes and get ahead fast is to *model the best* rather than trying to figure it all out for yourself. People who rely on experience alone are slow learners.

Study models, too, to understand what they did wrong and avoid the missteps that prevent people from achieving their desired outcomes. For example, if you want to become a better basketball shooter, you'll identify (a) the three most important things that good shooters do well and (b) the three most common errors poor shooters make. Rather than just shooting, without a deliberate focus, 1000 shots a day for a prolonged period, work on doing more of (a) while stamping out (b). Lots of shooting practice will probably work too, but which one do you think will get you to your desired goal faster?

How to build brand *you*

If you're selling to large enterprise clients, or any clients for that matter, having a compelling personal brand will help open doors to meetings with prospects, investors, potential partners and others. So how do you go about building your brand, network and credibility, often from a base of zero? This doesn't necessarily need to be a marathon-like effort. Yes, it takes time, but using today's tools you can 10X the pace at which you build your own brand.

Having a compelling personal brand is vital to opening doors. For example, my podcast was launched on a shoestring budget and in the space of 18 months opened doors to conversations and relationships with a wide range of influential thought leaders I might otherwise not have been able to get a direct line to.

The ever quotable Zig Ziglar said it best: 'You can have anything in life that you want, if you can just help enough other people get what they want'. When building your brand, especially through content, make it about *them*. All of my podcast guests are given an opportunity to promote their books to my audience. What's in it for them is a simple question you should answer whenever you approach anyone for help.

A number of tools exist to help you build your brand. By contributing regularly to platforms such as LinkedIn, Medium and Twitter, for example, you'll become more visible to people who matter, and when they are ready your name might already have some value in their minds. It's just like company branding. How many times have you been reminded of a brand through its marketing campaigns, but you weren't ready to buy until years later? When you finally reached that stage, you already had a shortlist of two or three companies, based on the visibility of their brand and its place in your subconscious.

If you've got a bit more time up your sleeve, start a podcast and invite influencers to appear on it. It's also a great way to build your network, learn more about your craft and improve your conversational skills. For more on starting a podcast, check out John Lee Dumas' free podcast course on Apple and Google Podcasts.

You need to tell a compelling story. Your brand should be about more than who you are; it should tell a story that resonates with people about why you do what you do, where you come from, where you're going.

Lawrence Levy, Pixar's former CEO and author of *To Pixar and Beyond*, says of the studio's purpose, 'It's not just about entertainment. It's about telling stories that audiences connect with emotionally'.

When I think of Apple, I don't just think of their products, but of their backstory of entrepreneurship and taking on IBM and Microsoft. I think about their quest for great design and great products that revolutionise the customer experience and the way we do things. I think of Steve Jobs being fired from Apple, and of his second coming more than a decade later, heralding the introduction of the hugely popular iMac, iPod, iPhone, iPad and new line of MacBooks.

PIG ISLAND

When I interviewed Paul Smith, author of *Sell with a Story*, he told me a fascinating story, which he calls an accidental sales story.

Paul was visiting an art fair in Cincinnati with his wife when he stumbled on a picture of a pig in the ocean. When he asked what the pig was doing in the water, the artist said that the picture was taken off an island called Big Major Cay, in the Bahamas.

Apparently, an entrepreneur had brought pigs to the island years ago to raise for bacon, but the island didn't offer the pigs much in the way of sustenance other than cactus, which pigs aren't very fond of.

However, a nearby restaurant soon started offloading its kitchen refuse offshore, and the pigs ultimately learned how to swim out to it to feed. Every generation of pigs since has learned how to swim.

The island is now known as Pig Island.

The story transformed an odd picture of a pig in water to a conversation starter and a lesson on geography, psychology and biological evolution.

People who tell good stories sell more than those who don't.

The key ingredients to any good story:

1. main character(s)
2. context
3. challenge or struggle
4. resolution.

So what's *your* story?

COMMON PITFALLS FOR ENTREPRENEURS TO AVOID

Following are some of the snares every budding entrepreneur should beware of:

1. Using a software development agency from day one, even though you have yet to nail your value proposition or find product/market fit.

2. Giving away too much equity for too little 'dumb money'.

3. Building something that's 'a little bit better' or 'a little bit cheaper'.

4. Falling in love with a solution instead of falling in love with solving a big enough problem or creating a lot of unique value.

5. Scaling prematurely, hiring the wrong team members or team members you don't need, and spending big on features and marketing campaigns that go nowhere.

---

12 RULES FOR MAINTAINING YOUR ENERGY AND ENTHUSIASM

Often when we first embark upon something, be it a new romantic relationship, or a new business, our dopamine receptors can be super-active, which cranks up our motivation. Over time, however, they get blunted and require a higher frequency or intensity of exposure to that thing that got us buzzing in the first place — also known as 'chasing the dragon'. So many entrepreneurs get excited when they start something but their motivation and effort tapers off after the initial buzz. With that in mind, how might you maintain the enthusiasm and energy required to make a sustained effort in your venture? Following are 12 rules I've found to keep the fire burning long after the proverbial honeymoon period has subsided.

1. A worthwhile 'why' underpinning what you do

When meaning underpins what you do, you'll be far more likely to ride the highs and, more importantly, the lows associated with pursuits of any kind and keep moving forward. If you don't believe in the underlying why, then you'll give up or slow down at the first sign of difficulty.

2. Novelty

Exploring new things that you can apply to your business, such as a new product line, marketing campaign or an experiment with a new sales tool, can keep things interesting.

3. Variety

Focus is important but, somewhat paradoxically, variety can help you focus for longer. Spending time podcasting, writing and keynoting, on top of my day to day, ensures no two days are the same and I don't get bored or uninspired.

4. Short-term goals an feedback loops

Capitalise on Parkinson's Law and engineer shorter term goals into your work year to ramp up focus and flow, rather than focusing on annual goals alone. Shorter term goals and smaller batch sizes in general translate into a shorter feedback loop, which Nicole Forsgren, co-author of *Accelerate: The Science of Lean Software and Devops: Building and Scaling High Performing Technology Organizations,* says helps to increase motivation and avoid burnout.

5. Constant learning

As your business grows, you might find your role will evolve with it — from a doer to a leader — and this requires learning what you need to thrive in your new role. Learning can be a source of ongoing reward.

6. Make time to flow

Find several hours of uninterrupted time each day to focus on tasks that require critical or creative thinking, tasks that make the rest of the world slip away and make three hours seem like 30 minutes. More on this in chapter 9!

7. Smell the roses

Celebrate and share the big and small values-aligned wins. This helps you to not lose sight of why you're doing what you're doing to begin with.

8. Develop your team

Take an active interest in your team's development, both as professionals and as human beings. This can be immensely rewarding.

9. Immerse yourself

When I watch a UFC fight card, I'm so much more motivated in the gym that week. Similarly, when I listen to an entrepreneurship podcast or talk to friends who are in the space, I'm also more motivated to invest the time and energy in my business. Immerse yourself in content and surround yourself with people who keep you motivated.

(continued)

12 RULES FOR MAINTAINING YOUR ENERGY AND ENTHUSIASM (*CONT'D*)

10. Aim to be better than who you were yesterday

It's not about comparing yourself with the next person — such thinking is a recipe for self-defeatism because we'll naturally overestimate their positive qualities and underestimate our own, leaving us feeling like shit. Instead, focus on what you can control — being better than you were yesterday.

11. Exercise and nutrition

Eat well, train well. More on this in chapter 11.

12. Rest

I used to subscribe to the Bon Jovi–inspired 'I'll sleep when I'm dead' philosophy, but it didn't take me long to realise that I'd be dead sooner than planned and so would my business if I didn't get enough rest and find time to play. Your energy levels (and your colleagues' opinion of you) will be all the better for it.

Call to action

1. Determine whether the type of business you want to build is a lifestyle business, a unicorn or, like most businesses, somewhere in between. This will inform how big or small you need to be thinking and subsequent decisions you'll be making.

2. Determine whether or not you really need investment (if so, what kind) or whether you can bootstrap. If your plan is for a lifestyle business, then you probably don't need much investment, if any.

3. Determine whether you need a co-founder or a team and what skills your team members need to complement your strengths. Identify people in your immediate network who can fill a role or introduce you to someone who can, and consider whether some 'hired guns', best found on online freelancer platforms, could help you through those early stages.

4. What models exist for what you are trying to achieve (people or businesses)? Reach out to them or Google them online to identify which of their steps you can replicate and which of their mistakes you should avoid.

5. Write your personal story, using the steps provided in this chapter, so when people ask you what you do, you can respond with something compelling and memorable, something that will leave them wanting to know more and perhaps to explore opportunities with you.

Chapter 8
TESTING YOUR IDEAS

'Success consists of going from failure to failure without loss of enthusiasm.'
Winston Churchill

We've already established that Moore's Law and the accelerating pace of change is making it increasingly difficult to predict what will give businesses a competitive advantage going forward.

The impact of change and uncertainty is manifest in two developments. First, 50 per cent of the companies on the S&P500 index will be replaced within the next 10 years at current rates of churn, with the average company lifespan expected to fall to under 15 years by 2030, from a high of 60 in the mid 20th century when the technology underpinning business moved at an exponentially slower rate.

Second, venture capitalists are taking the machine-gun approach. Despite the fact that investing in early-stage innovation is the mandate of most VCs, great ideas, great teams and all the due diligence in the world aren't enough to mitigate the uncertainty to a level where more than 10 per cent of VC investments amount to home runs. Venture capitalists invest across a number of startups and tend to hit one home run (a 100× return), a couple of base hits (10–20× returns) and seven strikeouts.

As already noted, market failure is the number one reason that startups fail.

'I just know this will work', 'I think this is a good idea' and statements to that effect are famous last words for many a failed entrepreneur. On this, Annie Duke, former World Series of Poker champion and author of *Thinking in Bets*, has this to say: 'Your intuition is generally not being challenged by people who think that another answer might be right, because it's generally just running on its own so it's not held accountable. The other thing that happens when you're relying on intuition alone is that it's harder to get to innovative solutions. It tends to encourage the status quo because intuition by definition is informed by the history of your experiences so it's not going to lead you to something like a paradigm shift'.

Don't rely on intuition or what some call professional judgement alone. Complementing what you think with customer-driven data and real-world opinions is an absolute must. Adopting an entrepreneurial mindset is key to succeeding in today's increasingly volatile environment.

Below I've built upon Alberto Savoia's 'pretotyping manifesto' to demonstrate what this mindset is all about:

- Execution beats ideation.
- Prototypes beat products.
- Doing beats talking.
- Simplicity beats features.
- Now beats later.
- Commitment beats committees.
- Data beats opinions.
- Failure is an option.
- Extreme ownership, not excuses.
- Long-term thinking, not short-term reward.
- Risk mitigation by doing, not analysis.
- Focus on the greater good, not what's in it for me.
- Adaptable, not inflexible.
- Measure outcomes, not inputs.

- Open and collaborative, not closed and secretive.
- Courage, not cowardice.

On the last point, Ben Horowitz puts it better than I ever could in his book *The Hard Thing about Hard Things*: 'Over the past ten years, tech advances have dramatically lowered the financial bar for starting a new company, but the *courage bar* for building a great company remains as high as it has ever been'.

You've got to be 10× better

If you're building something fundamentally new (remember, not just a simple lifestyle business), then being a little bit cheaper or a little bit better isn't anywhere near enough. People are hardly likely to take note of your product for a number of reasons, as Clayton Christensen, Karen Dillon and others noted in their seminal book, *Competing Against Luck*.

Here are eight reasons people won't care about your product unless you are fundamentally better:

1. People's habits of the present
2. 'I'm used to doing it this way'
3. 'I don't love the problem but I'm comfortable with how I deal with it' (On several occasions now I've contemplated switching to Android, only for my anxiety about leaving Apple to force me to stay and sign a two-year contract extension.)
4. Anxiety of choosing something new ('What if it's not better?' 'What if it's worse?')
5. Fear of loss
6. Switching costs
7. Budget constraints
8. Bad timing.

Richard Koch, author of *The 80/20 Principle*, echoes these sentiments in his book *Simplify*. He identifies two ways to simplify your business for competitive advantage: price and proposition. 'Be at least half as cheap or *one order of magnitude* better.'

This is where understanding your customer *jobs to be done* becomes important. Jobs to be done are the underlying tasks consumers are trying to perform in their lives. For example, a 24-year-old purchases a pair of Nike sneakers to satisfy a range of jobs, not only comfortably supporting their feet, but perhaps primarily expressing their style and signalling status. These jobs could have been satisfied in other ways, however — sneakers from Adidas or a niche brand, for example, or in the case of self-expression, a pair of distressed designer jeans or a zero-fade haircut with an elaborate quiff! Nike's competition in this instance goes way beyond just other footwear manufacturers.

I didn't grow my hair long as a teen because I wanted to save money on haircuts: I was expressing my non-conformist values and my love of heavy metal music (I guess not much has changed, except for the hair). I cut my hair at 21 and compensated by getting a couple of tattoos and wearing black T-shirts emblazoned with the logos of bands I was listening to at the time. The job to be done had not changed, but the means through which I expressed myself did. Tattoo parlours probably don't consider themselves competitors of hair salons, but they can be just that. A rebellious teen who has just discovered the punk stylings of NOFX or the Misfits is just as likely to turn up at home, much to the chagrin of his parents, in a lime green mohawk as with a tattoo on his arm.

Many people who have had a tough week look to gain some respite by downing a few glasses of whisky or wine, while others might hit the shopping malls for some retail therapy. Some might browse holiday spots on Expedia, while others seek out a cuddle from their partner or perhaps a romp under the sheets. All of these essentially serve the same underlying job to be done. Your competitors will go far beyond products or services that look just like yours. They extend to any product or service that helps customers get jobs done, whatever those jobs happen to be.

NO ROOM FOR MEDIOCRITY

Needing to be 10× better goes beyond products and brands, but also extends to brand *you*.

Alec Ross, author of the best-seller *Industries of the Future* and a widely respected futurist, believes there will be no room for mediocrity in the future. 'What previously would have been five anaesthesiologists inside five surgeries, it's now one anaesthesiologist managing five surgeries. Four anaesthesiologists have been displaced. So the one who remains, the one who monitors the five and goes into the room if there's a problem, they would be the best of the sample. It's making the labour more and more specialised, and it's punishing mediocrity. The future is going to be a terrible time to be mediocre.'

SETH GODIN ON THE PURPLE COW

In his book *Purple Cow*, celebrated entrepreneur, teacher and author, Seth Godin, urges would-be entrepreneurs to shoot for remarkable.

> When my family and I were driving through France a few years ago, we were enchanted by the hundreds of storybook cows grazing on picturesque pastures right next to the highway. For dozens of kilometers, we all gazed out the window, marveling about how beautiful everything was. Then, within twenty minutes, we started ignoring the cows. The new cows were just like the old cows, and what once was amazing was now common. Worse than common. It was boring.

> Cows, after you've seen them for a while, are boring. They may be perfect cows, attractive cows, cows with great personalities, cows lit by beautiful light, but they're still boring.

> A Purple Cow, though. Now that would be interesting. (For a while.) The essence of the Purple Cow is that it must be remarkable. In fact, if 'remarkable' started with a P, I could probably dispense with the cow subterfuge, but what can you do?

So how do you go about avoiding mediocrity and becoming remarkable? Instead of jumping to conclusions and building the first thing that comes to mind, or falling in love with your untested solution, or releasing a product that's a little better or a little cheaper, you need to find out what customers *really* want. What will make them say 'wow' and throw their cash, credit card or cryptocurrency at you. The challenge is, as Steve Jobs understood, customers often don't know what they want, so your job is to tease it out of them, and it's not as simple as asking.

Introducing design thinking

Design thinking is a human-centred design process that develops solutions for the problems humans encounter. The process starts with the people you are designing for and ends with the solution designed for these people.

The five stages of design thinking are collect insights, define the problem, ideate solutions, prototype and test. For the purposes of this book we will focus our attention on the first three phases.

COLLECT INSIGHTS

The highest quality solutions come from valuable insights into human behaviour. However, learning to recognise those insights is harder than you think.

First, engage. Traditional interviews often lead participants down a particular path and can return false positives, ultimately not unlocking new or unanticipated breakthrough insights. It's critical that you use open-ended questions and always ask 'why?' to uncover deeper meaning when having conversations with your customers.

Second, observe. Observing what people do and how they interact in their natural habitat gives you clues about what they think, feel and need that aren't revealed through conversations alone. Did you observe a customer performing some kind of workaround? You might be onto something. Ask them why.

Finally, immerse. What better way to understand what your customers go through than actually experience their journey first hand? Go through the experience they encounter and capture key aspects of this journey (what was expected, what was unexpected, how they felt etc.). For example, if you're trying to apply design thinking to the New York City subway, trace every step a customer might take from checking what time the train is coming while they're in the comfort of their home all the way to stepping into the office at the other end of their journey. What could be better? What were the pain points? What worked well?

DEFINE THE PROBLEM

Capture, consolidate and organise the insights gathered during the first phase into categories or themes. During this phase we're looking to define the overarching area we're addressing or the problem we're solving. What becomes powerful during this phase is the 'How Might We' question.

How Might We (HMW) questions provide a springboard to brainstorm innovative new solutions to problems identified. Here's an example:

- *Learning:* Adults spend a significant amount of time trying to find the right gift.
- *Theme:* We're looking at the time spent buying gifts.
- *Insight:* Time is an important consideration in the gift-buying process.
- *HMW:* How might we decrease the amount of time gift buyers spend trying to find the right gift?

IDEATE SOLUTIONS

If you're working alone or with customers, come up with as many solutions to your How Might We question as possible individually first. We call this 'working alone together' and it works to mitigate the effects of groupthink and anchoring to one of the first ideas that comes up.

Then present your ideas at the same time and group similar ideas. Discuss the different groups of ideas, then have each member of your team or each participating customer vote on their top three favourite ideas. This will help you to *diverge* across a massive pool of ideas but then *converge* on two or three to experiment with.

Timebox these sessions, go for quantity of ideas, remove judgement and encourage crazy ideas. It's easy to fall into the trap of shutting down ideas when you first hear them. ('That's not possible!' or 'That will never work!') When you hear an idea from a team member or catch yourself self-censoring, think 'Yes, and …' rather than 'But …' in order to maintain the momentum of the ideation session and to help generate as many ideas as possible. Bad ideas do exist, but sometimes they are the ones that lead to the breakthrough ideas. As Peter Diamandis says, 'The day before something was a breakthrough, it was a crazy idea'.

Taking this approach will help you avoid jumping to conclusions, get better at unlocking the true areas for value creation and ultimately land on a solution that wows, rather than one that just works. This is just one of many tools to help you come up with ideas.

For a comprehensive guide, download our free ebook, Design Thinking: Stop Talking, Start Making, at **www. employeetoentrepreneur.io/designthinkingbook**.

Design thinking is one of many ideation tools. Find a library of additional tools at **www.employeetoentrepreneur.io/resources**.

From idea to execution

You may have heard about the lean startup methodology. You may have even read the book and tried applying it. What I'm presenting here is a crash course in this methodology.

If you'd like to learn more, I've included some additional resources at **www.employeetoentrepreneur.io/resources**.

STEP 1: THE STARTING BLOCKS

In a world where technologies, business models and customer habits are changing fast, the assumptions underpinning our ideas are likely to be flawed, so it doesn't make sense to develop a 50- to 100-page business plan based on these flawed assumptions, complete with elaborate financial projections or prophecies. The thing about prophecies is that they usually don't come true, unless of course you happen to be an octopus named Paul. If you like wasting time, and telling people you're 'busy' makes you feel good about yourself, then go ahead, but if you're serious about taking a product to market that resonates with your target audience and makes money, then instead of an elaborate business plan, start with a single page (see figure 8.1).

PROBLEM	SOLUTION	UNIQUE VALUE PROPOSITION	UNFAIR ADVANTAGE	CUSTOMER SEGMENTS
List your top 1–3 problems.	Outline a possible solution for each problem.	Single, clear, compelling message that states why you are different and worth paying attention.	Something that cannot easily be bought or copied.	List your target customers and users.
	KEY METRICS List the key numbers that tell you how your business is doing.		**CHANNELS** List your path to customers (inbound or outbound).	
EXISTING ALTERNATIVES List how these problems are solved today.		**HIGH-LEVEL CONCEPT** List your X for Y analogy e.g. YouTube = Flickr for videos.		**EARLY ADOPTERS** List the characteristics of your ideal customers.
COST STRUCTURE List your fixed and variable costs.		**REVENUE STREAMS** List your sources of revenue.		

Figure 8.1: Ash Maurya's lean canvas

Source: LeanStack, used with permission from Ash Mauya

The lean canvas, popularised by Ash Maurya, is a single-page adaptation of Alex Osterwalder's business model canvas. It forces you to identify the key building blocks underpinning your idea and have a go at answering fundamental questions such as:

1. What's the problem you're solving?
2. How does your solution solve this problem?
3. Who will use your product (*not* 'everyone')?
4. Which channels will you use to get the product in the customers' hands?
5. How will you promote your offer?
6. What will it cost to do all this?
7. How will you make more money than you spend?

By completing a canvas, you'll be able to get a better feel for what your make-or-break assumptions are and get moving.

INTRODUCING THE MAKE-OR-BREAK ASSUMPTION (MOBA)

Take Uber's business model. There are a number of assumptions that underpin its success. For example, people will use smartphones and have access to the internet, they'll be happy to pay through their phones or they prefer not to use taxis and so on. But there is one leap of faith assumption underpinning Uber's success above all else ...

Trust.

Trust that the person picking me up isn't a serial killer, or that the person I'm picking up isn't going to pull a 1960s Robert De Niro mafioso-inspired move from the back seat and suck the life out of me with a garotte! Without trust, Uber's entire business model falls down faster than Apollo Creed in Rocky IV (sorry Creed fans, but it's hard to look past Ivan Drago as the coolest of all the fighters in the Rocky saga).

So your job, once you've completed your lean canvas, is to determine what your make-or-break assumptions are. It's easy to overdo it; don't.

- Limit your assumptions to those that have the greatest impact.
- Avoid paralysis by analysis.
- Focus on the *riskiest* assumptions only.
- Focus on what you don't know instead of falling into the trap of confirming what you already do know.

As an example of this last point, if you were building a wearable device, don't go testing whether or not people will use a device to monitor heart-rate as we already have enough evidence to suggest that they do this through existing products such as heart-rate monitors and Fitbits; similarly Apple didn't need to test whether customers would listen to music on the go, as the first Sony Walkman proved that a quarter of a century earlier.

PRIORITISING MOBAs

In order to focus your efforts on only the most risky and impactful assumptions, table 8.1 offers a simple approach to help you prioritise them. First, divide how impactful the assumption will be if it turns out to be true/false by how certain you are that the assumption is true. Second, take this result and divide it by whether or not the assumption is something that matters today, and that you can test today, to determine the final number. The higher the number, the higher the priority. This forces you to not only focus on the most impactful assumptions, but also on those that you can actually test today.

Table 8.1: how to prioritise your assumptions

	Step 1					Step 2		
	Low 0	High 10	Low 0	High 10	#	Today 1	Future 5	Rank
	Impact		Certainty			Time		
Assumption 1	9		3		3	2		1.5
Assumption 2	8		4		2	3		0.66
Assumption 3	7		5		1.4	4		0.35

For example, say I'm developing a fruit box subscription service. I have two assumptions: people will pay for a fruit subscription service and they will refer friends to that service to drive growth. In this case, we can test the former today, but the latter is something we won't be able to test until people have had an interaction with our service. So unless the first assumption is true, the second one doesn't matter.

STEP 2: PROTOTYPING

Once you've got to this point, then you want to create prototypes to start testing your assumptions and separating fact from fiction as quickly, cheaply and effectively as possible.

I like to categorise prototypes into the following categories.

1. HYPOTHETICAL

This is an improved version of asking people whether or not they'd use your product but doing so in a way that is designed to observe behaviour, rather than simply asking yes or no questions. The problem with leading questions is that it's much easier and rewarding for human beings to say 'yes', because we have an innate desire to avoid conflict, to conciliate, to be liked and not to hurt other people's feelings.

So how might we design this experiment? Well, if you were promoting, say, an 'Airbnb for Gyms' platform that gave young professionals with a heavy travel schedule casual access to gyms anywhere in the world, then you might camp outside gyms in your central business district and intercept your target market, probably between six and seven in the morning and six and seven in the evening. If you can offer them an incentive of some kind (maybe a protein bar or a shaker), they'll be more likely to spend a couple of minutes answering your questions. Try to actually sell a subscription to 'GymBnB', as if it exists. If they offer to sign up and pay, perhaps offer them a second protein bar or something altogether different as thanks and mention that the platform isn't yet up and running, but you'd be happy to take their details and get in touch as soon as it's live, and offer them a promotional discount.

2. WIZARD OF OZ

Remember Dorothy and her pals hop, skip and jumping along the yellow brick road, in search of courage, a brain and a heart, only to discover that the Wizard of Oz wasn't really much of a wizard at all, but just an old man hiding behind a curtain, pushing buttons to create the illusion of being a great wizard. As such, the Wizard of Oz prototype looks real from the outside, but if you peel back the cover you'll realise there's nothing much there.

3. MINIMUM VIABLE PRODUCT (MVP)

Finally, a minimum viable product has been defined as 'that version of a new product which allows a team to collect the maximum amount of validated learning about customers with the least effort'. It is a functional version of the product, but focuses on only the key features required to solve a problem or create value for the customer — that is, the minimum amount you need to build to compel a customer to pay you for said product. Just be wary of having an MVP hangover (introduced in chapter 7).

ON EARLY ADOPTERS

Remember, not everyone will be your customer from day one. You need to identify your early adopters, who usually make up about 15 per cent of the eventual market. These are the people who will become your early fans, keep your ship afloat and give you the cash flow and runway you need to build your product out over time to reach a wider audience. If you try to be everything to everyone you will ultimately wind up being nothing to everyone or, at best, mediocre and forgettable. Definitely not remarkable.

For example, when the iPad v1 came along, I recall how one of the directors at a government agency I worked for at the time bought one the day it was launched. He'd actually lined up to buy one. Many in the office poked fun at him: 'You're such a big kid!' and 'It's only a big phone, except you can't call or text people!' You might refer to my manager friend as a tech geek who loved to be on the cutting edge of things. Sure enough, though, I soon had a tablet of my own, because I found ways I could use it that would add value to certain aspects of my life. Reading books and blogs, browsing the web, watching video and playing mobile games were all way more conducive to a tablet screen than a smartphone screen.

This evolution from 'tech geek' to 'early adopter' is commonly how new innovations are received. Famous management thinker Geoffrey Moore even wrote a book about it called *Crossing the Chasm*. Here he shows that the technology adoption lifecycle starts with what he calls innovators ('tech geeks') to early adopters, the early majority, the late majority and, finally, the laggards (see figure 8.2). My old manager was in the 2.5 per cent of the eventual market for the tablet. I, like many of my colleagues, was an 'early adopter', making up about 13.5 per cent of the eventual market.

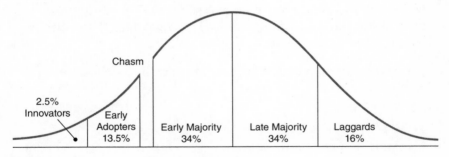

Figure 8.2: technology adoption lifecycle
Source: Geoffrey A. Moore, Crossing the Chasm

Sean Ellis, who had previously headed up Growth at Dropbox, told me that early customer surveys showed that about 80 per cent of people responded affirmatively to 'I like to be the first to use new technology', but before too long 80 per cent responded affirmatively to 'I like to use new products that add genuine value'. Dropbox was starting to acquire more 'early adopter' customers, representing a larger portion of the eventual market, as they made their way across the technology adoption lifecycle. But it all started with technologists who they found on online communities such as Digg (remember Digg? What was hip and cool yesterday can quickly become a footnote in history).

Identify and focus on early adopters, from the very get go. If you can pinpoint what your early adopters look like, you can focus your efforts on developing the features they *need* to justify paying for the product. In short, don't worry about all the bells and whistles. Get it right for a core group of early adopters first, then use the funding, experience and momentum generated to scale up.

12 TYPES OF PROTOTYPES TO TEST YOUR IDEA

'Fail fast and often' is an admonition we are no doubt used to hearing, and perhaps have become slightly sick of, like any advice that is repeated too often. Many people think a prototype is a proof of concept that usually takes several months to develop, costs tens of thousands of dollars — if not more — and is a functional product. Usually such prototypes go far beyond what's required and still don't serve the purpose of an early-stage prototype, which is to validate the problem, solution and proposed business model.

You can build many such prototypes in under an hour and for little or no cost.

1. Ads

Targeted ads on Facebook, Google, LinkedIn or any similar platform can help to quickly attract target customers to your offer and determine, based on click rate, how compelling your offer is. You'll end up paying anywhere from 10 cents per click up to $10 per click, and in a number of hours or days you can generate thousands or even tens of thousands of views. Further, Facebook offers the ability (thanks in part due to the kinds of practices that have got them into hot water lately) to target very specific groups of people based not just on demographics, but on past behaviour, so your ads are more likely to reach the right market.

2. Landing pages

When someone clicks on your ad, they hit your landing page — or you can use Facebook's built-in lead collection tool. If diverting clicks to a landing page, provide additional information on your offer. Your metric again is going to be clicks or sign-ups but could extend to your site's bounce rate or the amount of time a user spends on the page. Platforms such as LeadPages, Squarespace or the super-simple Launchrock can have you up and running in minutes.

3. Mobile app prototypes

Famous last words: 'We need an app!' How can you reduce the likelihood of your app ending up in the graveyard alongside hundreds of thousands of other apps that were also 'needed'? Online prototyping tools such as POP, Proto.io and Invision can help you quickly build and get functioning apps into your customer's hands. POP makes it as easy as sketching some screens by hand onto paper, taking photos with your smartphone then creating hotspots/links so you can navigate between screens and demonstrate to target customers what you're envisaging.

4. Concierge prototypes

Think Zappos, the online shoe company acquired by Amazon in 2017 for US$850 million. When they started out, they had an online store with a range of shoes in it. But when a customer bought something, they literally went down to the local shoe store, bought the shoes, packaged them up and sent them themselves. They didn't own any inventory or have a legitimate supply chain. They were purely testing genuine customer appetite in one of the cheapest, best and quickest ways possible.

(continued)

12 TYPES OF PROTOTYPES TO TEST YOUR IDEA (*CONT'D*)

5. Email marketing

If you've got an email database, you can send out emails to a select number of recipients to test appetite for a new offer. You could take this a step further and A/B test your offer — for example, include different solutions or price points in different emails — to test which offer resonates most.

Note: Although I don't spend too much time thinking or talking about regulation and compliance, I'll mention that the Global Data Protection Regulation (GDPR) went live in May 2018. Although an EU directive, it extends to companies doing business online everywhere, providing you collect information from EU citizens. Learn about what GDPR means for your marketing efforts before you find yourself on the wrong side of a €20 million fine.

6. Explainer video

When Dropbox was getting started, they developed a smoke-and-mirrors video demonstrating what Dropbox would do, and posted this on popular online communities where their target audience was hanging out. Literally overnight Dropbox earned itself 60 000 sign-ups, and the rest is history. Search for 'Dropbox explainer video' on YouTube and watch the four-minute video.

7. Paper prototypes

Don't know how to code? Want to speed up your build and learn cycle? Use paper to mimic the user interface and flow.

8. 3D printouts

When it comes to physical products today, we can print out almost anything we can imagine, at least as far as the physical form (sans functionality) is concerned. 3D printers are getting significantly cheaper and faster, and are fast becoming a viable form of hardware prototyping for companies great and small.

9. Cardboard

Don't have a 3D printer? Do you have cardboard? An employee at mail distribution company NeoPost used cardboard prototypes for a proposed packaging mechanism to win senior executive buy-in to build the real thing.

10. LinkedIn and email outreach

Today you can use countless 'growth hacking' tools to automate your identification of and outreach to target customers. You can leverage tools that automate messaging target executives, say on LinkedIn, to introduce them to your offer and gauge interest based on the number of people who accept and respond to your enquiry. Just don't start your message with 'We are a web development and SEO company'. Always make it about them! Check out tools such as MixMax for email or LinkedHelper for LinkedIn.

11. Crowdfunding

Not just a way to raise funds, crowdfunding is also a great way to test market appetite for your product without having to first invest in building it. Check out platforms such as Kickstarter or Pozible, but bear in mind that it's not enough simply to post a campaign — success requires that you do your bit to actively promote and best present your offer.

12. Hack it together

I often ask workshop participants how long they think it took Google to develop its first prototype for Google Glass, which is now finding joy in the enterprise market. The responses usually vary from three months to two years. The answer? One day. How? By using existing bits and pieces to hack together a very simple prototype; enough to gather valuable, informative and actionable feedback from customers, exactly what prototypes should do (see figure 8.3, overleaf).

(continued)

12 TYPES OF PROTOTYPES TO TEST YOUR IDEA (*CONT'D*)

Figure 8.3: the Google Glass prototype

Source: Tom Chi, formerly of Google X

By identifying the key assumptions underpinning your problem, solution or business model, then quickly and cheaply building prototypes to effectively test whether these assumptions are true or false, you're far more likely to invest time and money in what satisfies market demands and avoid investing in what doesn't.

STEP 3: SHORTLIST AND PRIORITISE PROTOTYPES

You've heard of return on investment (ROI), but what about learning on investment (LOI)?

Based on your make or break assumptions (MOBA), which type of prototype will you help you learn the most to prove whether your MOBA is true or false, with the lowest investment in time and money? To determine your prototype's LOI, simply divide the former over the latter and prioritise by the highest number. Table 8.2 gives some examples.

Table 8.2: how to prioritise prototypes

Prototype	Learnings	Investment	LOI
A	3	4	0.75
B	8	2	4 ☑
C	10	7	0.29
D	10	10	0.90

STEP 4: CUSTOMER ACQUISITION

Prototypes are useless unless your target audience is engaging with them and generating valuable data and actionable feedback for you. First, as part of your lean canvas you would have identified a number of customer segments. It's time to dig a bit deeper and identify the customer persona, in order to effectively target them and get more bang for your marketing buck.

Factors you might consider include age, gender, occupation, how they make decisions, where they hang out online, where they hang out offline, education, income, hobbies, passion, political persuasion, life goals, professional goals, who they are influenced by (both online and offline), media they consume, what products they've purchased in the past, how they dress, social groups they belong to, social media platforms they use and devices they use.

A WORD OF WARNING ON DEMOGRAPHICS

Who am I? I am a male. I am very wealthy. I was born in 1948. I grew up in England. I am a successful businessperson. I have been married twice. I have two children.

Not sure?

I could be Prince Charles ...

... but I could also be Ozzy Osbourne.

When using Google Analytics, you might find that the majority of your website visitors are 35- to 45-year-old females, even though your product is for 20- to 30-year-old males. This can mean one of two things. Either your marketing sucks (perhaps you have done a lousy job of targeting 20- to 30-year-olds). Or you should explore whether changing your target market, branding and so on to suit the 35- to 45-year-old female cohort bears fruit.

YOUR THREE ENGINES OF GROWTH

1. *Paid.* Paid advertising, that is. Make sure you track these all-important numbers. For example, you can turn your website URL into unique links using tools such as Bit.ly, so you can track the effectiveness of each campaign by viewing how many clicks a particular campaign received. For example, website.com becomes

website.com/emailpromo7, and by embedding this unique link into any hyperlinks you'll have a clear picture of how effective 'email promo 7' was in getting people to your website.

2. *Viral.* People love sharing what they love, and today we all have the power to share with hundreds, if not thousands, of people online. Word of mouth is sometimes referred to as the Holy Grail of marketing. In fact, 87 per cent of people who have a good experience with a product or service tell someone about it.

HOW VIRAL IS YOUR CONTENT?

To calculate how viral your product is, or isn't, you can use the following formula to determine what's called the 'viral coefficient'.

$$(\#) \text{ invitations sent per user} \times (\%) \text{ conversion rate} = (\#) \text{ viral coefficient (vc)}$$

For example, if my average user sends 10 invitations to their friends to join our service, and the conversion rate is 5 per cent, then our viral coefficient is 0.5. For a product to be considered viral, though, the vc must be greater than 1.

---

3. *Sticky.* Think magazine subscriptions, cosmetic boxes, Netflix and web hosting—all examples of products you need to keep paying for to keep receiving. To keep growing, all you need to do is add a small number of new customers, then what becomes of utmost importance, aside from retention, is your monthly revenue growth rate; a 10 per cent monthly growth rate results in a three-fold revenue increase in less than a year. Okay, so let's dig a little deeper on these engines of growth into the specific marketing channels you can apply to get customers to your offer.

MARKETING AND CUSTOMER ACQUISITION CHANNELS

Customer growth is everything for early-stage startups. It not only generates cash but is a key indicator that investors use to assess viability. In his seminal book on the topic, *Traction*, Gabriel Weinberg puts forward 18 channels. Peter Thiel proposes that if you can get just *one* of these channels to work for you, you've got a viable business. But don't fall into the trap of doing what most entrepreneurs do, which is focus on two or three channels and neglect the rest. Explore *then* exploit! You want to apply a process of rapid experimentation to your traction channels, as you do when finding product/market fit and testing your assumptions.

Following are 10 of the 18 channels.

For all 18 marketing channels, visit **www.employeetoentrepreneur. io/18marketingchannels/.**

1. VIRAL MARKETING

This consists of growing your user base by encouraging your users to refer to or share your offering with their network. Companies such as ThankYou Water, Twitter and Facebook have all grown virally through this channel. For example, ThankYou Water developed a Facebook campaign that ultimately went viral and called for 7-Eleven stores to stock the social enterprise's water. The campaign ultimately led to a meeting with the retailer and a decision to distribute their water nationally.

2. SEARCH ENGINE MARKETING OR 'SEM'

This is marketer speak for what essentially amounts to Google Adwords. Expect to pay anywhere between 10 cents and $30 for a click, depending on the search terms you target and how competitive they are.

Pro Tip: Don't target general, expensive keywords. For example, at Collective Campus we don't target general keywords such as 'business consultants' because not only would the cost per click be prohibitive, it would put us in a general bucket of searches, most of which would not bear fruit, so we'd be paying top dollar for useless clicks. We prefer instead to rank for what those in the space call longtail keywords such as 'corporate startup accelerator Australia'. Someone searching for such a keyword phrase is much more likely to be interested in our services, and given the more specific nature of the keyword, it attracts fewer searches and means we pay a pittance for each click (something like $1 instead of the $20+ you'd pay for 'business consultant').

For example, for every hundred $20 'business consultant' keyword clicks, we are likely to get maybe one genuine lead because of the generic nature of the search term. This means we've paid $2000 for that lead (100 × $20), which is simply not sustainable for us, especially if only something like one out of every 25 leads converts ($50 000 to acquire a customer using this term!).

For every hundred $1 'corporate startup accelerator Australia' keyword clicks, we are likely to get 10 genuine leads, so we've paid $10 per lead. This results in a $250 customer acquisition cost.

3. OFFLINE ADS

Think traditional media such as newspaper, radio, TV, billboards, magazines and flyers. Use offline ads where online isn't viable and/or your product has broad appeal. These channels are usually expensive, it's hard to measure their effectiveness and they don't provide for anywhere near the same degree of customer segmentation and targeting that you can achieve online.

Pro Tip: Find out when the hard cut-off date for ad submissions is by calling media outlets or publications you're interested in advertising in. Call media representatives a day before this cut-off date and suggest you're interested in advertising in the very next issue. If they haven't filled their allotment yet, they will be hungry to sell and earn their commissions. Push for a discount. Publishers will sometimes offer distressed ad pricing, which can be as little as 25 per cent of the normal price. They won't offer such pricing straight out of the blocks, but if you suggest that a rival publication has offered you an ad for half of what the publisher you're speaking to is offering, then you can play them against each other. Tim Ferriss suggests playing the 'let me check with my manager' card in response to a price point and coming back with something along the lines of 'I'm sorry, we've only got approval to spend $X, but I have authority to spend that *right now*'. Urgency, scarcity and fear of loss go a long way in negotiations of all kinds.

4. SEARCH ENGINE OPTIMISATION (SEO)

This channel is all about getting your website to show up on page one of Google. Fewer than 10 per cent of people proceed to page two of Google's search results. SEO can take time, months or even up to a year, to get you ranking for the right keywords, but it's worth the investment in time. You might want to use tools such as Moz or Ahrefs to help you optimise your website for SEO. If you're considering hiring an SEO marketing agency, be careful. Few do it well and you will need to work closely with them to better convey your value proposition and market.

Pro Tip: Most SEO agencies suck. Like app development agencies, most will ship work offshore but charge you developed world prices for what is often inferior work. To help offset the risk of engaging a lemon, ask SEO candidates (a) who they've worked for in the past, (b) what keywords they've got said companies to rank for, and (c) how profitable those keywords have been for those companies. Follow this up by speaking to their clients to see whether the reality is aligned with the story you've been told. I've seen prospective SEO managers of mine flaunt keyword rankings for words that either got few clicks or were the wrong keywords to go after in the first place, rendering the rankings useless. Not sure how many clicks you should expect for a keyword? Check out Google's free Keyword Planner tool.

5. CONTENT MARKETING

This essentially involves creating content and then sharing it to educate and acquire potential customers and generate traffic. This includes blogs, books/ebooks, white papers, infographics, videos, podcasts and more. I am a massive advocate of this channel, particularly if what you're selling is knowledge and/or you don't have lots of cash to burn on advertising or PR. The book you hold in your hands would not have been possible if I had not used a podcast, two self-published books, several ebooks and hundreds of blog posts to develop what book publishing houses call a platform or what you might better know as a following.

Pro Tip: Create some compelling content, make it downloadable, embed a pop-up on your website offering people the free download and capture their email. Ensure you've developed a drip feed so downloaders will automatically begin to receive a series of emails designed to nurture them towards taking the next steps. You can set up automated drip-feed campaigns with most modern email marketing platforms such as Mailchimp, Campaign Monitor and MixMax.

6. EMAIL MARKETING

This is one of the best ways to convert prospects while retaining and monetising existing ones. Despite the advent of social media and apps such as WeChat and WhatsApp, email is still the number one go-to form of online communication and engagement. According to Optimonster, of 2.6 billion email users, 58 per cent check it first thing in the morning and 91 per cent check it daily, which trumps any and every social media platform. Email addresses are golden.

7. TARGETING BLOGS AND COMMUNITIES

As discussed, this worked for companies such as Dropbox and Buffer. The key here is relevance of the product to the community.

For example, when I released my second self-published book, *The Innovation Manager's Handbook Volume 2*, I leveraged an online LinkedIn community group called Innovation Management Group. I had previously hosted the group's curator Paul Williams on my podcast, which served to develop a relationship. I asked him whether he'd be so kind as to send a direct message to his group's 40 000+ members to advise that my book had been released and was currently available via an introductory special offer on Amazon. He did so immediately. The next day more than 1000 copies of my book had been downloaded, a large number by members of Paul's group. This is the power of targeting existing communities.

8. SALES

The primary focuses here are on prospecting, setting up meetings, building relationships, learning what your prospect's pain points and desires are, and delivering solutions at a price they are willing to pay, at a margin that helps you achieve your goals. Customer relationship management (CRM) tools such as Copper or Hubspot Sales Hub can make your job easier, as can prospecting tools such as one of my personal favourites, LinkedHelper.

Pro Tip: Combining the power of LinkedIn's Sales Navigator and the third-party tool LinkedHelper, you can target members of LinkedIn Groups with direct, personalised messages. For example, if you're selling HR software, there are groups on LinkedIn for HR executives that are tens of thousands of users deep you can target.

I've deliberately not included a significant amount on sales in this book, as the book focuses on your transition from employee to entrepreneur and developing the mindset required to get to a product worth selling. There are endless resources on the market on sales, negotiation skills and influencing people. I've included my favourites in my online list of books and podcasts referenced in chapter 2.

However, it would be remiss of me not to include some sales strategies that I have found effective not only for my own business, but also for the many entrepreneurs and startups I've worked with, to help you hit the ground running when you're ready.

You'll find a range of resources, including email and direct message scripts, at **www.employeetoentrepreneur.io/sales**.

---

9. TRADE SHOWS

Trade shows provide companies in specific industries with a platform to physically show off their latest products, meet potential customers, learn more about the respective industry, and get feedback for an idea or product. From my experience, exhibiting at trade shows is a massive hit-or-miss proposition (more miss than hit, actually). Preparing for and successfully participating in a tradeshow requires days of effort and will probably set you back thousands of dollars, especially if there's travel involved. Your expenses will include space rental, transport and accommodation, booth displays, marketing collateral, prizes, branded materials, wi-fi dongles and most costly of all, employee time before (planning), during (delivering) and after the event (following up). Long hours staffing a booth at a trade show is hell on employees and can leave them so burnt out that they need a day or two to get back into the swing of things afterwards, costing you even more time.

More often than not, conferences are seeded with employees of organisations who are merely looking to earn some CPE (continuous professional education) points so they can tick that box as part of their next performance review when jostling for promotion. This is not to say that all conferences are a waste of time because they're not, but hocking your wares on a crowded convention centre floor with hundreds of other startups vying for attention is far from graceful, to say the least.

It's also easy to confuse movement or being busy with effectiveness, often to the detriment of your goals. If you're going to go down this road, you need to have a solid targeting, acquisition and conversion strategy. You need to ensure that decision makers of your target customer segment organisations will be present. Explore the possibility of running dedicated workshops or giving a keynote talk, which would give you an opportunity to put yourself forward as a thought leader and have customers come to you. And always, *always* have some kind of offer or lead magnet to help you collect emails, whether it's a worthwhile prize or a free trial of your product.

Pro Tip: Next time you're deliberating over whether or not to invest the time and money in a conference, perhaps email the conference organiser and ask for a list of attendees. Have your virtual assistant put together a list with the LinkedIn profile URL of each attendee, then import these URLs into LinkedHelper, which will send targeted, personalised messages to all relevant attendees via LinkedIn. This will save you heaps of time and money and help you better qualify prospects and pursue the ones more likely to convert. On conference days, get your VA to jump on Twitter and put a list together of who's tweeting. Do they fit your target customer segment? If so, repeat the steps above. The subject line? 'Sorry I missed you at conference *X*.'

10. SPONSORING OR RUNNING EVENTS

This can be an awesome way to get traction, because you're putting yourself forward as an authority in the space. For example, education boot camp General Assembly has scaled globally by partnering and sponsoring events hosted by local marketing agencies and the like on topics that align with GA's courses and workshops. The agencies tend to bring hundreds of people to these events through the strength of their brand name and existing email databases, while General Assembly gains access to all of the event registrations (including those near priceless emails) and can therefore begin to nurture these leads through their very deliberate marketing and sales funnel.

We adopted a similar tactic early in the life of Collective Campus when we offered to run a satellite event as part of the Australian federal government's Innovation Month. The session, dubbed Disrupt the Public Sector, was a relatively simple one-day event hosted at our office with a number of keynotes, panel discussions and short workshops taking place throughout the day. The government promoted the event through an online portal and it sold out, with more than 200 public servants RSVPing to attend. They had to RSVP through our event page, so we suddenly had 200 new emails to nurture. We've since run the event in a half-day format a further three times, in 2016, 2017 and 2018, and have worked with a number of public sector organisations as a result, including the Australian Securities and Investment Commission (ASIC), our equivalent of the US SEC.

A CRASH COURSE IN LEAN MARKETING

It's no longer enough to shout marketing slogans from the rooftops and expect people to buy your products, as today's customers have more power than ever because of the transparency delivered by the internet.

Traditional, long-term, above-the-line marketing campaigns are now mostly the domain of a few industry behemoths. The rest of us need to be more targeted and intentional with our marketing but with so many potential marketing channels to choose from, where do we even begin? Fortunately, we can adopt the approach to testing we outlined earlier in this chapter for marketing campaigns too.

Determine your target customer persona

Determine your customer personas, introduced in step 4 earlier in this chapter.

Define your objectives

Is it getting people to your website, extracting their email address or having them actually buy your product? What does success look like? Is it a 5 per cent click rate, for example? Understanding this will help you when it comes to measuring success or failure a little later in the process.

(continued)

A CRASH COURSE IN LEAN MARKETING (*CONT'D*)

Identify marketing channels

Select from the marketing channels introduced earlier.

Based on your target customer personas, identify which channels you think might apply. For example, if you're targeting seniors, you're unlikely to use social media channels such as Snapchat.

Develop channel strategies

You may have multiple strategies within each channel. For example, you may have different social media platforms to explore (Facebook, Instagram, Snapchat), paid ads or content and so on. If you wish to leverage existing platforms that already command a large audience, there might be many to choose from (such as Product Hunt, or The Hacker News), and if you're going for offline ads, are we talking community radio, flyer distribution, print ads, television or street posters, for example?

Prioritise strategies

Once you've developed a comprehensive list of potential strategies in your team, you need to prioritise these strategies. There are different approaches you might take, but in the interests of the weekly sprint, which is all about moving quickly, I prefer simply to divide the Likelihood of Channel Success by the Time Required to Test Strategy. It's all about optimising learnings in the least amount of time. For example, we could test some keywords in Google Search in a few days, but not necessarily a print ad in a quarterly magazine.

Sean Ellis proposes the following alternative method; just think Vanilla Ice:

- **I**mpact: the impact the idea could have if a win

- **C**onfidence: how confident you are it will result in a win

- **E**ase: how easy it is to test (think time, cost and technical implementation).

Rate each out of 10, calculate the average and prioritise by the highest number.

Run a sprint

Sprints are borrowed from the world of agile project management and Google. Jake Knapp, author of *Sprint: How to Solve Big Problems and Test New Ideas in Just Five Days*, has used sprints with more than one hundred of Google Ventures' investee companies, such as Slack, 23 and Me, Medium and Nest, to help them find product/market fit for new ideas and guide business strategy. A sprint, in our case, is simply a one-week test of your top five strategies by priority.

Measure and learn

Remember those success metrics we defined earlier? Well, after one week of testing we want to determine whether we're hitting those metrics. Where are we today, or what's our 'baseline', as Eric Ries says. It's important not to over-measure and identify what Ben Yoskovitz, co-author of *Lean Analytics,* calls our 'One Metric That Matters', which comes down to where we are in the marketing funnel.

You have three decisions to choose from at this point. You could make some changes to your campaign (that ad copy, imagery and positioning I mentioned earlier) to optimise results. Some strategies might require several weeks to truly determine whether or not they should be part of your ongoing marketing campaign. Or you could mark it as a win, promote it for subsequent testing and potentially throw more money at it. Or finally you could learn from your failures, cut your losses and promote an untested marketing strategy from the backlog you prioritised earlier.

(continued)

A CRASH COURSE IN LEAN MARKETING (*CONT'D*)

Oh, and don't forget, your *customer acquisition cost* (CPA) should always be less than your expected *customer lifetime value* (LTV), unless of course being a loss leader is part of your bigger picture strategy, which is not uncommon among many well-heeled startups today but unlikely to be your strategy if you're just starting out and not the recipient of a massive inheritance or some other capital injection.

Your critical path

After you've tested a number of strategies you should have a list of successful and failed options, so how much time and money do you allocate to each strategy? Ultimately, top-performing channels should command most of the spend, as any money diverted away from your better performing channels is effectively leaving money on the table. You might like to map out a *critical path*, which is a project management technique used to determine the minimum time needed for an activity, and subsequently the order in which to run your strategies.

For our marketing strategies we might use:

- the CPA:LTV ratio of a channel

- the number of customers we think are obtainable via a particular channel

- how many days it takes us to acquire X number of customers

- the number of days it might take us to exhaust a channel.

Note: these metrics are all living and breathing and likely to change over time.

There you have it: a quick guide to lean marketing that you can begin to use not only to determine which marketing channels might work best but also to test market appetite for new ideas.

GROWTH HACKING TOOLS

Lean marketing and 'growth hacking' can be used almost interchangeably; both are about applying rapid experimentation and a Socratic, innovator's mind to the testing of marketing channels that can help move the needle on growth. Growth hacking tools save you time doing things such as looking for emails of people in your target market and manually typing out each email individually (which for 50 emails could take you a few hours). Instead, you use tools such as LeadIQ or RocketReach to find the emails for you, then a tool such as MixMax to send 50 individual but personalised emails, bringing the time taken from several hours down to (no kidding) several minutes.

Get 100 free leads from LeadIQ at bit.ly/leadiqcc/.

Not only are you moving the needle on growth but you're also freeing up your time and yourself to focus on where you can add the most value, rather than engaging in mind-numbing, process-oriented tasks that anyone with half a brain and a keyboard could do for you. That's not how you distinguish yourself.

There are a multitude of growth hacker tools on the market, so kick things off by perusing the list at **www.employeetoentrepreneur.io/growthhacks/**.

STEP 5: METRICS

INTRODUCING PIRATE METRICS

I'll let you figure out why this funnel, illustrated in figure 8.4 (overleaf), is often referred to as 'pirate metrics'.

Here, in a nutshell, are the five types of validation levels this funnel addresses:

1. *Rate of Acquisition — validating the problem*
   Do people click through to a website via, say, an advertisement?
2. *Rate of Activation — validating the solution and features*
   Do people leave their email address on said website or contact the company?

3. *Rate of Conversion — validating the revenue and pricing model*
   Do people ultimately pay for a product or service?
4. *Rate of Return — validating stickiness and engagement*
   Do people come back?
5. *Viral Coefficient — validating viral qualities*
   Do people refer friends and family?

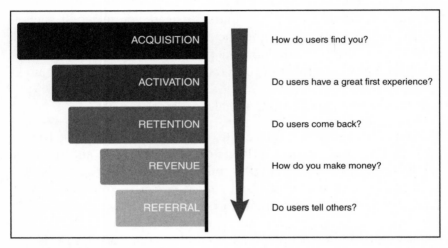

Figure 8.4: pirate metrics funnel

Initially, you will focus on acquisition and activation. For example, what percentage of people who see your ad click on it (acquisition) and what percentage of people who click on it elect to join your waiting list (activation)?

FOCUS ON ACTIONABLE METRICS, NOT VANITY METRICS

Actionable metrics are stats that teach you something you can act on to improve your business. *Vanity metrics* are stats that are all style and no substance, such as the number of likes your latest Instagram post got!

Cohort analysis breaks users into related groups for analysis — for example, the percentage of users returning to your website week on week — rather than looking at users as a whole. This tells us more about the data and the stickiness or quality of our customer retention activities.

In web analytics, split testing, or *A/B testing*, is a controlled experiment with two variants, A and B. For example, you can A/B test variants such as price, copy and imagery on your website. Each subsequent person who visits your site will see either A or B (or the proverbial C, D and E), and after you have enough visitors to constitute a meaningful sample size, you get a better picture of which variant performs better and make that your default for all to see.

NORTH STAR METRIC

The North Star Metric, coined by Sean Ellis of GrowthHackers. com, is considered by many to be the metric that best captures your product's value. It helps teams move beyond driving fleeting, surface-level growth to instead focus on generating long-term retained customer growth.

A word of warning on NSM. The risk of focusing on one metric only, as Ash Maurya reminded me on *Future Squared*, is that it can often come at the expense of others. For example, if Airbnb focused only on nights booked and not on nights returned, it might soon find that most of its customers have such a lousy experience that the well eventually runs dry. A focus on sub-metrics is key. In this case, Airbnb would focus on nights returned, among other sub-metrics.

BASELINE AND TARGET METRICS

Now you have a handle on basic metrics, you'll want to define where you are today based on your key assumptions in order to determine whether or not the different tweaks you'll employ are moving the needle.

'Help, I'm losing track!'

It's time to introduce you to the validation board (see table 8.3).

Table 8.3: validation board

Leap of faith assumption	Test hypotheses	Pirate funnel stage	Prototype	Target metric
Customers will trust an alternative to taxis that connects local owners of vehicles with riders.	Customers will enter a vehicle after they have become familiar with our driver screening method.	Activation	A manual version of Uber, connecting drivers with people waiting in a taxi queue.	Percentage of people who agree to pay for a local driver after being shown relevant driver screening documentation.

STEP 6: MEASURE, LEARN AND ADAPT

During the Vietnam War, the United States had inferior F86 fighter planes, while the North Vietnamese fighters flew Soviet MIG15s. On paper, the MIG15s were superior to the F86s and should have wiped the skies clean of them, but they didn't. Top Gun Naval Fighter Weapons School training aside, there were two key reasons for this. First, the MIG pilots had limited vision (the F86s featured a relatively clear bubble canopy unlike the MIG15s with their panes and struts). Second, the MIG15's throttle was only semi-hydraulic and required lots of physical exertion to control (pilots did weights in training to control the throttle, whereas the F86's throttle was fully hydraulic and therefore allowed pilots to transition faster between manoeuvres).

The outcome was that the American pilots were able to observe and orient faster thanks to their better vision and, more importantly perhaps, they were able to decide and act on that information faster owing to their fully hydraulic throttle. This beautifully captures the OODA concept which was born out of the US military:

1. Observe
2. Orient
3. Decide
4. Act
5. *Repeat, fast.*

Best-selling author Tim Harford said recently that Donald Trump, inadvertently or otherwise, made use of the OODA loop to help him win the US presidency. The OODA loop is a term coined by John Boyd, the late US Air Force fighter pilot and Pentagon consultant. Boyd, known for challenging convention and authority, was an influential thinker and his ideas have been adopted in the sports and business domains. One of his enduring insights is that if you can continuously disorient your opponent, you can gain a big advantage.

To disorient your opponent, move quickly and be unconventional. A confused opponent needs to orient themselves, again and again, while you race ahead. You're effectively 'inside their OODA loop'. Donald Trump moved fast, with unconventional tactics, during the primary campaign, and while his adversaries were discussing their response with advisers, Trump had moved on to talking about the next thing. He was inside their OODA loop.

Just as in the military, startups that learn (and act) fastest, while also disorienting their opponents, are more likely to win. This is why you need to measure, learn and adapt—fast.

ANALYTICS TOOLS

Google Analytics is one of the most widely used tools to help you monitor your website and your visitors. You can build a clear picture of which channels and which marketing campaigns are delivering the most traffic, how many people visit your site, what percentage come back, visitor demographic information and a hell of a lot more. It's the logical first step in anyone's foray into the world of analytics and as far as 80/20 goes, it gets you 80 per cent of the way.

Leadfeeder is another analytics tool that allows clients to track the movements of individual visitors through a website. We use this tool at Collective Campus to identify what individual visitors appear to be interested in. For example, I can use it to determine that the Head of HR from a large FMCG company spent 30 minutes on our website, reading all about design thinking. That's our cue to get in touch and have a conversation on the topic. Again, this is 80/20. It means spending your time with prospects who are much more likely to convert because their behaviour suggests they have an appetite to buy. This kind of thinking offers you a departure from the traditional spray and pray you find in boiler-room operations resonant of Stratton Oakmont, made famous in *The Wolf of Wall Street*.

Hotjar uses heatmapping to give you a picture of what your website visitors are actually doing on your site; where they're moving their mouse, where they're clicking, how far down the page they're scrolling. Are all your customer testimonials and 'call to action' buttons too low on the page, past the point people scroll to? Are visitors clicking on unlinked text? Do customers appear to get confused on your website and just up and leave as a result? Heatmapping tools such as Hotjar help you find the answers.

SEMrush, an intelligence-gathering tool for online marketing, helps you with SEO, search engine marketing (SEM) and social media. Find out what keywords your competitors are targeting, what they're ranking for in Google and more. As Sun Tzu said, 'Know your enemy'.

Backed by what it calls 'the largest community of SEOs on the planet', *Moz* builds tools that make SEO, inbound marketing, link building and content marketing easier. I've talked with Moz's founder and former CEO, Rand Fishkin, on *Future Squared* a couple of times. Check out the podcasts if you'd like to learn more about building a company from the ground up as well as get some pointers on content marketing.

PIVOT OR PROCEED

After a number of cycles — maybe hundreds — of building, measuring and learning, you have to make a call on pivoting (if something fundamental needs to change, such as your target customer or distribution channel), persevering (if you've managed to demonstrate something amounting to traction) or quitting (if better opportunities lie elsewhere or you've lost the desire to go on).

PIVOT STORIES

PayPal

PayPal started out as a mechanism to beam IOUs from PalmPilot to PalmPilot (remember them?). It didn't work, so the fledgling startup pivoted towards a mechanism that supported the transfer of money via email — as it turned out, just when both email and a little company called eBay were enjoying exponential growth. As of this writing, PayPal is worth US$91 billion.

Slack

Today's beloved instant messaging and collaboration platform started out as a failed video game venture called Glitch. The team behind Slack fell into the concept because of a communication platform they had developed to support them during Glitch's development. The platform was a customised version of IRC (internet relay chat; think mIRC, or ICQ if you're over 30). Slack's founder, Stewart Butterfield, tells of how this communication platform made the team 'very efficient in being unsuccessful to make the game'. As of this writing, Slack is worth more than US$5 billion.

Nintendo

Nintendo began life as a playing card company way back in the 1880s. In the mid 20th century, as the demand for playing cards waned, Nintendo explored a number of different alternatives including a taxi company, instant rice and even hourly hotels (wink wink). It also took an interest in the growing popularity of video games on the back of the success of MIT's Spacewar, and negotiated the rights to distribute the first video game console, the Magnavox Odyssey, in the early 1970s. It released its first console in 1977 and a stocky Italian plumber and his carb-conscious brother entered our lives shortly thereafter.

Play-Doh

Play-Doh began life in the post-Depression 1930s as a wall cleaner, designed to pick up the black residue that coal heaters left on walls. Less than two decades later, as oil and gas heaters made commercial inroads, Kutol found that demand for its product went the other way. Scrambling for direction, one of the founders learned that his sister-in-law, a teacher named Kay Zufall, had been using the product in arts and crafts class where the children made ornaments with it. They explored distributing the product to kindergartens. More than two billion cans of Play-Doh have since been distributed worldwide. Play-Doh is now owned by toy company Hasbro, which boasted a market cap of US$11.3 billion at the time of writing.

Deciding whether to persevere, pivot or quit calls for what Ben Yoskovitz calls a healthy balance of data (leading indicators) and gut (intuition and judgement). Using data alone is not enough, because it reflects the data you collect, how well you clean it and how effectively and objectively you interpret it. You also might not have a clear picture of the underlying drivers of the data. This is why complementing data with professional judgement and intuition, based on past experience, can help offset some of the challenges of using data alone.

LEAN STARTUP WALKTHROUGH

Mary works for a large life insurance company. She has an idea for a holistic health management app that satisfies the disruptive innovation litmus test we provided earlier. She has received $1000 seed funding to explore the problem and solution and has decided to use the lean startup methodology. To test the problem and solution she will use a combination of a lean canvas, online ads and landing tools, and acquisition rate and activation rate metrics.

Step 1: She completes a lean canvas (see figure 8.5).

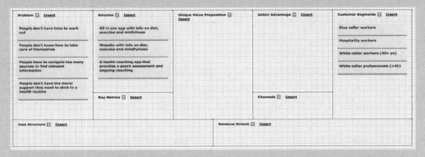

Figure 8.5: lean canvas example

For simplicity's sake, this canvas focuses only on the starting blocks: problem, solution and customer segment. We can see that Mary has made a number of assumptions around the problem and customer segment that need to be tested.

Step 2: She pulls the riskiest assumptions from the lean canvas. She is first going to test the assumption that people don't have time to take care of themselves. She will test this across the different customer segments identified to see if it resonates with any particular group more than others.

Step 3: She builds online ads and a landing page targeting the customer segments to determine what the initial acquisition and activation rates look like (see figure 8.6).

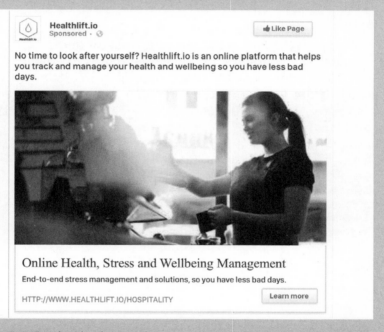

Healthlift.io
Sponsored · ⊘

👍 Like Page

No time to look after yourself? Healthlift.io is an online platform that helps you track and manage your health and wellbeing so you have less bad days.

Online Health, Stress and Wellbeing Management
End-to-end stress management and solutions, so you have less bad days.

HTTP://WWW.HEALTHLIFT.IO/HOSPITALITY

Learn more

Figure 8.6: Facebook ad example
Image source: © GaudiLab/Shutterstock

What we want to measure early on in the innovation lifecycle is learnings. To validate that the assumptions underpinning an idea or business model are flawed or valid, we must experiment, learn and iterate relentlessly in order to move closer to product/market fit. You might use pirate metrics to map out metrics at each stage of the funnel. Initially, you might simply want to

(continued)

LEAN STARTUP WALKTHROUGH (*CONT'D*)

test under acquisition 'percentage of target customer clicks on Facebook ad for problem assumption is above X per cent'.

Testing acquisition in practice with a Facebook ad, Mary's target customer segment is hospitality workers. The problem she is testing is 'People have no time to take care of themselves'; her metric is the percentage of targeted people who click on *Learn More* in the ad.

Table 8.4 shows the results of the campaign. She has spent between $68 and $337 testing assumptions across the respective customer segments, averaging about ten dollars per 1000 impressions (or ad views) and $1.24 per click. Her reach exceeded 140 000 impressions and generated almost 1400 site visits in under two weeks. Already we can see that the problem appears to resonate more with blue-collar workers, who clicked on the ad at a rate of 3.17 per cent, as opposed to 0.54 – 1.27 per cent for the other segments.

Table 8.4: Facebook ad campaign results

Customer segment	Impressions	Clicks	Cost per click	Acquisition rate (%)	Total cost ($)
White collar	16 550	210	1.64	1.27	68
Blue collar	10 505	338	0.99	3.17	334
Hospitality	54 574	519	1.29	0.95	671
Freelancers & entrepreneurs	58 747	316	1.07	0.54	337

Note: These are actual results from a similar campaign.

Step 4: She measures the activation rate of subsequent interactions with the landing page from people who clicked on the ad.

Testing activation in practice with a landing page (see figure 8.7), Mary's target customer segment is hospitality workers; the solution tested is online stress management and resilience training; and the metric used is the percentage of visitors who click on *Get Early Access*. Note the hospitality-specific imagery.

Figure 8.7: landing page example

Image source: © Dean Drobot/Shutterstock

Table 8.5 shows the results. Again, the blue-collar customer segment comes out way in front in terms of receptiveness to the proposed solution, with 7.4 per cent of website visitors from this customer segment signing up for further information. It's worth noting that the others also performed reasonably well, given that average conversion rates for successful online platforms hover at around 2 to 3 per cent.

Table 8.5: landing page test results

Customer segment	Site visits	Sign ups	Activation rate (%)
White collar	210	4	1.90
Blue collar	338	25	7.40
Hospitality	519	11	2.12
Freelancers & entrepreneurs	316	9	2.85

(continued)

LEAN STARTUP WALKTHROUGH (*CONT'D*)

Step 5: She updates her ads and landing page to reflect assumptions based on learnings.

At this point, she might again make some tweaks and perform some further testing. She might reach out to the 25 blue-collar users who signed up for more information and engage them with problem and solution interviews to better understand their problem and home in on a solution that would truly resonate. She might start exploring elements of the business model with them too, such as the pricing model, which she could subsequently test online using the approach we've provided.

Whatever the case, Mary is racing ahead, learning a lot about the proposed concept and its associated customer segments, problem and solution, and can make much better decisions based on real, actionable, customer-driven data, significantly increasing her likelihood of success.

By amping up the pace at which you learn about all of the assumptions that underpin your idea's problem, solution, product features, business model and so on, you'll radically increase your likelihood of getting to breakthrough success before you run out of money, time, patience, energy or enthusiasm. Fast learning and more importantly, adapting, will help you to avoid the graveyard where 96 per cent of new businesses reside, and is your key to thriving in the land of the living.

Call to action

Speed is fundamental to success. With this in mind, complete the following 10 steps in the next week — yes, the next seven days!

1. Complete a lean canvas at www.employeetoentrepreneur.io/leancanvas/.

2. Identify key assumptions underpinning your idea.

3. Identify and prioritise potential prototypes.

4. Identify and prioritise potential marketing channels.

5. Define key metrics and analytics tools.

6. Promote and test your idea.

7. Learn from customer interactions.

8. Update key assumptions and prototypes.

Rinse and repeat until you decide to pursue, pivot or abandon your idea.

Chapter 9

STRENGTHS AND WEAKNESSES

*'Know your enemy and know yourself and you can fight
a hundred battles without disaster.'*
Sun Tzu

I often tell people that while I spent a total of 13 years at university obtaining multiple degrees and cutting my teeth in the corporate world, I learned 10× more in half the time as an entrepreneur (okay, so that's an arbitrary 10×, but you get the idea.) Not only did I learn about business but I had to learn about and develop philosophies that shape how I show up each day, in and out of the office.

Having said that, many of the character and workplace attributes I developed during my time in the corporate world were transferable and gave me a huge advantage over entrepreneurs who had never walked the halls of a large organisation, especially if looking to sell to one.

Lessons learned

For example, thanks to the time I spent in corporate gigs, I've found it easier to develop relationships with and sell to large enterprise companies. My years in that world gave me a better understanding of how internal sales processes work, how business unit budgeting and corporate cost allocation works, and how there's usually more than one person or functional department to get on the bus before the proverbial John Hancock comes out.

FROM DIFFERENT WORLDS

Many first-time B2B entrepreneurs I've worked with who lack corporate experience seem dumbfounded by just how slow large organisations move and by the time it takes them to sign up to what the entrepreneur imagines is the centre of their universe. Demonstrating that you can deliver value is often not enough to get the deal across the line. The decision to work with your company is just one of many your prospect has to contend with. Often, when it comes to B2B sales, all the stars must align, including people, timing, budgets and strategic objectives. I make sure my team understands everything they need to know about what they're up against when selling to a large organisation. This gives them the best chance of avoiding the trap of using tried and true B2C SaaS sales strategies to sell an enterprise deal, as so many of the less informed do.

Having spent time on both sides of the fence, and now operating at the intersection of the two through our corporate startup accelerator programs, I can say that corporate cultures and startup cultures could not be more different.

'Startups that learn the fastest win,' asserts Eric Ries in *The Lean Startup*. This is even truer today than it was when the book was released in 2011. Startups rely so much on speed that entire industries have popped up, seemingly overnight, to support the 'optimisation' of almost everything—from food consumed and calories burned to ketone and blood oxygen levels, sleep patterns, moods, brainwaves, fitness levels, productivity, distance jogged and more. The desire to measure and manage is perhaps highest among startup founders and employees. This extends to the use of automation and outsourcing tools that help startups 'go to eleven', to quote the delightful Nigel Tufnel from mock rockers Spinal Tap.

BORN OF NECESSITY

If you've gone to college, scored a gig with a large investment bank, then quit to follow your dreams and work for a fraction of what you were making at a large firm, and your business only has six months of runway before it begins its rapid fade into oblivion, then you'll do whatever it takes to make things work. If you've got only five employees, you'll monitor and optimise so that five operate as though they were 10, 15 or even 20 equivalent full-time employees at a large organisation. At least, that's what you should be doing. It's not a case of 'build it and they will come'.

This is what the entire growth hacking movement was born out of. Necessity. If you don't have bags of cash to throw at expensive (and often underperforming) above-the-line advertising and public relations campaigns, you'll find other ways of getting the word out, such as leveraging the audiences of influencers for free by providing some form of non-monetary value in exchange. Having said all of that, you would have acquired different skills, strengths and accidental weaknesses in the corporate world to bring to the startup world.

Character and workplace attributes

In *New Power: How Power Works in Our Hyperconnected World*, Jeremy Heimans writes of how our ubiquitous connectivity makes possible a different kind of power from the one we've known. It is open, participatory and peer-driven and it is changing the way we work, think and feel.

To harness this new power and the opportunities offered by the third industrial revolution, you need to become conscious of the character attributes that support or hold you back from doing so.

Strengths (traditional workplace character attributes that transfer reasonably well into the world of entrepreneurship) include:

- networker
- intelligence gatherer
- door opener (In the early days I would namedrop past employers such as EY and KPMG to build credibility and secure meetings.)
- sales oriented (If selling to established organisations, appreciating how sales works internally can help you operate effectively from the other side of the fence.)

- effective communicator
- professional
- influencer and negotiator.

Weaknesses (traditional workplace character attributes that don't transfer well into entrepreneurship) include:

- outsources accountability ('Let's set up a workgroup!')
- gets things perfect before showing to a customer
- slow moving, excuse making, procrastinating
- compliance-centric
- intellectual property-centric (Today speed, not patents or trademarks, is usually your greatest ally.)
- scared to fail or take risks
- market research mindset (The problem with market research is that it's based on the past; in a fast-changing world we can't rely on such research alone to make good decisions.)
- analysis paralysis (Refer to the decision-making tips provided in chapter 4.)
- failure to build personal brand (Some in the corporate world are great at this, but most people don't build or promote their personal brands as an entrepreneur is encouraged to.)
- no strong point of view
- poor time management (A common tendency is to default to busy instead of effective; pursuing 'inbox zero' is a classic example of this.)
- risk management by analysis instead of by doing (Everyone has a plan until punched in the face. A 10-page 'risk and control matrix' is no match for getting out of the building with a real-world prototype from day one.)
- 'we know best' mindset (Insular thinking is going to put you at a disadvantage and result in minimal customer engagement.)
- short-termism and ROI-driven mindset (If you want to deliver short-term revenue and ROI, then you're probably not going to be thinking all that big or doing anything all that different, which is fine if you're pursuing a lifestyle or a moderately successful service business but not much more.)

- thrives only on certainty (Corporate executives tend to make decisions from a place of certainty, with well-etched plans to give them a sense of stability. Today's world is far from certain, however, so learning how to navigate ambiguity and make decisions without all the information is key.)

ABUNDANCE AND SCARCITY

In life and business, whenever you have an abundance of one thing, it tends to mean there is scarcity elsewhere. Similarly, when it comes to transferable character attributes, too much of a good thing is still too much. The following three tools can be effective allies in your quest for entrepreneurial success; however, taken to the extreme they can be a significant detriment.

Processes and *systems* should be in place to support the delivery of your goals, but once they impede speed and the realisation of your and your team's talent, they stop serving their purpose.

Then there's *planning*. We've been raised on the belief that if you fail to plan, you plan to fail, but there is a fine line between planning for success and planning for paralysis analysis. Remember, speed is fundamental to success, and in those early stages you can only plan so much around untested assumptions underpinning your idea or product. By all means plan, but be aware of when the law of diminishing returns kicks in.

ON UNDERSTANDING YOUR STRENGTHS AND WEAKNESSES

John Lee Dumas, who hosts the *Entrepreneur on Fire* podcast, admits self-awareness has played a big role in identifying his own limitations. 'I have to know my limitations, so I can hire others to fill those gaps, and I have to know my strengths, so I can focus on them and them alone.'

Amplify and capitalise on your strengths, but be conscious of weaknesses that could be your undoing in the world of entrepreneurship. Find ways to mitigate, delegate or offset them. Don't spend an inordinate amount of time trying to personally resolve your weaknesses, as all that will do is bring you up to everyone else's level. It won't give you an *advantage*.

217

Call to action

1. Review this chapter and write down which character attributes might hold you back from success as an entrepreneur.

2. Develop an action plan to replace those attributes with their startup equivalent.

3. Identify your strengths and weaknesses.

4. Put together a plan to offset, mitigate or delegate your weaknesses.

5. Double down on your strengths.

Chapter 10

10× YOUR OUTPUT

In three years, I built a seven-figure business that has worked with a formidable line-up of large companies, including some of the world's corporate heavyweights, in Australia, Singapore, Hong Kong, Frankfurt, Paris, London, Amsterdam, New York, Washington DC and Lincoln, Nebraska! Our children's entrepreneurship program, Lemonade Stand, has been delivered to more than 1000 kids across Australia and Singapore, and we released the online version in late 2018.

I have self-published two books, one of which topped the Amazon charts in a number of categories, such as technology and startups, then secured a book deal with Wiley for this, my third book. I've written more than 250 blog posts. I've launched and hosted an award-winning podcast, which is now more than 300 episodes strong.

I've also delivered more than 50 keynote presentations to audiences of between 50 and 400 people, and mentored more than 50 startups.

I'm often asked, 'How do you manage to get so much done?' I credit my output to:

- having purpose and a worthwhile mission at the centre of everything I do
- my awesome team
- automating as many repeatable tasks as possible
- delegating and outsourcing repeatable tasks that can't be automated

- using the 80/20 principle
- applying agile task management tools
- creating a distraction-free environment
- knowing how to get myself into flow, or 'the zone'
- subscribing to philosophies that help me stay focused
- meditation and mindfulness practices
- an awareness and appreciation of Parkinson's Law
- effective partnerships and networks
- knowing and doubling down on my strengths
- taking a serious interest in my health and fitness (this is perhaps most important of all and is the focus of chapter 11).

Having seen how slow most corporate teams move, I often say that while our team at CC is only seven deep, we move as fast as most corporate teams I've come across that are three, four or even five times our size. Napoleon Bonaparte, one of history's greatest military leaders, once said, 'The moral is to the physical as three to one'. By this he meant that having purpose and a 'worthy cause' at the centre of what his *Grande Armée* did so increased motivation and team morale that they could topple armies three times their size on the battlefield.

Purpose aside, we keep the 80/20 or Pareto Principle at front of mind in everything we do and constantly reassess what we're spending our time on (product, geography, customer segment, marketing channel, sales strategy and so on). We outsource basic tasks to virtual assistants overseas for a fraction of what we'd pay their local equivalents. We automate anything that can be automated using online tools such as Zapier. We use agile workflows to keep up a fast cadence of delivery and tap into productivity hacks (batching tasks, checking email infrequently, keeping prioritised to-do lists and turning off notifications, for example). We do what we can to get shit done fast and well.

People striking out on their own or in a small team generally don't have lots of resources. That's why optimising every hour is key to building a competitive advantage and making every ounce of effort go further. When you get started, you need to find ways to optimise your use of your time and limited resources and stretch your runway as far as it will go.

Cal Newport, in his best-selling book *Deep Work*, says that producing at an elite level and mastering hard things, both quickly, are two core attributes that will set winners apart in the new economy. In order to produce at an elite level, you need to get into flow, or 'the zone'.

INCREASE YOUR PRODUCTIVITY BY 500 PER CENT

Flow has been defined as a mental state of operation in which a person performing an activity is fully immersed in a feeling of energised focus. First coined by Hungarian-American psychologist Mihaly Csikszentmihalyi in 1975, it is often referred to as 'the zone'. What is less widely understood is that it is in fact a physiological state. A 10-year McKinsey and Co. study on flow and productivity found that top executives are 500 per cent more productive when in flow!

The flow state

The human brain utilises five different types of electric patterns, also called 'brain waves', across the cortex. C Wilson Meloncelli defines the five brain waves as follows:

1. Delta — experienced in deep, dreamless sleep

2. Alpha — dominant during quiet thought or light meditation, or while daydreaming

3. Beta — associated with normal waking consciousness

4. Theta — associated with intuition and processing information above and beyond normal consciousness

5. Gamma — for higher processing tasks and cognitive functioning.

The flow state is activated when the alpha and theta brain waves merge, essentially at the border between the conscious and subconscious mind.

(continued)

INCREASE YOUR PRODUCTIVITY BY 500 PER CENT (*CONT'D*)

Picture for a moment a lone surfer about to hurl himself up onto a six-metre wave near a treacherous, shallow coral reef. In that moment, his mind is processing information above and beyond normal conscious thought. Intuition (theta) takes the driver's seat while the rest of the world simply slips away (alpha), allowing the surfer to focus on just one thing — catching that wave. According to Steven Kotler, bestselling author of *The Rise of Superman* and co-founder of the Flow Genome Project, 'If we are hunting the highest version of ourselves, then we need to turn work into play and not the other way around ... unless we invert this equation, much of our capacity for intrinsic motivation starts to shut down. We lose touch with our passion and become less than what we could be and that feeling never really goes away'.

In order to be our best at anything, we need to pursue our passions and activate a sense of play; otherwise we will never perceive work as anything but that, and we'll struggle to tap into the flow state that sees free solo rock climbers (that's climbing with*out* a safety harness) scale and survive 600-metre-high cliff faces. When it comes to pushing human limits, it's often a case of *flow or die*.

Triggering the flow state

So you've never caught a wave, climbed a cliff face or base jumped. Have you ever been so immersed in an activity that time just seemed to stop and you put in hours of work, effortlessly and blissfully, while the rest of the world seemed to just slip away? That's flow. Did you find that state productive? Do you want to get into that state more often? According to Kotler, there are a number of ways to activate the flow state across psychological, environmental and social lines.

Psychological triggers

Intense focus on a single task demands no distractions, no multi-tasking and often, solitude. With *clear goals* and calm, the mind doesn't wander and can stay focused on the present moment and action.

Riding a wave, the surfer adapts and adjusts based on *immediate feedback* from the wave itself. The mind stays present, knowing how to improve performance in real time. The *challenge/skills ratio* is another trigger point. Research shows that tasks that are 4 per cent more challenging than our skills are capable of meeting strike a chord at the midline between boredom and anxiety—this is the sweet spot to maximise attention and flow.

Environmental triggers

Where decisions and tasks have *high consequences*, elevated risk levels keep us focused. There's no trying to get in the zone when it's life or death, success or failure. A rich environment with lots of novelty, unpredictability and complexity can also focus our attention, and not knowing what is coming next can activate flow.

Social and group triggers

Think of a basketball team focused on sinking the game-winning shot with five seconds left on the clock. *Serious concentration*, a *clear shared goal* and *effective communication* will get them there.

Familiarity means a common language and a shared knowledge base, with everyone on the same page. Professional athletes will soon be bored playing with amateurs, who themselves will be frustrated by the experience. *Equal participation and equivalent skill levels* best trigger the flow state.

Without skin in the game, be it monetary, mental, physical, creative or social, there's no *risk* in failure. Yet failure underpins

(continued)

223

INCREASE YOUR PRODUCTIVITY BY
500 PER CENT (*CONT'D*)

innovation and creativity. Ever played poker without money on the table? No doubt you were 'all in' on many an occasion when you normally wouldn't be with real money down.

Some other triggers to explore

Meditation and mindfulness calm the mind and help you think clearly and stay present on the task at hand. If you've never meditated before, the Headspace and Calm mobile apps are a great place to begin. For reluctant starters, try taking six deep, mindful breaths, which should take you no longer than a minute but can go a long way to changing your mental state for the better before you commence a task requiring mental focus.

First discovered in 1839 by physicist Heinrich Wilhelm Dove, *binaural beats*, involving the coalescence of different audio frequencies in each ear, can help trigger brain activity in the flow state. You can listen to some beats at MyNoise.net and Brain.FM the next time you're doing something that requires your full concentration. Matt Mullenweg, founder of WordPress, believes listening to the same song on repeat gets him into the flow state, an idea supported by the research of Arkansas psychologist and musicologist Elizabeth Hellmuth Margulis, as discussed in her book *On Repeat: How Music Plays the Mind*.

Smart drugs, known in Silicon Valley as 'nootropics', are cognitive enhancers that support focus, memory, creativity and motivation. UFC commentator, stand-up comedian, entrepreneur and podcaster extraordinaire Joe Rogan claims he won't do anything that requires focus without nootropics. Popular products worth checking out include Onnit's Alpha Brain (Joe Rogan co-owns Onnit), Four Sigmatic's Mushroom Coffee and Bulletproof Coffee's Brain Octane. Or just mix a tablespoon of emulsified MCT oil into your coffee.

Tim Ferriss popularised *batch processing* in his bestseller *The 4-Hour Workweek*. The idea is to select times of day to batch certain processes, such as checking email, which he limits to once or twice a day. This way, you reduce distraction and stop chasing supposedly shiny objects down a rabbit hole.

Flow state busters

When I asked one of America's most popular personal trainers, Ben Greenfield, what his biggest productivity killer was, he replied without hesitation: 'Push notifications, bar none'. There's no shortage of things that get in the way of flow each day. Some of the more common busters are:

- a lack of passion or enthusiasm for your job

- a lack of underlying purpose

- no tangible, measurable or visible outcomes (or a very long feedback loop)

- the distraction of checking email

- notifications on your desktop or smartphone

- interruptions by colleagues in an open-plan office, phone calls, texts and the like.

It's worth mentioning the cognitive switching penalty. The time it takes to get back into flow after being interrupted might be as short as a few minutes or as long as 45 minutes. If your day is littered with interruptions, then do the math and the numbers start to look very ugly very quickly.

The modern mind tends to be messy; clouded with work, social, monetary, emotional, psychological and physical pressures; and rarely focused on one task at a time. This means most people spend little time in flow, which too often results in sub-par performance and creative endeavours. Eckhart Tolle, author of the mindfulness bestseller *The*

(continued)

225

INCREASE YOUR PRODUCTIVITY BY 500 PER CENT (*CONT'D*)

Power of Now, observes, 'Because we live in such a mind-dominated culture, most modern art, architecture, music, and literature are devoid of beauty, of inner essence, with very few exceptions. The mind left to itself creates monstrosities, and not only in art galleries. Look at our urban landscapes and industrial wastelands. No civilization has ever produced so much ugliness'.

Many people claim they have their best ideas while in the shower after a gym workout or while going for a run. This is because such activities tend to calm the mind and free it from the noise of the world, allowing us to see things more clearly.

Getting into a flow state is a powerful way to not only increase productivity, but also increase creativity and innovation, which is key to your not only bringing something new into the world but maintaining your competitive edge.

My smartphone addiction and how I overcame it

The biggest flow state buster of all, in my opinion, is your smartphone.

On 23 October 2001, using the slogan 'one thousand songs in your pocket', Steve Jobs introduced the original iPod and ushered in a new age for music lovers. Six years later, the launch of the iPhone would fundamentally change the way we interacted with the world around us.

Today we can communicate, check email, consume media, find our way around, find a date, check the weather, call a cab, buy clothes, take notes, do our banking, pay bills, take selfies, order food, settle disputes, track our steps and more via these shiny little pocket devices of ours. Unsurprisingly, many of us have grown psychologically dependent on them; there's even a clinical term for it: *nomophobia* (short for 'no mobile phone-phobia'), which has been proposed as a specific phobia in the *Diagnostic and Statistical Manual of Mental Disorders*. So this *is* a mental disorder.

A TOOL IS ONLY AS GOOD AS HOW YOU USE IT

Are you using your phone for a specific reason, with a desired outcome in mind, or are you mindlessly scrolling through whatever attention merchants such as Facebook throw at you in today's news feed, ultimately, to sell ads? Since the launch of the iPhone 10 years ago, it has become clear that a growing proportion of the population is not using the tool all that well. Recent research from dscout found that the average person touches their phone 2617 times each day, with extreme users doing so more than 5400 times a day!

Nir Eyal put forward a product design strategy in his influential book *Hooked: How to Build Habit-Forming Products*. At a high level, the elements underpinning Nir Eyal's model and the addictive quality of our apps are internal and external triggers such as notifications to get you to open an app, variability (not knowing what you're going to get, rather like a slot machine), investment (effort or monetary, such as the time spent building your Instagram profile and following) and reward (the tiny dopamine hit you get from a little red notification on Facebook, for example).

Tactics like these have contributed to the recent backlash against tech companies.

Notable criticism has come from the likes of:

- Salesforce CEO Marc Benioff, who proposed that we 'regulate Facebook like tobacco'
- Tristan Harris, former design ethicist at Google, whose TED talk on the topic has received 2 million views
- WhatsApp co-founder Brian Acton, who started the Twitter hashtag #deletefacebook
- Napster founder and former Facebook board member Sean Parker, who expressed concerns that Facebook was 'exploiting a vulnerability in human psychology'
- Adam Alter, author and professor of psychology, whose book *Irresistible* looks at the rise of addictive technology and the business of keeping us hooked.

Interestingly enough, the designers of these addictive apps often don't let their kids use them, for obvious reasons. In fact, Steve Jobs never let his kids use an iPad.

IMPLICATIONS OF SMARTPHONE ADDICTION

'So what,' you say. 'My smartphone enriches my life.' While there can be no disputing the value the utilitarian smartphone features have created, the adverse implications of smartphone addiction are significant and can be debilitating, potentially leading to:

1. *Crappy relationships*. It affects our relationships. How often, when you are out to dinner with friends or simply at home with family, do you catch yourself spending a little too much time checking your Instagram feed or saying, 'I just want to quickly check…'?

2. *A lesser experience of life*. Our experience of life suffers as we spend more time looking for that perfect selfie to share later (often taking 20 or more shots of what is essentially the same photo so we can be painted in the best possible light), rather than simply enjoying the sunset, the live band or the hike.

3. *Depression*. A recent study at Baylor University found that heavy smartphone users tend to be moodier, materialistic and temperamental, resulting in an inability to focus.

4. *Lost productivity*. In a recent conversation with Alter, we discussed tech addiction and touched on author Cal Newport's concept of 'deep work', which is a synonym for flow. Checking our phones, even for just a few seconds, can take us out of flow, and have us suffering the dreaded cognitive switching penalty.

TAKING A STAND

Given that my work, relationships and experience of life are all important to me, I recently decided to take a stand as I felt I was spending too much time on my phone! These fears were confirmed when I started using the Moment app to track the time I spent looking at my screen (oh the irony!). Turns out I was spending more than two hours on my phone each day, which for my money was at least an hour too long. I felt a little better about myself, and a little worse about humanity, when I learned that the average Moment user spends 3 hours and 50 minutes a day looking at their screens ('Holy Oleo Batman!') — and these users have an obvious predisposition towards wanting to use their smartphone less.

The average user? Analytics firm Flurry found that the average American spends up to 5 hours a day staring at their smartphones; this doesn't even include laptops or tablets. To put these numbers into perspective, figure 10.1 shows a simple visual I developed on what the standard work week might look like for the typical Moment user.

Figure 10.1: the typical smartphone user's week day (toilet optional)

The assumptions here are an eight-hour work day, with four hours on the phone each day. But wait … if we include weekends, figure 10.2 shows what it looks like over the course of the year.

Figure 10.2: the typical smartphone user's year

This assumes no work on weekends. Almost nine weeks staring at our device, without even including desktop, laptop or tablet time.

So what did I do about it? First, I set a goal: less than 60 minutes a day of screen time. Second, acknowledging that old habits die hard, I set out to change my environment so looking at my phone would be harder. For example, if you want to eat fewer potato chips, not having them in the house is more likely to work than simply fighting temptation.

This prompted me to buy a clock radio to replace my smartphone as an alarm clock. This way, I was able to leave my phone in another room while I slept, which meant no looking at it before bed, if I happened to wake up in the middle of the night or first thing in the morning. I worked towards developing a habit of not looking at my phone until after I had completed my morning routine. Basically, I'd be a good 90 minutes into my day before checking email or social (I'd only use my phone to tee up a podcast or music for my morning gym session).

Third, I turned off all notifications so I would not be sucked back into any apps.

This left me with much more mental clarity as I got on with my day. But still, during the course of the day, particularly as the day became night and my willpower was progressively depleted, I could feel myself reaching for my phone more often, not to do anything in particular, but simply to dive into the bottomless pits that are Twitter and Facebook feeds.

So I needed to dig deeper and ask myself some questions. Such as why am I checking my phone? (Was it merely habitual or from a need for social connection? Was my brain hungry for a dopamine hit or was I just bored?) Is there utility in doing so? Did I check it five minutes ago? What can I do instead right now? For example, if I'm in transit or on the train, I'll read a book or listen to a podcast or audiobook, or maybe just give my mind some time and space to think as I stare out the window.

It took me three weeks of concerted effort to form new habits, as illustrated in the screenshots in figure 10.3.

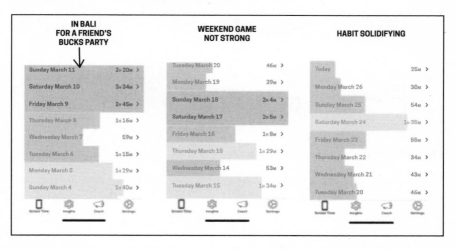

Figure 10.3: hitting my target consistently took almost three weeks
Source: 'Moment' app screenshots reproduced with permission from Kevin Holesh.

DON'T EXPECT TO CHANGE ENTRENCHED HABITS OVERNIGHT

Each week I've made more progress, despite catching myself out sometimes, perhaps taking too many photos during a friend's wedding or succumbing to the willpower-depleting effects of one too many Bintangs during a friend's bachelor party in Bali (okay, so it was probably one too many vodka soda limes).

But more often than not, I now find myself a lot more self-aware when it comes to how I use my phone. I'm no longer on autopilot. When I use it, I use it deliberately to do whatever I need to, then get off as soon as I'm done. No more just checking email or Twitter or my crypto portfolio (which, like most, has lost 90 per cent of its initial value at the time of writing).

As a result, I feel much better, calmer and more clear headed. I have more breakthrough ideas, more time for actual conversations, more time to read and learn. I get more high-quality deep work done. (I wrote this late at night when I might once have been checking my phone every 10 minutes, compromising my ability to get into flow.) It almost makes me wish I hadn't signed up to a two-year contract for the iPhone X, as it is now wasted on me.

I've since revised my target from under 60 minutes to under 30 minutes, as illustrated in figure 10.4.

| 17.3 WEEKS | 12.4 WEEKS | 21.2 WEEKS |

Figure 10.4: a typical year at 30 minutes a day of screen time

That's an extra eight weeks of living each year for the four-hour-a-day smartphone user—unless you consider being on Snapchat living! For a 35-year-old like me, assuming a life expectancy of 74, that's an extra 320 weeks, or six years, of life!

THE END IN MIND

When it comes to habits, it's often a case of LIFO (last in, first out), so beginning with the end in mind and reminding yourself of the following question can help you stay the course.

'What will I wish I had done differently when lying on my death bed?'

Here's what I won't be saying: 'Damn, I wish I had spent more time on Facebook'. I'm more likely to say I should have spent more time with family and friends, more time exploring the world, less time caring what people think and more on leaving my mark on the world.

As Hunter S Thompson once put it, 'life is not a journey to the grave with the intention of arriving safely in a pretty and well preserved body, but rather to skid in broadside, thoroughly used up, totally worn out, and loudly proclaiming—WOW—What a Ride!'.

FINISHING KICKS

Research on athletic performance by Ross Tucker and colleagues at the University of Cape Town compared the pacing strategies used by champion men's distance runners historically. In the 5000 and 10 000 metres, the first and last parts of the race were consistently the fastest.

Reviewing these results, Alex Hutchinson, an award-winning journalist and author of *Endure: Mind, Body, and the Curiously Elastic Limits of Human Performance*, writes, 'There are a number of different ways of looking at this. It could be a result of the psychology of pacing: the farther away the finish line is, the more conservative you're likely to be. Or it could, as Tim Noakes and others have argued, reflect some sort of hardwired protective mechanism in the brain: no matter how hard you try, it's only when you're about to stop that you're allowed to access your emergency reserves'.

The tendency to speed up as we approach the finishing line is called 'the finishing kick', and it can be found not only in endurance sports, but in weightlifting—and, if you look closely enough, the workplace too.

We often double down as a deadline approaches or when the financial year end looms large and bonuses and promotions hang in the balance. Time, and our perceptions of it, clearly play a part in influencing how we perform. Imagine if we could perform at a finishing kick pace more often; what might it mean for our output levels, the results we achieve and our ultimate success? Take compounding effects into account and we're talking proverbial light years between here and where we'll end up in a few years' time.

So how might you hack your environment to induce a finishing kick more often?

(continued)

FINISHING KICKS (*CONT'D*)

At Collective Campus, we run something we call 13-week years. Rather than focusing on annual goals, we have quarterly goals, and for each goal we have a number of ambitious tasks that need to be completed before the quarter ends, tasks that will move the dial a considerable way forward to help us achieve said goals. This experiment has been paying such impressive dividends that very soon we may tinker with four-week years.

The great Chinese military strategist Sun Tzu knew all about hacking the environment for performance. He wrote, 'When your army has crossed the border, you should burn your boats and bridges, in order to make it clear to everybody that you have no hankering after home'. If retreat isn't an option, to advance is imperative, and in such an environment you've no choice but to go all in!

Virtual assistants 101

By using a virtual assistant, you can focus on value-adding tasks, rather than routine, process-oriented, soul-sucking administrative ones. VAs are being used increasingly in entrepreneurial circles owing to both time and capital constraints that come with the territory. I've used them for several years; they are indeed one key reason why I can maintain my output level.

WHY YOU SHOULD USE A VA

What makes someone successful and sets them apart is their strengths. Whatever their magic formula or secret sauce, *that's* what they need to spend most time doing, rather than engaging in process-oriented tasks that take them away from doing what creates the most value and leaves them feeling unfulfilled.

Outsourcing obviously saves us not only time but also money, particularly if offshoring to countries with a significantly lower cost of living and minimum wage. Ultimately, outsourcing allows us to do more of what we love and to create more value.

Basically, if you are capable of generating at least $20 an hour doing what you love, putting your best skills to use, then you should make no bones about paying a virtual assistant $10 an hour to do what you don't love, what you're not great at.

Table 10.1 shows a handy chart from Perry Marshall's highly recommended book *80/20 Sales and Marketing*. If you find yourself wrestling with $10-an-hour tasks, then you're not using your time effectively. You can get a VA (or a personal assistant) to do many if not all of these tasks. You should be spending your time on high-value activities and slowly transition from $100-an-hour tasks up to $10 000 an hour as your business and team grows.

If you spend 'just two hours a day' on $10-an-hour tasks, instead of $50-an-hour tasks, the cumulative effect over the course of a year is huge.

Table 10.1: tasks you can outsource to a VA

$10 per hour	$100 per hour	$1000 per hour	$10 000 per hour
Running errands	Solving a problem for a prospective or existing customer	Planning and prioritising your day	Improving your USP
Talking to unqualified prospects	Talking to a qualified prospect	Negotiating with a qualified prospect	Creating new and better offers
Cold calling (of any variety)	Writing an email to prospects or customers	Building your sales funnel	Repositioning your message and position
Building and fixing stuff on your website	Creating marketing tests and experiments	Judging marketing tests and experiments	Executing 'bolt from the blue' brilliant ideas
Doing expense reports	Managing pay-per-click campaigns	Creating pay-per-click campaigns	Negotiating major deals
Working 'social media' the way most people do it	Doing social media well (this is rare)	Doing social media with extreme competence (this is very rare)	Selling to high-value customers and groups
Cleaning, sorting	Outsourcing simple tasks	Delegating complex tasks	Selecting team members
Attending meetings	Customer follow up	Writing sales copy	Public speaking

Source: Perry Marshall, *80/20 Sales and Marketing*

Value of $10 tasks at year end: $4800

Value of $50 tasks at year end: $24 000

So what's the value of $1000-an-hour tasks at year end?

$480 000.

Got a team of 10 and a culture where people spend 'just two hours a day' on $10-an-hour tasks? *That's $4.8 million over the year.*

This doesn't even take into account the compounding effect of higher value creation tasks, neither does it take into account the cognitive switching penalty incurred by shifting your focus from deep work to lodge an expense report or change the colour of a button on your website. The value of focusing solely on high-value tasks goes far beyond these numbers.

Of course, the brain can handle only so much deep work each day. When I spoke with clinical psychologist Sherry Walling, who also hosts the *ZenFounder* podcast, she suggested that the average person can manage about four to five hours of deep work each day. However, rather than spend the rest of the day on menial, repetitive tasks, you and your employees would be far better off delegating or outsourcing this work and taking a break, so you'll be fresh to tackle the higher value tasks later and also be able to sustain your efforts longer.

BE EXPLICIT

You really can't leave anything to chance as far as your instructions go. The key is never to assume! Be explicit about every element if you expect your hired gun to deliver what you envisage in the dark corners of your mind. For example, our VA used to curate a weekly email we'd send to our database that was based on 14 pages of instructions (that's a 2000-word, 10-point Google Doc, complete with screenshots, arrows and bubbles).

TYPES OF TASKS

So what kinds of tasks might you outsource? They might, for example, include content creation, curation and distribution, bookkeeping, payroll, conversion optimisation, reporting, scheduling and administrative tasks, research, data entry, presentations, graphic design, web development, call answering, email management or social media marketing. At its core, anything that can be effectively codified into a clear, actionable step-by-step process, and that doesn't come with unacceptable privacy or quality risks, can and should be outsourced

I outsource:

- curation of weekly email to database
- podcast guest shortlisting, outreach and scheduling
- podcast editing, mixing, publishing and distribution
- infographic creation
- conference speaking gig research and outreach
- lead generation
- video development
- content distribution (podcasts, blogs, infographics, ebooks etc.)
- social media management and influencer outreach
- research and execution of growth hacks (but not their review and selection)
- analytics reporting

WHERE TO FIND YOUR VIRTUAL ASSISTANT

Really, just Google 'virtual assistant' and you will find countless places.

My preferred approach is to find someone on a platform such as Fiverr or Upwork, evaluate them based on past work, buyer feedback and an interview, then engage them on short projects where I pay by the hour.

You've got to cut them some slack initially and give them a little time to find their groove. After a few weeks, either I'll look for ways to formalise the arrangement and incentivise them accordingly, or if I'm not happy it's back to the drawing board.

Remember, mastery, autonomy, purpose. I strive to make a virtual assistant feel like part of the team and remind them of their why, and also surprise them with random bonuses or gifts that they tend not to expect. The investment you make in your VA will be repaid in droves. For example, my VA didn't just read this entire book and put together a list of permissions I needed from third parties mentioned in the book; she also went above and beyond to identify inaccuracies and grammatical errors that I was unwittingly sleeping on.

Figure 10.5 shows a note from our Philippines-based VA Paulina in response to a handwritten note and gift bag we sent her.

Figure 10.5: note from our VA based in the Philippines

80/20 baby!

The Pareto Principle, which derives its name from Italian economist Vilfredo Pareto, suggests that 80 per cent of effects come from 20 per cent of causes. This applies to revenue, products, distribution of wealth, land title holders, software bugs, employees and exercise, among many other things.

The thing about 80/20 that's often overlooked, though, is that if you break it down (providing your numbers are big enough):

- 64 per cent of your revenue is attributable to just 4 per cent of your customers
- 51 per cent of your revenue is (or should be, according to the principle) attributable to less than 1 per cent of your customers.

This also suggests that 4 per cent of your customers are willing to spend 16 times more than the rest of your customers. If you can identify them and put premium packages together to appeal to them, you'll be much better off investing your time in these few high-value clients than many low-value ones, especially over the long term, when you take account of the cost of customer acquisition and customer relationship management.

Marketing guru Perry Marshall made the case in *80/20 Sales and Marketing* that if 50 000 sports fans are willing to spend $100 each on tickets, food and refreshments on game day at the stadium, then 238 will spend more than $10 000 (think corporate boxes). According to *Forbes* magazine, the total revenue of the Chicago Bears in 2010 was US$416 million, but only US$75 million of this came from gate receipts; the rest would have come from media rights, corporate boxes, brand licensing, and food and beverage and merchandise sales.

So here are three questions to think about:

- What 20 per cent of your tasks create 80 per cent of the value?
- Who might your 4 per cent customers be?
- What might your equivalent of a stadium corporate box be?

For more on this, work out what your highest value customer might be worth by checking out Marshall's 80/20 Power Curve at 8020curve.com.

Agile time management

In order to get the most out of every day, a certain amount of process will help guide your efforts so you're more deliberate about how you're spending your time. Consider using agile management techniques such as the following to get the most out of your and your team's days.

MANAGING TEAMS

More isn't always better. In the words of late rapper the Notorious B.I.G. aka Biggie Smalls aka Big Poppa, 'Mo money, mo problems'. When it comes to products, more features usually translates to greater complexity, cost and confusion on the part of the customer. Similarly, more people on a project doesn't necessarily mean more work will get done.

According to Brooks' Law, teams of three to seven people require about 25 per cent of the effort of groups of nine to 20 people to get the same amount of work done. Why? The number of relationships you need to manage in a team increases dramatically with every person you add. For example, a team of five has only 10 team member relationships to manage, while a team of nine has 36. Adding four people added 26 new relationships for the team to manage communication between. What about a bloated team of 20, the kind you might find sitting around a boardroom table in a large organisation? That's 160 relationships! This is why agile team sizes are usually capped at nine team members.

Want to figure out how many relationships you need to manage in your team? Use the simple formula below.

$$X = N\ (N-1)/2$$

where:

N = number of team members

X = number of team member relationships.

THE NEED FOR *SPEED*

I've stressed that speed is absolutely fundamental to success, but I'm not talking about the kind of speed that simply has you doing what you're currently doing but at an increased keystroke pace or talking to your team at 2×. No, I'm talking about a different kind of speed.

During agile projects, sprint retrospectives are performed at the end of every cycle of development and delivery of the product, which is usually between one and four weeks long. The purpose of this is to consolidate learnings around what could have been done better to incorporate into the subsequent sprint.

Agile teams ask themselves key questions: Is there anything we don't have to do? Are there any impediments to remove or items to offload? Are there any people/procedural/policy/systems impediments we can address that are slowing us down? By getting into the habit of asking questions like these, either of yourself or of your team, you'll find you progressively work on more high-impact work and less low-value work. Productivity, after all, is really about what you don't do.

KANBAN BOARDS

Something as simple as a Kanban board shown in figure 10.6, which will give you clear visibility of your to-do list, what's currently in progress and what's completed, can go a long way to managing workflow. This applies especially if working on a team, as it helps identify bottlenecks and keeps people accountable; there's nowhere to hide, particularly if the Kanban board is clearly visible in the office and colour coded by team, deliverable or team member. It's easy to default to online spreadsheets and the like, but unless these are religiously referred to each day by every member on your team, and discussed in daily or at least weekly stand-ups, it's easy for things to fall through the cracks.

You can use online tools such as Trello or Asana to set up a simple Kanban board that will also help you allocate responsible persons and due dates to tasks and/or projects so you can better monitor and manage workflow.

Figure 10.6: organised chaos: a project-centric Kanban board at Collective Campus HQ

DAILY AND WEEKLY STAND-UPS

On accountability, three times a week at Collective Campus we run a stand-up, where each member of the team quickly advises (1) whether they got through their to-dos yesterday and if not, why not (is there anything in their way or anything we can help with?), (2) what they're working on today and (3) if they foresee any challenges or need assistance.

This helps keep everybody on the same page and avoids issues blowing up and costing us a lot more time and resources than we can afford further down the line. We use a stopwatch and limit these sessions to 15 minutes. If anything requires more time than that, then it's discussed between the relevant parties after the stand-up.

STRATEGY QUADRANT

Every quarter, my team and I sit down to assess how we're tracking. We simply draw up a four-quadrant chart on a whiteboard with more, less, start and stop in each quadrant (figure 10.7). We think cycle through product, sales, marketing, target market and other areas to determine what we need to stop allocating resources to if it's simply not working or what we could be doubling down on.

This keeps us from doing 'what we've always done around here' and ensures we maintain a culture of experimentation, optimise our allocation of resources and move forward.

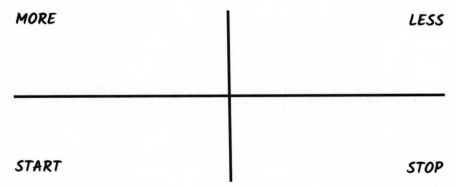

Figure 10.7: strategy quadrant

It's critical that everyone feels comfortable sharing their thoughts during these sessions to avoid groupthink. Have people write their own ideas on Post-it notes for each quadrant across each area, then have them add their Post-it notes to the board at the same time, grouping any similar ideas and opening the floor for discussion.

You can also apply this tool to your personal life.

I, Robot

Anything that can be codified without compromising quality should be *automated*. In some cases, a small dip in quality is also okay if the negative impact isn't material. Today you can use an API (application programming interface) to get different applications to talk to each other — and no, you usually don't need to develop these APIs yourself. You can leverage off-the-shelf providers such as Zapier to get your apps to talk to each other and save you time in the process. For example, if someone signs up to an ebook on the Collective Campus website, they are automatically added to our email database. Thereafter, they automatically receive a welcome email and, depending on how they interact with that first email, they get fed into a subsequent, tailored email 'dripfeed'.

These apps can save you precious time, and there's no shortage of them. For example, Zapier supports more than 1000 apps. Popular 'zaps' help you:

- share blog posts to your social channels (auto share to Facebook, Twitter and RSS feeds, for example)
- keep your notes with your tasks (create Trello cards from Evernote or Asana tasks from Evernote, say)
- create an email list (such as adding subscribers to Mailchimp from Google Sheets, Typeform or Facebook Leads).

Other tools in this category worth exploring include Integromat, Microsoft's Flow, PieSync, CloudHQ and WappWolf. If you're not automating it, you're stuck doing it.

Perhaps you baulked at the time required to set up the systems for automating and outsourcing tasks in the first place. At this point, I'll defer to former US President Dwight D. Eisenhower, who once said, 'I have two kinds of problems: the urgent and the important. The urgent are not important, and the important are never urgent'. He used this principle to organise his time. There's no point being efficient at the wrong things.

By prioritising the important over the urgent, we can minimise the stress of having too heavy a workload, too many tight deadlines and too much rudimentary and unfulfilling 'firefighting' to do. As Michael Gerber put it in *The E-Myth Revisited*, 'The key to real prosperity in business is to work *on* your enterprise, not in it'.

10× your sales pipeline

No matter how good your product, you've still got to convince the buyer, and often that will require good old-fashioned sales techniques. Depending on what you're selling, how effective your targeting and qualifying is, and what industry you're in, an average sales conversion rate (the percentage of leads you are able to convert from prospect to sale) can vary from as little as 1 per cent to as much as 20 per cent or more in some cases.

Chances are, if you *do* have a product worth selling, you'll be looking at about a 5 per cent conversion rate. This means that for every 20 qualified leads, you'll convert *one*. If you're selling to large organisations, the sales cycle can be looooong — three to 18 months in some cases — so in order to offset the risks, increasing the number of legitimate leads in your pipeline is key.

Fortunately, there are a number of tools and techniques you can use to do just that, including the following:

Sales Navigator. LinkedIn's sales and prospecting tool helps you find and target leads based on variables such as location, industry, company size, seniority, title, company name and more. Not only that, but you can send messages to people based on relevant media mentions or new roles they might have just stepped into, increasing the likelihood of a response.

LinkedHelper. This tool enables you to safely send up to 150 targeted, personalised messages via LinkedIn each and every day.

MixMax. Like LinkedHelper but for email, MixMax helps you set up sequences of personalised emails, sent at predefined dates, to a list of recipients, saving you lots of time typing out individual email addresses. Notably, it's not until the third email (usually the 'breakup email') that I get most of my responses.

Facebook Lead Ads. Whatever your philosophical stance on Facebook, Lead Ads are a powerful way to generate leads. Simply put, if someone clicks on your ad, a pop-up form will appear that encourages them to send you their pre-populated details, such as their name and email address, with the click of a button. This reduces friction and increases the likelihood of their sending you their details.

LeadIQ. This browser plugin that works with LinkedIn is loaded with features, my favourite of which is scraping LinkedIn people search results to find their email addresses. When used in conjunction with a tool such as MixMax, this becomes incredibly potent. Speaking of finding email addresses, you can also use tools such as *RocketReach* to find an individual's professional and personal email address or *Hunter.IO* if you want to generate a list of all email addresses in use at an organisation.

For additional tools and sales resources to help you 10x your pipeline and convert more customers, head over to **www.employeetoentrepreneur.io/sales**.

Use your calendar

Jordan Harbinger, former host of *The Art of Charm* podcast, believes using his calendar effectively has helped him become more productive than most people.

> I just put everything on my calendar. What's on the calendar gets done, what's not on the calendar does not get done ... Every to-do lives in a place in my calendar so it has a time to get done and if I move something I don't just say well I'll do it later, I actually physically move it on the calendar and it takes up an appropriate amount of time so that stops me from getting a backlog of things I need to do someday and it also makes sure that every day I'm actually moving forward. And that's been shockingly simple in making me become more productive than what seems to be most people.

Turn bad habits into good habits

A guest on the *Zig Ziglar Show* podcast, recalled how, when asked at a conference in Australia what he believed was the fastest path to success, he said simply: 'Replace bad habits with good habits'.

This struck a chord with me. As an avid experimenter, I decided to spend some time thinking objectively about what my bad habits were and how to replace them with good habits. From the following list of good habits I worked to instil, you can easily infer which bad habits I sought to replace!

1. Do the most challenging and highest impact things first.
2. Check email and social media only three times a day (at 8 am, at 12 pm and finally at 4 pm).
3. Commit to at least one outing each weekend with friends and/or family.
4. Don't make plans I can't keep, and keep plans I've made.
5. Judge less, with a view to not judging at all. Our annoyance with others reflects something we are unhappy with in ourselves.
6. Resist FOMO (fear of missing out) and create time for solitude, and for learning and growth, to become more introspective and self-aware.
7. Don't pursue the deceptively 'greener' grass.
8. Don't eat after 8 pm.
9. Don't waste time on people I see no future with, whether on a personal or a professional level.
10. Go first! Greet strangers when going for a walk, making eye contact.
11. Attend at least one meetup or networking event a week, and introduce myself to at least five people.
12. Spend more time speaking about and asking questions of others—listen more and talk less.
13. Stop chasing that toxic relationship.
14. Keep cheerful around friends, family, colleagues, clients and strangers.

15. Turn complaints into opportunities for improvement.
16. Turn impatience into time to reflect and breathe.
17. Accept what I can't control, seek to influence only what I can and recognise the difference.
18. Whenever I get the urge to do something that is ultimately junk food for the soul, choose to do something positive instead, such as go for a walk, read, watch a TED talk, go to an open mic night, call a friend or family member I haven't spoken to in a while, listen to an audiobook or podcast, make dinner plans, spend quality time with a significant other, meditate, stretch, reflect ...
19. Show gratitude for five things, no matter how great or small, *every night*.
20. Notice negative thoughts as just that—passing thoughts, usually involuntary, and not an extension of my mind. Watch them come and go; don't identify with or become them.
21. Don't drink a single drop of alcohol on Monday, Tuesday or Wednesday.

Of course, like any behaviour, whether good or bad, it takes time for it to become a habit. Conventional wisdom has it that 21 days of successive behaviour is enough to form a new habit, but factors such as intensity of action, original motivation and other circumstances will affect this, and we'll rarely ever 'arrive' completely.

Sometimes you will slip up. Be kind to yourself and accept it when you do. Even the habit of consciously *trying* to right all of these purported wrongs has a positive impact. Put together your own list of good and bad, then revisit it weekly, monthly or (as in my case) quarterly. Like going to the gym regularly, building positive habits is an intentional practice. Sure, you might miss the occasional gym session, but if you go more days than you miss, you're in a good place.

As human beings, it's easy simply to accept our bad habits as 'just the way I am', but the way we are is something we can change. The first step is to determine who we *want* to be, what the bad habits preventing us from getting there are, and what good habits we might want to replace them with to become that person.

Parkinson's Law

Cyril Parkinson said, 'Work expands so as to fill the time available for its completion'.

Give a person three months to do something and they'll do it in ... three months. Give a person three days to do something and they'll do it, as best they can, in ... three days.

Set a realistic amount of time to do a good job but a short enough time to make it challenging and avoid procrastinating.

Extreme ownership and accountability

You can make excuses all day. You can externalise all you like and blame extenuating circumstances or people for why you haven't achieved your goal or done what you set out to in the time you had planned. Making excuses is easy, and it feels good because it takes the onus off us. Teenagers know this well. Trying harder means falling harder, so in the face of failure they lower their efforts and expectations and say, 'I didn't try anyway'.

But in the long term, making excuses sabotages the achievement of our goals and robs us of the gift of living a life of learning, growth and fulfilment. Ultimately, making excuses leaves us with a victim mentality, which strips us of our power to do anything about it. The opposite of a victim mindset that externalises is a mindset of extreme ownership, one that internalises.

When you take ownership for whatever goes wrong or whatever is standing in your way, it empowers you to identify the problem and do something about it, no matter how daunting. Whether or not you come out the other side successfully is beside the point. Making excuses leaves you standing still. Taking ownership moves you forward, even if it does not seem like it at the time.

When you apply extreme ownership to your business and life you'll wind up much further ahead than your victim-minded peers in the long term. See it as a form of compound interest.

Radical transparency

Did you hear about the manager who would scold underlings who came bearing bad news? Eventually he stopped hearing bad news, but unfortunately for him it wasn't because there was none to report. Such managers are fired ostensibly because they aren't able to identify and respond to threats in a timely manner, but really because they're terrible communicators and lack emotional intelligence.

The best way to address challenges and threats is to identify them as early as possible. To do this, a culture of radical transparency and objectivity, both with yourself and with your teammates, goes a long way. Radical transparency is essentially about thoughtful disagreement and the free exchange of ideas in the best interests of the company and its people, free of remorse, hurt feelings and lingering grudges.

Growth and comfort don't coexist, so it would be tragic to let a desire to avoid conflict get in the way of your own success, especially when you might have one real shot at it. Yes, you might hear some things from colleagues that you'd prefer you hadn't. It might be difficult to be radically transparent with them. But ultimately, by identifying and responding to issues earlier, you're helping your company and everyone who works in it to learn and grow. If people have a problem hearing the truth, then consider the implications of this and whether you want such people on your team.

Of course you could tell someone that their jacket is ugly, but that would just make you an asshole. Radical transparency requires us to empathise and give feedback related to performance, not personal attributes or fashion taste.

Call to action

1. Turn back to table 10.1 on page 235. How many of the $10-an-hour tasks do you do? Outsource them to a VA now.

2. Are there any other tasks you could ultimately write a step-by-step instruction document for? Outsource those too. Now.

3. Create a strategy canvas for how you spend your time and objectively determine and action the tasks you will do less or more of, and the tasks you'll stop doing.

4. Aside from outsourcing, can any of your tasks be automated? Check out the list of apps at Zapier.com that you can configure to speak to each other and save you time.

5. Write down a list of your bad habits and identify good habits to replace them with. The little decisions you make every day dictate where you end up in life.

6. Turn off all notifications (including on your smartphone and desktop).

7. Set up time in your calendar for uninterrupted deep work, and put yourself in a physical environment to support this.

8. Review and test the tools at www.employeetoentrepreneur. io/10xtools/.

9. Whenever you allocate a task to yourself or a team member, remember Parkinson's Law and don't allocate more time than is really necessary.

Chapter 11
POWER UP!

When I started working out in my early twenties, let's be real, it was so the opposite sex would be more receptive to my advances (then at music festivals and nightspots). But today it's mostly to maintain a reliable foundation that keeps me at the top of my game, not only physically but mentally and emotionally. People sometimes ask me, 'Do you do any exercises for your brain?' The best brain exercises are essentially no different from the physical ones. Physical exercise changes your brain chemistry for the better, aiding memory, recall and critical thinking, and delaying the onset of the cognitive decline that comes with ageing.

You can increase your productivity and output by an order of magnitude by investing just a little time in your health and fitness, which, paradoxically, will give you more time for other things, because you will be more focused and effective at what you do. I rarely work more than 50 hours a week and sometimes work less than 40, a far cry from the 80-hour weeks often associated with entrepreneurship.

Far too many people insist that they don't have time for exercise or self-care. I say they don't have time *not* to invest in themselves. Exercise, sleep and eat well, and you will not only be more productive and effective, moving you closer to your goals, but you will live a richer, more rewarding life. It will make you a better friend, lover and family member, and quite simply a better person.

Rock that body

So what do the experts say on the link between physical health and productivity?

DO YOU EVEN LIFT?

The old adage, 'Why work harder when you can work *smarter*?' extends to physical fitness. Fast Company's Josh Davis believes, 'Done right, a good workout can affect how you feel emotionally, your energy level, and how you think that very same day'. Exercise also has same-day effects on cognition, making it easier to engage in key executive functions such as self-control, decision making and handling conflicting needs. When people say they are too busy to exercise, what they really mean is they aren't *prioritising* exercise. 'I'm too busy to exercise,' the self-aggrandisement goes.

Whenever you work out, serotonin is produced and released in the brain, and that not only makes you feel better but improves your state of mind, making the stresses of work easier to handle, and strengthens your immune system, which means fewer sick days. It reduces our risk of heart disease, diabetes and obesity, all of which can run riot in our work.

Interestingly, serotonin is also released in the gut, where an enormous number of micro-organisms, known as the microbiota, influence your decision making and behaviour thanks to a communication system between the digestive and nervous system called the gut–brain axis.

THE EARLY BIRD GETS THE WORM

One of America's most celebrated personal trainers, Ben Greenfield, recommends starting each day with 30 burpees and a two-minute cold shower. 'Everything seems doable after that.' Working out before work has many benefits, including freeing up time for family and social activities after work, as well as increased focus and cognition when you get to work. According to Bodybuilding.com's Melih Cologlu, it will also 'help to boost your metabolism, allowing you to burn more calories for the rest of the day. This phenomenon is called excess post-exercise oxygen consumption, or EPOC'.

Tom Corley, author of *Rich Habits*, spent five years studying 233 rich people and 128 poor people. He found that most rich people get up three hours before actually 'starting' their day, during which they partake in at least a 30-minute exercise routine. Sherry Walling, a clinical psychologist who works with entrepreneurs and hosts the *ZenFounder* podcast, advises a minimum of three 30-minute workouts a week.

You don't need to join a CrossFit gym or sign up for a triathlon. If you're not already working out regularly, start by walking and perhaps explore different forms of physical exercise over time to find something you can see yourself doing long after the novelty wears off. Yoga, pilates, gymnastics, strength training, CrossFit, powerlifting, swimming, running, Spartan Races, cycling, surfing, soccer, basketball, tennis, boxing, martial arts, rock climbing... the world is your gym.

For me, getting up early and hitting the gym is a form of priming. It's about overcoming that little voice in your head that says, *Let's just stay in bed another hour, it's so warm and cosy in here.*

SICK AND TIRED OF FEELING SICK AND TIRED

Sick days cost the Australian economy $30 billion per year, about 62 per cent of which ($18.6 billion) are taken for legitimate reasons. They cost the United States economy US$576 billion.

How many legitimate sick days have you taken in the past year? How often have you felt unwell? How has this affected your productivity, not just when you were away from work but during the onset and recovery from illness while in the office?

COLD SHOWERS

MedicalDaily reports that a cold shower increases alertness, improves immunity and circulation, stimulates weight loss, speeds up muscle recovery and soreness (to keep you from skipping tomorrow's workout), eases stress and can relieve symptoms of depression.

Nobody *wants* to have a freezing cold shower, but life doesn't always give us what we want, and to be successful we need to do the hard things. By starting your day with a personal, private win like this you set yourself up for taking on the hard things of the day. A 60- to 90-second blast of cold water is all it takes to start reaping the benefits. As Ryan Holiday says, 'the obstacle is the way'.

TAKE A STAND

We're all aware, at least we should be, that sitting all day is damaging our bodies in various ways. According to the health and wellness website Authority Nutrition, standing lowers your risk of weight gain and obesity, lowers blood sugar levels, lowers your risk of heart disease, reduces back pain, improves mood and energy levels, boosts productivity and focus, and ultimately helps you live longer. One American study has found that reducing sitting time to three hours a day would raise the average American's life expectancy by two years.

In addition, standing for a couple of hours each afternoon burns more than 150 calories, accounting for almost 1000 calories a week, equivalent to a kilogram lost every seven weeks, and according to the UK's *Daily Mail*, getting up from your desk for just two minutes every half an hour can slash your risk of diabetes.

Consider investing in a standing desk, which can be purchased for a few hundred dollars from Ergotron or Kogan. Or, if you're feeling really game, people such as XPRIZE founder Peter Diamandis and author Gretchen Rubin swear by the treadmill desk.

Speaking of walking, Lifehacker's Thorin Klosowski sees the case for walking more throughout the day as pretty simple. 'All the movement you do throughout the day, from getting up to grab a glass of water to doing the dishes, burns calories and increases metabolism. Even if you're exercising daily, sitting all day counteracts that. Walk more. The goal is to hit about 10,000 steps a day.' This could be during commutes, while talking on the phone, even in meetings. Go for a walk on your lunch break. There are so many opportunities to get your step count up and reduce your sedentary state, and *they all add up*!

You might be familiar with the Pomodoro technique, a time-management method founded by Francesco Cirillo in the late 1980s that breaks work down into chunks of 25 minutes separated by short, three- to five-minute breaks. After four rounds, the technique suggests, take a longer, 15- to 30-minute break. Why? Because intense focus and flow is finite and breaking up your work into chunks of intentional, focused time, free from distractions, with frequent reward mechanisms built in, can help you to churn out more hours of deep work. Michael Todasco, PayPal's Director of Innovation, calculates it takes him 16 minutes to walk around PayPal's campus in San Jose. 'So if I have 18 minutes until my next meeting, I'll get up and walk around campus.' You'll find yourself feeling mentally clearer.

FUEL FOR YOUR ENGINE

Health, fitness and physique are said to come down to 80 per cent diet and 20 per cent exercise. The jury may be out on these figures but whatever the ratio, it's clear that diet is the major contributing factor. There's little point in exercising each day if you're just going to stuff your face with simple carbs such as sugars and starch, food prepared in toxic vegetable oils, and packaged goods that list more chemicals than natural ingredients on their label.

What should you eat to support a productive lifestyle? Low GI carbs, good fats and lean proteins are fuel for the productive go-getter. Moderation is key. Some subscribe to the 80/20 principle here, which suggests that if you eat healthy foods 80 per cent of the time you can indulge in your favourite treats 20 per cent of the time.

Rand Fishkin might swear by his morning exercise and clean diet these days, having recovered from a debilitating bout of depression that he opened up about on *Future Squared*, but he has no issue with the occasional indulgence, having shared with the Twitterverse a happy snap of himself posing with a ramen noodle burger!

STOP CUTTING THE FAT

Fat has got a bad rap in the past, but new US dietary guidelines suggest it's been wrongly accused all these years, prompting Weight Watchers to add fatty foods such as eggs and salmon to its 'zero point foods' list—that's food that doesn't need to be tracked or weighed. When carbohydrates are severely restricted, the body turns to fat metabolism, or 'ketones', for a source of slow-release energy, which also helps you burn fat and stay trim. Compare this with carbs that have you crashing shortly after you've consumed them, leaving you raiding the office pantry for whatever additional sustenance you can find—okay, often a Tim Tam.

On supplements, each morning I'll drink a glass of water with some sea salt in it and pop a multivitamin (which I concede is probably a placebo, but I've been doing it for so long now...), down some Omega-3 fish oil (to aid immunity, blood flow and concentration), magnesium chelate to aid youthfulness, glutamine to assist with muscle recovery and vitamin C to ward off the cold. I'll occasionally lace my coffee or tea with a teaspoon of emulsified MCT oil, which is converted to brain-boosting ketones in the liver. Other supplements I occasionally dabble with include cognitive enhancers such as Onnit's Alpha Brain and Four Sigmatic's Mushroom Coffee.

As Zig Ziglar once said, 'You are who you think people think you are'. Looking and feeling good go a long way towards influencing how people treat you. This can be the difference between open and closed doors. Dario Maestripieri, a professor of evolutionary biology and neurobiology at the University of Chicago, believes attractive people tend to have desirable personality traits, such as greater self-confidence. 'People's self-confidence manifests itself in their behaviour, so that their looks are rated more highly, and their self-esteem makes them more desirable.'

You can access an eating plan I developed for a colleague at bit.ly/2IgMLKu. *Note: I am not a nutritionist and while it works for me, it doesn't necessarily mean it will work for you.*

CUT EVERYTHING INTERMITTENTLY

The benefits of intermittent fasting are increasingly recognised. Many heavy-hitting entrepreneurs, athletes and influencers credit it with giving them more energy, a trimmer waistline and, above all, a healthier disposition. I decided to try fasting and haven't looked back. I tend to fast for 14 to 16 hours, two or three times a week, which isn't that hard (stop eating at 8 pm, and have your first snack at 10 am the next day).

The practice of abstention, whether from food, sex, warm showers or many other of life's pleasures we might take for granted, makes them all the more rewarding and appreciated when we return to them.

Fasting:

- burns fat by facilitating a drop in blood insulin levels (instead of using carbs for energy, it uses your existing fat stores)
- aids cellular repair
- increases human growth hormone production, which has a number of benefits (especially for males)
- lowers the risk of developing Type 2 diabetes
- reduces stress and inflammation in the body, which builds resistance to various diseases
- reduces risk factors for heart disease (cholesterol, blood pressure, triglycerides)
- boosts brain health and focus (especially if your body experiences *ketosis* by generating ketones, which your brain uses as a better, much more sustainable source of energy than carbs)
- checks neurodegenerative diseases such as Parkinson's and Alzheimer's.

The bottom line: intermittent fasting helps you live a longer, healthier, more focused and happier life.

NOW I LAY ME DOWN TO SLEEP

The health and wellness industry, with its spas, aromatherapy oils, meditation retreats, yoga classes, sports supplements and nootropics, is worth more than US$3.7 trillion globally, yet the ultimate bio-hack doesn't cost a cent.

You're far more likely to be productive if you're well rested and firing on all cylinders than if you're burning the candle at both ends and showing up, mostly in the physical form only, for 16 hours a day. Lack of sleep, while okay in short spurts when you need to crank out 60 or more hours a week (I call these spurts 'the playoffs'), is simply unsustainable and will result in burnout, so you should do your best to get the minimum dosage of high-quality sleep every night. You can't crush it when you're crashing.

The US National Sleep Foundation recommends at least seven hours of sleep a night and no more than nine. Try to keep your distance from anything that will get your mind racing within an hour of bed so you're more likely to fall asleep easier; that includes the bright blue light of your smartphone, and stimulating or unfamiliar movies and television programming, as your brain needs to make sense of new contexts and characters when it is exposed to something new.

IF YOU CAN MEASURE IT, YOU CAN MANAGE IT

Peter Drucker's famous dictum, 'If you can measure it you can manage it', is perhaps truer today, in this age of real-time data capture and analytics tools, than ever before. It is especially true in an age when wearable devices make it easier for us to track calories consumed and burned, steps taken and so on. If you know your smoothie actually contained eight teaspoons of sugar, would you drink it again? 'Not my smoothie,' you say? Well, according to its website, a 610 mL Passion Mango Classic smoothie from Boost Juice will set you back 84.9 grams of sugar; that's over 21 four-gram teaspoons of sugar!

Better check the nutritional stats of your 'healthy' smoothie online if they're available, or ask your local juicer what they actually put in your smoothie outside of kale. Sidenote: is that kale even cooked or is it raw? If the latter, it's doing you more harm than good.

If you knew you were getting in only 4000 steps a day, would you be more motivated to clock up the additional 6000? Baselines are important in business and in life. If you know where you want to go, you need directions on how to get there. But those directions must start from where you are today. If you haven't defined your baseline, where you are today, then getting to your destination becomes exponentially more difficult because essentially you have no feedback loop.

Consider investing in a wearable device such as a Fitbit or use your smartphone's free apps, such as the iPhone's Heart app, to count steps, and download a nutrition app so you can get an idea of what you're really consuming.

Mind over matter

In his bestselling book *A New Earth*, Eckhart Tolle tells the story of being a student at the University of London, riding the Underground and noticing a woman in her early thirties talking to herself incessantly in a loud, angry voice. He proceeded to follow her at a safe distance into the university's central administrative building and library (let's ignore for a moment the fact that he was stalking a stranger). It was here that he came to the realisation that while her behaviour seemed insane, she was simply thinking out loud rather than, as most of us, doing so in her head.

Are we any less crazy and controlled by involuntary thoughts that ultimately serve to root our thinking in the past or build anticipation of the future, limiting the amount of time we stay truly present and focused?

GRATITUDE

According to research by psychologist Robert Emmons, expressing gratitude improves mental, physical and relational wellbeing, and also impacts the overall experience of happiness, the effects of which tend to be long-lasting.

A common method of cultivating gratitude is keeping a gratitude journal. Quite simply, write down three things you are grateful for each day. It could be the pleasant conversation you had with your local barista or something greater such as your health or the opportunities you've been given in life. Recording what you're grateful for boosts your enthusiasm, determination and energy.

Dale Carnegie declared in *How To Win Friends and Influence People*, 'Once I did bad and that I heard ever. Twice I did good, but that I heard never'. People are hard-wired to focus on the negatives and we hold onto negative experiences longer than positive ones. All the more reason to make time to acknowledge the positives. If you record your positive experience for just two consecutive weeks, the enduring positive effects of being more aware of such experiences as they happen are said to last for up to six months. Not only will journaling help to inject you with a positive attitude, but by putting stuff on paper you're getting it out of your head and signalling to your brain that it's time to sleep, helping you get a better night's rest in the process.

MINDFULNESS

I like to think of mindfulness as a form of meditation that you can practise throughout the day without anyone even noticing. It's about recognising involuntary thoughts and distractions as they arise and releasing them.

When the mind wanders it is not present; when it is not present it is often anxious about the future or depressed about the past. Being grounded in the present means it can't be either of those things. How many of your thoughts would you choose not to think if you had a choice? Becoming more mindful means you will more often respond from a place of voluntary reason, not impulse and involuntary reaction.

Relationships

The quality of our relationships is the essence of what allows us to be fulfilled on both a professional and personal level. Sometimes these relationships hold us back from living a life true to ourselves rather than as others expect of us, and sometimes they can empower us.

My colleague Shay joined the team shortly after getting married, plus one on the way. His most important relationship is the one with his wife Priya. He had plenty of deliberations before joining our team: '*I am going into a new role*', '*I'll be paid less and will be working late hours*', '*This is the last thing she wants to hear*'...

Her response was worlds apart from what he had imagined. She threw her support behind him. She gave him permission to leave a successful career in top tier management consulting and pursue his passion. And that support continues unabated.

It is possible to have a family and chase your dreams, but as with any stakeholder buy-in conversation, involve them early. Happiness in your professional life often feeds into your personal life, and relationships can play an integral role not only when making the leap from corporate employee to entrepreneur but, more importantly, while staying the course.

Having said that, being deep in the trenches of entrepreneurship is no excuse for neglecting your loved ones. As Steve Blank puts it, he doesn't want his epitaph to read 'He never missed a meeting'. He wants it to read 'He was a great father'.

Quality, not quantity

The Roman philosopher Epicurus is remembered for putting pleasure above all else. 'Pleasure,' he wrote, 'is the beginning and the goal of a happy life'. Many have misinterpreted his teachings, as manifest in our notion of over-indulgent Epicurean delights.

However, as philosopher Alain De Botton observes in *The Consolations of Philosophy*, for Epicurus a happy life came down to four elements: *friendship, freedom, food* and *thought*. Epicurus and his friends removed themselves from Athenian society so they would not have to work for people they didn't like or respect. They would have none of the trappings of wealth but would be free to live according to their principles. They built what was essentially a commune with a garden that provided them with fruit and vegetables that were by no means abundant or luxurious, but were nutritious and fresh. 'The wise man,' said Epicurus, 'chooses not the greatest quantity of food but the most flavoursome'.

Where do you prioritise quantity over quality in your life? When you find yourself yearning for more, take a moment to reflect on what you already have: the food you can order up whenever you want, the friendships you sometimes take for granted, the freedom you enjoy. Nelson Mandela said he always felt free, even behind bars where he spent almost three decades of his life. That's because freedom is more than a physical state; it also means freedom of thought, and that is largely a matter of personal judgement.

Call to action

1. What do you need to be content? Write it down.

2. What aspects of your diet are not serving you? Replace them.

3. Take as many of your meetings and phone calls standing up or walking as possible.

4. If you're not already working out, make a plan to start. Begin by walking at least 10 000 steps a day, before exploring other forms of exercise. Anything is much better than nothing.

5. Think your significant other or family obligations will get in the way of your dreams? Have that conversation.

FINAL THOUGHTS

When you near the end of your journey and, reflecting on the life you've lived, ask yourself, *What do I wish I had done differently?*, will it be that you had challenged the status quo more? Will you wish you had challenged *yourself* and broken out of your comfort zone more? Will you regret not spending more time with family and friends and on the important relationships in your life? Or not being more adventurous in exploring the world?

I doubt you'll regret you hadn't worked harder. But entrepreneurship isn't really about working harder. It's about living life on your terms; it's about spending your life doing work that matters, work that makes a difference in the lives of others and leaves this world just a little better than you found it.

Here's what I won't say during my final days:

'I wish I had spent more time watching Netflix.'

'I wish I had spent more time shopping.'

'I wish I had spent more time on social media.'

'I wish I had spent more time watching the news.'

'I wish I had spent more time drinking.'

'I wish I had had more stock options.'

'I wish I had bought more real estate.'

Yet this is how so many people spend their 'spare' time today. On stuff that is easy and comfortable in the moment, but leaves us feeling unfulfilled and miserable later on, with all the trappings of wealth but devoid of the joy that the simplest of things can deliver.

Polishing off an entire bag of potato chips might give us a fleeting pleasure high, but it leaves us feeling not only physically sluggish but, more often than not, guilty and hating our lack of self-control.

Life's most rewarding experiences are those that push us beyond our comfort zone, that drive us to answer questions we don't know the answer to, that force us to learn something new, to face adversity and come out the other side a better version of ourselves, looking back on the experience, not with resentment or sadness, but with fondness.

You might not know what your 'why' or purpose is. You may have just read this book cover to cover and not yet applied anything you've learned here. Even if you have, maybe your why still isn't clear ... and that's okay. Sometimes by starting on a 'what', any 'what' for that matter, the work you subsequently do will reveal new opportunities and bring you closer to a 'why' you truly believe in. Don't let not knowing what to do, or not having 100 per cent conviction in your idea, stop you from taking that next step. In Paulo Coelho's novel *The Alchemist*, Santiago, a young farm boy, sets off on a grand journey across the desert to the Egyptian pyramids in search of treasure, only to find that the treasure was at his feet the whole time. Sometimes the answer is right in front of you but you need to go on a journey to see it.

Genius is the ability to see what others don't, and the ability to see requires that you get moving and start collecting dots. Then, and only then, will the opportunities and path present themselves.

When I set off to build Hotdesk all those years ago, I had no idea I would wind up working on concepts such as a children's entrepreneurship program or a blockchain-based platform to help make home ownership accessible to more Australians, or even writing this book, only a few short years later. Identifying this opportunity came organically, thanks to the work I was doing, the conversations I was having, the books I was reading and the people I had developed relationships with. Ultimately, it came down to the law of momentum, one of John Maxwell's irrefutable laws of leadership.

So my challenge to you is to stop procrastinating, stop waiting for the elusive and subjective 'right time', and build momentum. Put this book down, or give it to a friend who could benefit from it, and take that first step, no matter how small, today. Go and register a domain or business name. Declare to the world what you're doing. Register for an entrepreneurship meetup. Complete a lean canvas for an idea you've been toying with. Register a domain name with GoDaddy. Whatever it is, whatever you can do ... do it, but *do it today*. And make time to do something, anything, every day from here on. The small act of doing something will not only build momentum, but lead you to do progressively more, and form a habit, and once formed, like most habits, it will be incredibly hard to kick.

Entrepreneurship is a state of mind. Start building yours, then for guidance refer back to this book and the resources I've made available at www.employeetoentrepreneur.io.

A well-known aphorism, first attributed to American humourist and actor Robert Benchley in 1920, proposes, 'There are two kinds of people in the world: those who divide everybody into two kinds of people, and those who don't'. I guess I'm in the former camp then, because what I've come to know of readers of books such as this one is that there are indeed two kinds: those who apply what they read and those who don't.

You might be feeling a sense of accomplishment and be enjoying a serotonin hit from having finished this book. If you want to build a life of sustainable contentment, meaning and accomplishment, though, you need not only to think bigger but to back up your thinking with action.

Whether it's on the path to entrepreneurship or following one of the other avenues I've outlined in this book, take that first step. It's time to stop just doing something and get busy *being* something. The world needs you.

INDEX